Japanese Bakehouse

Japanese Bakehouse

Satoshi Narusawa

The Art of Shokupan
and Other Classic Recipes

Smith Street Books

SHOKUPAN
NAMA CHOCO
BLACK SUGAR

HOJICHA
RAISIN
MATCHA

BENCH COFFEE CO.
LITTLE CARDIGAN

I never planned to be a baker. I was backpacking through Europe when I saw Asako's email saying she was pregnant. My friends discouraged me from returning, but I did what I thought a man should do: go home, become a salaryman and care for my family.

Before I discovered baking, I was an expert in recovering from after-work drinking sessions. The blur of bowing twelve hours a day, the nights of cheap booze, then catching the train to start it all again the next morning. Before I knew it, our daughter Yuma was walking and talking, and I was never home. I'd had enough. With zero experience, I walked into a bakery and asked for a job.

If I become a baker, I can work anywhere, I thought; however, nothing prepared me for the heat of an oven at 3 am or the aching back from hauling 20-kilogram (44-pound) tubs of dough. But there was an honesty to baking that office life could never touch. Dough doesn't care about feelings; it waits for no one. You learn its rhythm, or you fail. At the end of the day, you have something real – something customers can see, smell and touch.

When I moved to one of the bigger French bakery chains in Tokyo, I saw the future of commercial baking: dough arriving frozen on a truck from a factory, ready to be baked by staff following standard procedure. I was promoted to train new bakers who came and went. I was becoming detached, mentally and physically. That's when I typed 'overseas baker' into a search engine and booked the first flight out.

I never planned to migrate to Australia. In the city of Cairns, I learnt that bread means something else entirely. A loaf of sourdough wasn't just an accessory to a meal; it was the meal. It made me question: what was bread really for?

Asako and I visited a friend in Melbourne and fell in love with the city. Turns out, I was right – you can work anywhere as a baker. Eventually, I found my feet at Loafer Bread in Fitzroy North. Andrea ran her bakery on a different principle. Customers knew her by name. Farmers dropped off flour in person. People stopped to chat when buying bread. They didn't complain about the rustic shapes; they said it was character.

I never planned to make shokupan or start my own business. A local Japanese cafe asked if I could bake a few loaves for their menu. Then another cafe called Saint Dreux became popular and asked me to bake bread for them, too. Soon, I had to ask Andrea to use Loafer's oven to keep up. I was baking after hours, delivering at night, then back to my usual shift. A few years later, I partnered with Bench Coffee Co., and we took over a space in Brunswick.

I met Harvard at a friend's Christmas barbecue. He lives on Little Cardigan Street in Carlton. He's a photographer who also likes to cook, and he invites us for dinner often. He likes to talk about food and design, and he made me try Musang King durian for the first time. When it came to naming my business, I wanted something that gave a warm feeling – like people coming together. So we called it Little Cardigan.

I never planned to write a book about Japanese baking. Harvard introduced me to chef Brendan Liew, who recommended us to the publisher. When it came to writing, I thought, 'Harvard has to tell this story.' His wife is Japanese, so he can explain and translate well for non-Japanese readers. He also helps with our bread deliveries, so he understands the business. He can make the connection. Connection is the most important ingredient, like gluten in bread.

Our aim in this book is not perfection. If you want perfection, just go to a bakery chain. We want you to think about who you're baking for and the conversations that might happen over a slice of toast. Enjoy the process, then return to it. Be happy with the repetition. Have a go. See where it takes you. Maybe your life will change. Sometimes, things don't go as planned. That's okay. That's life.

I met Satoshi ten years ago when I was trying to break into food photography. (I'm still trying now, but I was trying back then too!) Being a chef is hard, but being a baker is harder. Not only do they work behind the scenes, they also start at 3 am and never see customers' expressions when they bite into their creations. You can't improvise with baking – it's science: scales, repetition, shaping, third-degree burns. It's about getting the timing right.

Satoshi likes to stress he's not a traditional Japanese man, but that's what all traditional Japanese men say. Sure, he rides his bike to work in Brunswick, drinks oat lattes, still has a full head of hair, but underneath that smile is a set of adamantium bones supporting an even tougher spirit.

He asked if it was okay to use my street's name, 'Little Cardigan', for his business.

I laughed. I'm not the city council; I don't own the rights to my street. He didn't need my 'permission'.

'Are you sure?' I asked. 'Do you want to think of my street every time you bake?'

'Why not?' he replied. 'We feel happy and relaxed when we visit.'

I want to set the record straight: I don't host dinner parties in a Victorian townhouse with swan napkins. When I first met Satoshi, our leaky two-bedroom apartment was a constant mess with no natural light (it still is, to be honest).

The Chinese have a saying: 'Neighbours are worth more than relatives afar.' Not having nine-to-five jobs meant we didn't have work–life balance, but we had the opportunity to make homemade noodles, experimental assam laksa, countless attempts at Japanese cotton cheesecake, kombucha and, eventually, Satoshi's first batch of shokupan.

Satoshi is a doer. He takes pride in his work, but he's also extremely humble. I'm pretty sure he was the first to bring shokupan into Melbourne's zeitgeist. The idea of 'white bread' had been around, but he made it artisanal, with local organic wheat flour and cultured butter, combining the shokunin (artisan) discipline from his experience in Japan with the sensibility he learned at Andrea's Loafer Bread in Melbourne's Fitzroy North. (I cherish my memories there with my daughter reading *The Tiger Who Came to Tea* to go with her babycino. Thank you, Andrea.)

If Satoshi were more vocal, he could've had more exposure, wholesale clients, online orders, expansion, franchises, workshops – even a Lamborghini. But I can almost hear his thought: 'What's the point? That's why I left Tokyo.'

Still, he's always the first to arrive at work. I know because I deliver bread for him (a favour he asked of me and another story altogether). If it's Satoshi's shift, the shokupan will be ready by 8.10 am. If you ask him why he works so hard, he'll say, 'I don't know.' Maybe don't ask too many questions. Maybe figure it out yourself. Him the iron chef, me the clueless commentator Fukui-san.

Let me translate: he wants to do better, but he wants it to be organic, like his baking process. Like all good things, it's about getting the timing right.

The second time he asked for a favour was to write this book with him.

'Are you sure?' I asked. 'What do you want out of this?'

'To acknowledge everyone who's helped me along the way,' he said.

It doesn't matter if he's a traditional Japanese man or not – Satoshi is part of Melbourne now, and Melbourne is lucky to have him. This book is about his experience, memories, sacrifice, talent and often underrated contribution to the baking community.

The city smells better with Little Cardigan. The joke's on me: now every time I see my street name, I think about bread.

PANYASAN AND THE RELEVANCE OF THE JAPANESE BAKEHOUSE

SATOSHI NARUSAWA

I grew up in Tokyo in the late 1970s and the 1980s, a time when Japan's rapid postwar economic growth had begun to settle. Most neighbourhood shops were still small, family-run businesses. The only chains were supermarkets, and a few upscale department stores near major train stations. Convenience stores were brand new then – so unfamiliar that most people weren't sure what purpose they served. (Fun fact: Japan's first 7-Eleven opened in 1974 in Toyosu, Tokyo.)

Naturally, shoppers still linked the personality of a shop to the face behind the counter. Among these local shops, the panyasan (bakery) held a special place in my heart. Even as a child, I found them warm and inviting. A tiny shop filled with trays and tongs, rows of shelves lined with beautifully browned, glossy loaves, and a blend of yeast, butter and savoury aromas carried in the air. Unlike the grocer or the butcher, the bakery had a gentler atmosphere – casual, unpretentious, warm. When my mother asked what I would like, I always chose a tuna sandwich or a curry pan and, of course, an an-doughnut – her favourite.

Today, Japan's bread culture has evolved beyond anything imaginable back then. The quality has improved remarkably, and the variety is endless. From croissants made with French butter to artful Danish pastries designed for social media, and rustic country loaves baked in wood-fired ovens with natural yeast – the world of bread has flourished alongside technology and globalisation. This is not unique to Japan; it's part of a worldwide transformation in how bread is made and enjoyed.

In this landscape, the traditional Japanese bakery has become something nostalgic – 'retro', 'old-fashioned', or simply fading away as owners age and successors are scarce. Yet for many of us, these bakeries hold a quiet place in our collective memory.

When I was invited to create a book on Japanese bread, what first came to mind were the breads of those small neighbourhood bakeries from my childhood. I can still recall their smell so vividly, and I picture the bakers working before dawn in their narrow kitchens. Now, as a baker myself, I want to honour those who inspired me – and to preserve memories that may someday disappear with time.

The breads featured in this book form a continuous thread connecting my family and childhood memories in Japan with my present life as a baker in Melbourne. I hope they will continue to resonate with people living in 2026 and beyond.

I spent seven years at Loafer Bread in Fitzroy North. I started on pastry, then moved to bread, working alongside Andrea, who built the bakery on her own values: honesty, patience and no cutting corners. Back then, coming from a commercial bakery, I was surprised by how much she made from scratch. In Japan we have so many ready-made ingredients, so many shortcuts if you want them – but at Loafer, nothing was ever done the easy way. That changed the way I bake.

But what stays with me most is the neighbourhood. Almost everyone lives nearby. They come in every morning, almost by instinct – pick up their bread, say hello, grab a pastry, have a coffee. They don't care about the shop's name; it's simply their bakery. The shop is small, in a good way, and you feel the intimacy as soon as you step inside.

It reminds me of the bakeries I grew up with in Japan. When I was a kid, we'd walk into a panyasan and know immediately what was baking from the smell alone. Freshly baked loaves stacked on the racks, trays of pastries still warm and the excitement of choosing what you want (I can still hear my parents saying, 'Pick only three!'). The bread was soft, warm, unwrapped, alive. That freshness is something you can never get from supermarket bread.

Loafer gave people in Fitzroy North that same feeling. A place woven into daily life, where bread is not just food but a ritual. For me, it became the Melbourne version of the neighbourhood panyasan I knew as a child.

Andrea is one of the most honest bakers I've met. Nothing was ever rushed. Nothing was ever done halfway. She helped many young bakers, including me, when we were starting out.

WHAT I LEARNT AT LOAFER

- Integrity in baking: No shortcuts. If something can be made properly, then that's the only way to do it.
- Community matters: A bakery isn't only about the product. It's about being part of people's daily rhythm.
- Freshness is a feeling: Bread made for the neighbourhood tastes different from bread made for a supermarket shelf.
- Supporting others: Andrea helped new bakers find their way. That generosity stays with me.

Japan has long exported its culture – food, fashion, design – but what's fascinating is how often those exports come back home, slightly changed, carrying a foreign accent. This loop is called 'gyakuyunyu', or 'reverse import', and it's one of the most interesting engines of Japanese taste.

Bread is no exception.

Shiopan, born in a small bakery in Ehime, a prefecture on Shikoku Island, migrated across Asia. In Korea and Singapore it evolved into salt-butter bread – shinier, richer, even more buttery. Those versions came back to Japan, inspiring a new wave of glossy, laminated rolls that now dominate bakery displays.

Sweetcorn buns made a similar journey: a simple Shizuoka invention reborn overseas with cheese and chillies, such as jalapeno, before reappearing on Japanese menus as 'new flavours'.

Karepan – the curry-filled doughnut – is another traveller. It left Japan, found new spice blends and breading styles in places like Los Angeles and Bangkok, and returned home with crispier shells and heavier curries.

Then there's an butter. Japan's Tokai TV station traced its modern boom to ogura toast from Nagoya, then spread nationwide by Komeda's Coffee chain. Korean cafes picked up the red-bean-and-butter idea and turned it into 'ang butter' culture – pairing it with baguettes, croissants and cookies – before Japan re-imported it as a fashionably rustic trend.

To see reverse import as a simple copy and paste misses the point; it's about having a dialogue in which Japanese bakers send their ideas into the world, watch them change and welcome them back like old friends who've learnt a few new tricks.

Essential tools

STAND MIXER

Shokupan is an enriched, high-hydration dough that really benefits from consistent, intensive mixing that only a stand mixer with a dough hook attachment can do. For that long, soft, stretchy chew, the dough needs to pass the windowpane test (stretching it thin enough to let light through without tearing) – and achieving this by hand can feel like wrestling a sumo made of mochi.

Using a stand mixer keeps things cleaner, too. Less flour drifting around the room, less dough glued between your fingers, and a final product that actually matches the recipe's hydration.

HIGH-PRECISION DIGITAL SCALE (0.1 G INCREMENTS, UP TO ~3 KG/6 LB 10 OZ)

A digital scale is the most important tool in baking. Percentages matter. Measurements matter. Consistency matters. A digital scale does all three.

INSTANT-READ DIGITAL THERMOMETER (WATERPROOF)

A digital thermometer helps you hit your target Desired Dough Temperature (see page 27) every time.

ROUND DOUGH SCRAPER

Use a round dough scraper for removing dough from bowls, dividing portions cleanly and keeping your bench tidy. A pliable plastic scraper is the best option.

ROLLING PIN

For shaping rolls, buns, logs or laminated-style pastries, Japanese doughs respond well to a wooden rolling pin with some weight.

WOODEN SPATULA

A wooden spatula is essential when making yudane (see page 23), as it won't scratch your bowl and gives better control over the paste.

SILICONE NON-STICK MAT

This multipurpose work surface is non-slip, dough-friendly and easy to clean. It also helps to stabilise your stand mixer on the kitchen bench.

Baking tools

PULLMAN LOAF TIN (SHOKUPAN TIN)

A Pullman loaf tin is the secret to a perfect square loaf. It helps produce a thin, even crust and the classic Japanese bread profile. The tin's dimensions should ideally be 196 × 106 × 110 mm (7.72 × 4.17 × 4.33 in) with lid.

CREAM HORN MOULD

This conical metal mould is used to shape cream horns and cornets and create their distinctive spiral shape. Having eight 30 × 138 mm (1.18 × 5.4 in) moulds on hand will allow you to efficiently make a batch.

BAKING SHEET/BAKING TRAY

A heavy-duty, aluminium or steel rimmed tray distributes heat evenly and prevents scorching on the base of shiopan or melonpan. The typical household baking tray size measures 30–35 × 25–30 cm (12–13¾ × 10–12 in).

BAKING MAT (SILICONE OR TEFLON)

Ideal for shaping and baking, a silicone or Teflon baking mat is a reusable alternative to baking paper with even heat distribution and no waste.

WIRE COOLING RACK

Leaving bread on a hot tray softens the base. A wire cooling rack lets steam escape so bread and buns set properly.

Preparation tools

BOWL

A large glass, stainless steel or ceramic bowl is ideal for mixing and storing sponge dough.

BALLOON WHISK

A balloon whisk is useful for making custard.

SILICONE FLAT SPATULA (HEAT-RESISTANT UP TO 260°C/500°F)

Also for making custard, a heat-resistant spatula won't melt at high temperatures.

GRATER (FINE/MICROPLANE)

A fine grater or microplane is ideal for zesting yuzu or other citrus, grating nutmeg and adding micro-flavour accents to doughs and fillings.

MESH STRAINER

Use a mesh strainer for sifting flour, dusting icing (confectioners') sugar and straining creams, custards or anko (red bean paste) for a smoother finish. It should ideally be 25 cm (10 in) in diameter with a medium mesh (as opposed to a very fine mesh).

Optional but helpful

MEASURING CUPS, SPOONS AND JUGS

Even though everything in this book is weighed in grams, measuring cups, spoons and jugs are still helpful for liquids, *mise en place* and quick preparation.

SPRAY BOTTLE

Spray water on the surface of doughs to keep them hydrated during proofing and to add steam during the first seconds of baking. Use a spray bottle with a fine mist and ensure it is food-safe.

THERMO-HYGROMETER

If you bake in a climate with mood swings, this handy device helps you understand your room's temperature and humidity instantly.

OVEN THERMOMETER

Most home ovens lie. An oven thermometer tells you the truth – crucial when baking at exact temperatures like 185°C (365°F) or 200°C (392°F).

OFFSET SPATULA

Use an offset spatula to smooth creams, fillings and anko, or to glaze with precision. A small one works best.

PASTRY BRUSH

A pastry brush is useful for applying egg wash, melted butter and syrups, or for brushing excess flour off dough. I prefer to use one with natural bristles, so that I can apply egg wash gently.

INGREDIENTS USED IN THIS BOOK

FLOUR

Most of the flour used in this book is bread flour, which contains about 12 per cent protein. In comparison, plain (all-purpose) flour contains around 9 per cent protein, which produces a softer, more cake-like crumb. You can check the protein level of your flour by looking under 'per 100 g (3.53 oz)' on the nutritional label of the packaging.

SUGAR

RAW (DEMERARA) SUGAR brings a subtle caramel flavour and mellow, rich sweetness. In buttery, rich doughs, it enhances the depth of flavour.

KOKUTO (OKINAWA BLACK SUGAR) offers a mild, complex sweetness that enhances baked goods. If kokuto is not available in your area, you can substitute it with panela sugar (a South American unrefined cane sugar), jaggery (commonly used in India and Southeast Asia) or muscovado sugar. Each will provide a slightly different, unique flavour.

FINE SEA SALT

I use naturally harvested additive-free Australian sea salt, which has a gentler flavour compared to table salt.

CREAM (40 PER CENT MILKFAT)

Freshness is key. I use locally sourced cream in my recipes.

FULL-CREAM (WHOLE) MILK

I'm fortunate to live in Australia's top dairy-producing state, which allows me to use very fresh milk. I always use full-cream (whole) milk.

YEAST

I use both osmotolerant instant dry yeast and regular instant dry yeast in this book. Osmotolerant yeast is designed for doughs with high sugar and fat contents, such as sweet and enriched breads, where it provides a reliable and even rise. Regular instant dry yeast is best suited to lean and lightly sweetened doughs, as its activity can slow in high-sugar environments. Using the right yeast helps ensure consistent fermentation and good volume.

SALTED, UNSALTED AND CULTURED BUTTER

I use salted butter in savoury recipes and unsalted butter in sweet recipes. Cultured butter adds depth and gives bread a richer, more aromatic taste.

CHOCOLATE

I buy my chocolate from a local chocolate maker in Melbourne who sources their ingredients directly from growers.

DUTCH COCOA POWDER

I use Dutch-processed cocoa powder in this book, which has little effect on bread fermentation compared to natural cocoa. For recipes with dark chocolate, I use 55 per cent dark chocolate.

DRIED FRUIT

Dried raisins, yuzu peel, figs and apricots are good staples to have on hand.

I didn't know about tangzhong when I was baking in Japan. Back then, the bakery I worked for used different techniques: a liquid sourdough starter and old dough starter ('rou mén' or 'lao mian' in Chinese) – similar to a poolish that you rest so it develops flavour. The idea was to make bread taste better, not softer. It was Andrea – my ex-boss and owner of Loafer Bread in Fitzroy North, Melbourne – who told me to look up tangzhong.

Same flour, same leavener – but suddenly the dough felt different. The bread stayed moist for days. Now, of course, bakeries around the world use tangzhong. But when I was learning, hardly anyone did. I learnt it from an Australian.

The science of 'fuwa fuwa'

Every loaf of bread is built on starch. In its raw state, starch exists as microscopic granules – tight, crystalline, stubborn things that resist water. When you heat flour and water together to 65°C (149°F), those granules swell and burst, absorbing more water. The paste thickens like pudding: this is gelatinisation.

Flour that's been pre-gelatinised can hold roughly twice as much water as raw flour. Because so much of the moisture is now 'locked in', the dough feels supple rather than sticky – high-hydration yet easy to handle. In the oven, those swollen starches act as tiny water balloons. They keep the crumb open, moist and resilient, while the gluten network – now stronger and more elastic – traps the gas from fermentation, creating that even, shreddable structure that defines shokupan.

The benefit of tangzhong doesn't stop at texture. By holding on to moisture, it dramatically slows staling – the process known as starch retrogradation – where bread firms up as water migrates out of the crumb. A tangzhong loaf can stay soft and fluffy (fuwa fuwa) for three or four days without additives.

Finally, tangzhong allows gelatinised starch to break down more easily, releasing a mild, natural sweetness.

You may be thinking: if tangzhong is so great, why not make a full loaf of tangzhong, rather than 5–10 per cent of the total volume? That's because cooking the flour with hot water denatures (destroys) the proteins needed to form gluten. If all the gluten turns to gel, there will be no structure, no network and no bread.

From yudane to tangzhong: a breadcrumb trail

Tangzhong's story began in Japan. In the 1960s, postwar Japan was chasing a new idea of softness – a bread that could comfort like rice. Industrial bakers experimented with yudane (湯種製法): scalding a small portion of flour with boiling water to form a gelatinised paste that kept bread moist for longer.

When Japanese-style bakeries spread across East Asia in the late twentieth century, local bakers adapted the same idea but began cooking the flour-and-water mixture gently on the stove, rather than scalding it with boiling water. The result was smoother, easier to portion and more consistent in warm, humid kitchens.

Over time, the method became widely known as tangzhong (湯種) – the same characters, new pronunciation – and in 2004, baking writer Yvonne Chen brought it into the mainstream with her influential book *65°C Bread Doctor*.

Chen didn't invent the technique, but she gave it a language. By naming it, quantifying it (65°C/149°F, the exact point of starch gelatinisation) and explaining it to home bakers, she gave the method a life of its own. From there, it spread through bakeries in Hong Kong (China) and Korea, found its way into cookbooks and classrooms, and eventually circulated back to Japan and beyond.

Yudane vs. tangzhong

There is no single answer as to which method is superior; the choice depends on the baker's priorities. However, some technical bakers argue that yudane may produce a slightly lighter loaf. This is because the scalding process may not fully denature the gluten proteins in the flour (change their structure through heat), whereas the sustained cooking of tangzhong does.

FEATURE	TANGZHONG	YUDANE
Origin	Popularised in Taiwan, China (from Japanese method)	Japan
Technique	Cooked to 65°C (149°F) on the stovetop	Scalded with boiling water
Ratio	1 flour : 5 liquid	1 flour : 1.5 liquid
Texture	Smooth, paste-like	Dense, dough-like mass
Use	4–10% of total flour	10–25% of total flour

For many, the decision comes down to practicality. Yudane is often considered more convenient, as it's faster to prepare and involves less clean-up.

On the other hand, the tangzhong method offers more precise control. By using a thermometer and actively managing the cooking process, a baker can ensure that the starches are fully and perfectly gelatinised every time, removing the variability that can occur with yudane depending on ambient and hot water temperatures. When made correctly, tangzhong should form a smooth, slightly loose paste that slowly drips from a spoon while still holding together. If the mixture is too runny, it is likely under-gelatinised; if it becomes overly stiff or dry, it has been overcooked.

HOW I MAKE YUDANE

Yudane is made using 1 part flour to 1.5 parts liquid, with the optional addition of raw (demerara) sugar.

For the standard loaves in this book (made with 294 g/10.4 oz flour, yielding roughly 600 g/21.16 oz total dough), use 59 g (2.08 oz) flour and 88 g (3.1 oz) boiling water or very hot milk. If using milk, heat it until steaming and near-boiling, about 90–95°C (194–203°F), to avoid scorching.

FLOUR (59 G/2.08 OZ)

Use the same flour as your base dough, usually bread flour

LIQUID (88 G/3.1 OZ)

Water for a neutral dough

Milk for added richness

Soy or oat milk for vegan alternatives

METHOD

1. Warm a bowl with hot water, then discard the water. (This prevents the mixture cooling too quickly and helps the starch gelatinise evenly.)
2. Place the flour in the warmed bowl and mix well.
3. Add the boiling water or hot milk in one swift motion, ensuring it evenly coats the flour.
4. Mix the flour and liquid with a wooden spatula for 30–60 seconds, until the yudane forms a thick paste, similar to mashed potato. If it feels too dry, add 1–2 teaspoons of hot water. If it seems too wet, mix in a small pinch of flour.
5. Cover with plastic wrap, pressing it directly onto the surface of the yudane to prevent a crust forming.
6. Once cooled to body temperature (about 37°C/99°F), refrigerate overnight to rest.
7. Yudane can be stored in the fridge for up to 3 days.

HOW I MAKE TANGZHONG

Tangzhong is made using one part flour to five parts liquid, and is cooked gently to form a smooth starch paste.

For the standard loaves in this book (made with 294 g/10.4 oz flour, yielding roughly 600 g/21.16 oz total dough), use 15 g (0.53 oz) flour and 75 g (2.65 oz) liquid to make the tangzhong. This yields about 90 g (3.17 oz) tangzhong paste.

FLOUR (15 G/0.53 OZ)

Use the same flour as your base dough, usually bread flour

LIQUID (75 G/2.65 OZ)

Water for a neutral dough

Milk for added richness

Soy or oat milk for vegan alternatives

METHOD

1. In a small saucepan, whisk the flour and liquid together while cold, until completely smooth and free of lumps.
2. Place the saucepan over medium–low heat and whisk continuously as the mixture warms.
3. Continue whisking until the mixture thickens into a paste, lines of paste remain visible when you drag the whisk along the base of the pan and the temperature reaches 65°C (149°F) on a digital thermometer.
4. Remove from the heat and transfer the tangzhong to a small bowl.
5. Cover with plastic wrap, pressing it directly onto the surface of the tangzhong to prevent a skin forming.
6. Allow to cool to room temperature before using in your dough.
7. Tangzhong can be stored in the fridge for up to 2 days.

In Japan, bread-making methods are often categorised as:

1. **JIKAGONE-HO**
   The direct method, where everything is mixed in one go.
2. **NAKADANE-HO**
   The sponge, or intermediate starter method: a pre-dough is made first, allowed to ferment, then mixed into the final dough mixture.

Sponge dough is a type of pre-ferment, but the fermentation time is shorter than poolish or biga. The sponge develops flavour and structure quietly in the background. By the time you mix the final dough, the yeast is awake, the gluten relaxed and the bread is already halfway to fluffy.

It's not yudane or tangzhong, which rely on cooked starch for softness, but the idea is similar – to give the dough a head start. It's a slower way to bake, but the payoff is in the texture – that fine, creamy crumb that makes Japanese rolls so distinct.

HOW I MAKE SPONGE DOUGH

Sponge dough is a simple pre-ferment made from flour, liquid, sugar and yeast. It helps develop flavour, improves texture and strengthens gluten before the final dough is mixed.

For the standard portions in this book (500 g/17.64 oz total dough, yielding 8 rolls), use 125 g (4.41 oz) bread flour, 8 g (0.28 oz) raw sugar, 3 g (0.11 oz) instant dry yeast and 100 g (3.53 oz) lukewarm full-cream (whole) milk.

FLOUR (125 G/4.41 OZ)
Use the same flour as your base dough, usually bread flour

LUKEWARM LIQUID (100 G/3.53 OZ)

Milk for richness and softness

Water may be substituted for a leaner dough

METHOD

1. Place the flour, 8 g (0.28 oz) sugar and 3 g (0.11 oz) instant dry yeast in a bowl and mix to combine.
2. Add the lukewarm milk and stir until no dry flour remains and a smooth, thick batter forms.
3. Cover the bowl with plastic wrap or a clean cloth and leave at room temperature until doubled in size and bubbly, about 1 hour.
4. Once fully risen, refrigerate overnight (up to 16 hours) to develop flavour and structure before using in the final dough.
5. The sponge dough is ready to use when it has risen well, smells lightly sweet and yeasty, and shows small bubbles on the surface.

Bread reacts to time, temperature, humidity and sometimes to our own mood, and over the years I've developed certain rules and habits. Every variable has a reason. You don't have to follow the below exactly, but these are the conditions that work for me. Understanding them will help you find your own way.

Mixing

The dough in this book is made using a KitchenAid stand mixer. It allows for consistent kneading and helps control dough temperature.

WHAT TO LOOK OUT FOR

Planetary mixers generate friction heat, and the dough hook can raise your dough temperature by 8–12°C (46–54°F). Too warm, and the dough ferments too quickly and loses flavour. Aim for a final dough temperature of 25–28°C (77–82°F).

Mixers can also wobble or 'walk' across the bench when working a heavy dough. Make sure the head is locked, the bowl is seated properly and the machine is sitting on a stable surface. A silicone mat placed underneath the mixer works wonders.

MY MIXER BASELINE

1. Mix dry and liquid ingredients on a low speed until a rough dough forms.
   OPTIONAL: Rest for 30 minutes – an autolyse that jump-starts gluten.
2. Mix on speed 6 (medium–high) for 20–25 minutes. You'll know you're close when the dough slaps the bowl and pulls cleanly away from the side.
3. Add soft butter (cut into 1.5 cm/½ in cubes), making sure it is absorbed into the dough completely.
4. Stop when the dough is glossy, elastic and reaches 25–28°C (77-82°F) on a digital thermometer. If the dough reaches temperature but doesn't look glossy and elastic yet, prioritise the look and feel of the dough over the temperature. The fermentation time can be adjusted as long as the dough temperature is not too far from the DDT (desired dough temperature; see page 27).

Hand-kneading

Yes, you can hand-knead shokupan – it just takes time, rest and patience. Think of it as meditation with gluten on a quiet afternoon. Techniques like Rubaud mixing and slap-and-folds help you work with wet dough efficiently without throwing flour everywhere.

Hand-kneading does come with a small cost: dough sticks to hands and the bench, so the final yield drops by around 15 per cent. If you're hand-kneading, increase your ingredient quantities accordingly.

HAND-KNEADING GUIDE

1. **COMBINE AND REST** Mix dry and liquid ingredients to form a shaggy dough in the bowl. Rest for 15 minutes.
2. **RUBAUD MIX (ABOUT 5 MINUTES)** Scoop, lift and let the dough fall back into the bowl. Rest for 5 minutes, then repeat.
3. **SLAP-AND-FOLD (3–6 MINUTES)** Place the dough on a clean surface, lift it up and slap it down while stretching the end towards you. Fold the dough over itself and repeat the motion until it becomes smooth and stops sticking to the surface. Rest for 5 minutes.
4. **BUTTER INCORPORATION** Once the dough is cohesive and the gluten has started to develop, incorporate the butter in small portions. At first, the dough may become sticky and break apart, but keep kneading until it comes back together. Knead until the dough is smooth and elastic.
5. **CHECK** Look for a thin, elastic 'windowpane' in the dough by pinching a small piece and stretching it between your fingers to see if it is thin enough to let light through without tearing. The dough should feel bouncy and slightly tacky – not gluey. Keep the dough between 25°C and 28°C (77°F and 82°F), using shorter kneads and longer rests on warm days.

PRACTICAL TIPS

OIL A light film of oil keeps the dough manageable without stiffening it. I recommend using an oil that is very low in trans fat, such as rice bran oil or avocado oil. Oil your hands lightly to prevent the dough from sticking.

WORK-REST RHYTHM 3–5 minutes of kneading followed by a 5-minute rest is far more effective than one long slog.

Understanding the baker's percentage

In bread-making and professional baking, the baker's percentage (also called the baker's per cent) is a standard way of expressing ingredient quantities relative to the weight of the flour.

WHAT THE BAKER'S PERCENTAGE MEANS

- Flour is always 100 per cent.
- All other ingredients are expressed as a percentage of the flour weight.
- This makes it easier to scale recipes up or down and compare formulas.

For example, if a recipe calls for:

- 500 g (17.64 oz) flour (100%)
- 325 g (11.46 oz) water (65%)

The water percentage (65 per cent) tells you the dough's hydration level.
To scale the recipe up to 1000 g (35.27 oz) flour, simply do the following calculation:

1000 g × 65% = 650 g (22.93 oz) water

This system allows bakers to maintain consistent ratios regardless of batch size, making it invaluable for both home bakers and professionals.

Temperature and environment

ROOM TEMPERATURE

When I state 'room temperature' in the recipes, I mean 20–26°C (68–79°F). At this range, the dough ferments steadily – not too fast, not too slow.

If the weather is cold, things will take longer. If it's hotter, you may need to shorten the resting time. Rather than watching the clock, learn to watch the dough.

INGREDIENT TEMPERATURE

All ingredients should reach room temperature – ideally 20–24°C (68–75°F) – before mixing. At this temperature, the fat and water components form a smooth, stable emulsion that supports even gluten development. A consistent temperature also improves aeration: as the dough ferments, these fine air pockets expand uniformly, giving the bread its light and elastic crumb.

In winter, slightly warm the room or the mixing water. In summer, cool the water a little to keep the dough within range. Bring butter, cream and eggs to room temperature too – dough likes it when everything's the same temperature.

DESIRED DOUGH TEMPERATURE (DDT)

After kneading, I aim for a dough temperature of around 26°C (79°F). Use a digital thermometer to check the dough itself, not the bowl or the bench. This temperature helps the yeast and gluten develop in balance. If your dough is warmer or cooler, simply adjust the proofing time by small amounts.

As a general guide, cooler dough ferments more slowly and needs longer resting, while warmer dough ferments faster and needs less time. If your dough is around 22°C (72°F), expect the first proof to take roughly 30–40 per cent longer. If it's closer to 28°C (82°F), it may take about 25–30 per cent less time. For the final proof after shaping, cooler dough usually needs an extra 10–20 minutes, while warmer dough may need 5–15 minutes less. These are starting points only – always let the dough's look and feel be your final guide.

Proofing

FINAL PROOFING

For the final rise before baking, I aim for about 30°C (86°F) with around 75 per cent humidity. If your oven has a proofing function, that's ideal. If not, place a bowl of hot water inside the oven to create a warm, slightly humid environment. When the dough looks light and full, it's ready to bake.

FINGER TEST

Purpose: To check whether the dough is properly proofed.

HOW TO DO IT

- Lightly flour your finger.
- Gently poke the dough about 2 cm (¾ in) deep.
- Observe the dough's reaction.

RESULT	MEANING
Indentation springs back slowly	Dough is properly proofed
Indentation springs back immediately	Dough is under-proofed → needs more time
Indentation does not spring back	Dough is over-proofed → may collapse or bake poorly

The recipes in this book were tested in a 450 g (1 lb) Pullman tin (volume: 2285 ml/77.27 oz), but it's easy to adjust the quantity of ingredients for any tin you have at home. Here's how:

1. **Measure your tin's volume**

   BY SIZE (QUICK METHOD)

   For a fast approximation of your tin's volume, measure its internal dimensions with a ruler or tape measure.

   Multiply the tin's dimensions: length × width × height (in cm) to ascertain its volume in cubic centimetres (cc), which equals millilitres (ml). For example, my tin is 19.6 × 10.6 × 11 cm (7.72 × 4.17 × 4.33 in) = 2285 ml (77.27 oz)

   This technique is most accurate for Pullman-style tins with straight sides and sharp corners. While this method is less precise for tins with slanted sides, it's the perfect way to get a reliable figure in seconds without needing a scale or water.

   BY WEIGHT (MOST ACCURATE METHOD)

   The most accurate way to measure volume is with water.

   1 Place your empty bread tin on a digital kitchen scale and set it to zero (tare).
   2 Fill the tin to the very brim with water.
   3 The weight of the water in grams (g) equals your tin's volume in millilitres (ml).

   For example, if the water weighs 2285 g (80.6 oz), your tin's volume is 2285 ml (77.27 oz). (If your scale has a weight limit, you can do this in batches and add the weights together.)

2. **Choose the volume ratio**

   The volume ratio tells you how much dough to use in relation to your tin's size. A higher number means less dough; a lower number means more dough.

   The ratio depends on the style of bread you're baking:

   - Pullman (square) loaf: 3.8–4.0
   - Domed (mountain) loaf: 3.5–3.7

   (Lower ratio = denser bread; higher ratio = lighter bread)

   These ranges exist because different tins and loaf styles need different amounts of dough. Open tins need more dough to rise upwards and form a dome, while lidded tins need slightly less dough so the loaf expands neatly to fill the square shape without overflowing.

   If your loaf struggles to reach the lid or lacks height, try a slightly lower ratio (more dough). If it rises too much or overflows, use a slightly higher ratio (less dough). Over time, you'll learn how small adjustments affect both the shape and texture of your bread – and how to tailor each bake to your tin and your preferences.

3. **Calculate total dough weight**

   Dough weight (g) = tin volume (ml) ÷ volume ratio

   Example for a 2285 ml (77.27 oz) tin for a square loaf:
   2285 ÷ 3.8 = 601 g (21.2 oz) of final dough.

4. **Determine flour weight**

   Use the total baker's percentage from the recipe.
   Flour weight (g) = dough weight ÷ total baker's percentage

Example: The flour weight for a 601 g (21.2 oz) dough with a total baker's percentage of 209% = 601 ÷ 2.09 = 287 g (10.12 oz) flour.

5. **Calculate each ingredient**

   Ingredient weight (g) = flour weight × ingredient's baker's percentage

   Example using 287 g (10.12 oz) flour:

INGREDIENT	BAKER'S PERCENTAGE	CALCULATION	WEIGHT (G)	WEIGHT (OZ)
Bread flour	100%	287 × 1	287	10.12
Raw (demerara) sugar	8%	287 × 0.08	23	0.81
Water	80%	287 × 0.8	230	8.11
Cream	10%	287 × 0.1	29	1.02
Salt	2%	287 × 0.02	5.7	0.2
Butter	8%	287 × 0.08	23	0.81
Yeast	1.2%	287 × 0.012	3.4	0.12
Total dough weight			≈601	≈21.2

Round the numbers where it makes sense – a few tenths of a gram won't change the taste or texture noticeably.

This same method works for most recipes. Once you know your tin's volume and your recipe's total baker's percentage, you can adapt your dough to any tin size.

Happy baking.

CHAPTER ONE

SHOKUPAN

CHAPTER ONE

SHOKUPAN

食
パ
ン

Written as 食パン (eating bread), shokupan is the thick slice of toast under a slab of butter and anko (red bean paste) in a kissaten (coffee shop); the neatly wrapped loaf carried home from a neighbourhood bakery, each family loyal to its own for reasons no one can quite explain; the softness, the crust, the taste that reminds them of childhood.

Shokupan's story begins in the Meiji era, when bakers like Uchiki Pan in Yokohama tried to bake something familiar for foreign settlers. But its popularity was forged later, in the rebuilding of Japan after World War II. With rice in short supply, bread became a lifeline. Soft white loaves made from imported American wheat appeared in kyushoku (school lunches), feeding a generation that didn't choose bread but was raised by it. For them, shokupan wasn't a novelty or a Western import; it was comfort, survival and, eventually, the taste of home.

That emotional connection, the pursuit of 'fuwa fuwa' (fluffiness) and 'mochi-mochi' (soft-chew), lingers in every loaf. Shokupan is all about that dimple when you press your thumb into it. The key is the tangzhong or yudane method (see page 22), a cooked flour paste that locks in moisture, and the relentless kneading that builds a dough so strong it can be stretched thin enough to become see-through.

There are two archetypes: yamagata (山型), the round-topped mountain loaf, meant for tearing and toasting; and kakugata (角型), the square, lidded Pullman loaf, designed as the foundation for the perfect sandwich. There's even a persistent wartime urban legend that the kakugata's square shape was born from soldiers baking dough inside rectangular battery cases. While the military did indeed invent a method for 'electric bread' (a technology that actually gave birth to panko breadcrumbs), the square shokupan is simply a descendant of the American Pullman tin, originally designed to stack efficiently in railway dining cars.

Shokupan is such a big part of daily life in Japan that people even have strong preferences about the thickness of the bread slices. Whether you buy it pre-sliced or have it sliced at the shop, the standard thicknesses are always the same: 4-slice, 6-slice or 8-slice. Ask any Japanese person, 'Which slice thickness do you like?' They will almost certainly answer with one of these three options. (My favourite is 8-slice – it gets nicely crisp when toasted while maintaining that good bread texture.)

This chapter is about mastering the foundation of the loaf that helped build postwar Japan, an icon that remains the soul of the Japanese morning.

SHOKUPAN

SHOKUPAN

食パン

In Japan, breakfast traditions typically fall into two camps: bread or rice. My family was firmly on team bread, and shokupan was always on our table. On weekends, we would pick up a fresh loaf from the bakery and have it for breakfast. The flavour and texture were so satisfying that I often ate several slices just as they were: no butter, no jam – the way you might savour a freshly made shio onigiri (salted rice ball).

This shokupan uses the yudane method (see page 22) – a simple scalding technique that keeps the bread soft for days without additives. Unlike tangzhong, yudane requires no saucepan or thermometer – just boiling water poured straight over the flour.

MAKES 1 STANDARD LOAF

YUDANE (MAKE AHEAD)

59 g (2.08 oz) bread flour	(20%)
6 g (0.21 oz) raw (demerara) sugar	(2%)
88 g (3.1 oz) boiling water	(30%)

FINAL DOUGH (ADDITIONS)

29 g (1.02 oz) cream (40% milkfat)	(10%)
147 g (5.19 oz) water	(50%)
235 g (8.29 oz) bread flour, plus extra for dusting	(80%)
18 g (0.63 oz) raw (demerara) sugar	(6%)
6 g (0.21 oz) fine sea salt	(2%)
4 g (0.14 oz) osmotolerant instant dry yeast	(1.2%)
24 g (0.85 oz) unsalted butter, softened	(8%)

(Values in parentheses indicate baker's percentages)

TIN DIMENSIONS WITH LID

196 × 106 × 110 mm (7.72 × 4.17 × 4.33 in)

Day 1

MAKE THE YUDANE

1 Warm a bowl using hot water, then dry it thoroughly.

2 Place the flour and raw sugar in the bowl and mix well. Add the boiling water in one swift motion, ensuring it evenly coats the flour.

3 While the bowl is still warm, mix the dough with a wooden spatula until it comes together into a cohesive lump.

4 Cover the bowl with plastic wrap, pressing it directly onto the surface of the yudane to prevent a crust forming. Once cooled to body temperature, refrigerate overnight to rest. (Yudane can be stored in the fridge for up to 3 days.)

Day 2

MIX THE FINAL DOUGH

5 Place the yudane, cream and water in the bowl of a stand mixer fitted with the dough hook, followed by the flour, sugar, salt and yeast. Mix on speed 3 (low) for 5 minutes. Increase to speed 6 (medium–high) and mix for 20 minutes, or until the dough starts coming together. Gradually add the softened butter and continue mixing. In the final stage of mixing, the dough will come together into a lump and begin slapping against the bowl as it separates from the side. The finished dough should be glossy and pass a windowpane test (stretching it thin enough to let light through without tearing).

Desired final dough temperature: 26°C (79°F).

FIRST PROOF

6 Cover the bowl with a damp tea towel and proof the dough for 30 minutes. Perform a fold by stretching one side of the dough up out of the bowl and folding it down over the remaining dough in the bowl. Cover and proof for another 30 minutes.

DIVIDE AND REST

7 Turn the dough out onto the bench and divide into two equal pieces. Round each piece gently by placing your palm over the dough and rolling it taut against the surface of the bench. Cover with the tea towel and rest on the bench for 20 minutes to relax the gluten.

↓ RECIPE CONTINUES

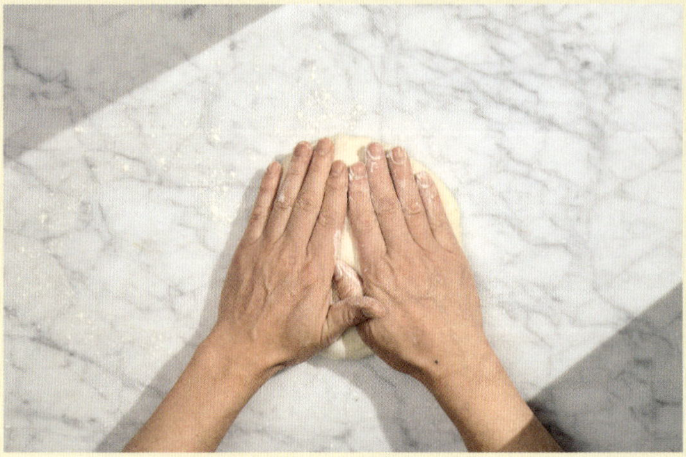

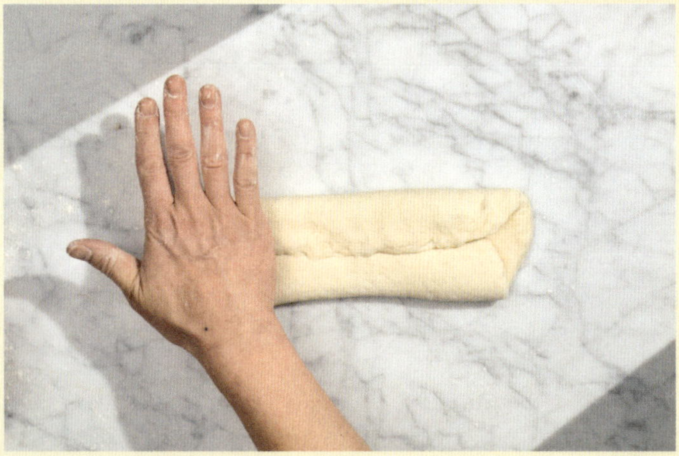
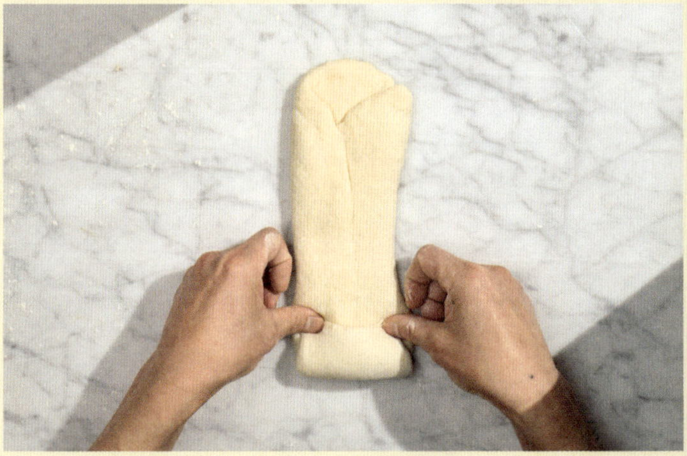

SN2066
450g

SN2066
450g

SN2066
450g

SN2066
450g

SHAPE

8 Lightly flour the bench and place the dough seam side up. Working with one piece of dough at a time, press down gently to release any air, then roll the dough into a rectangle about 30 cm (12 in) long (roughly three times the width of your loaf tin).

9 With a long edge facing you, fold the dough into thirds like a letter. The ends of the folded piece should be slightly narrower than the width of your tin (about 10 cm/4 in for the tin used in this book).

10 Press your palm along the length of the dough to help seal it, then roll it up into a log with moderate tension – not too tight and not too loose. The dough should feel springy but not stretched. Pinch the end to seal, then repeat with the remaining piece of dough.

11 Place both logs of dough seam side down and with the coils facing outwards in a greased 196 × 106 × 110 mm (7.72 × 4.17 × 4.33 in) Pullman loaf tin.

FINAL PROOF

12 Close the lid and proof at 30°C (86°F) for 60–90 minutes (see page 27), until the dough reaches about 8.5-tenths of the tin height.

BAKE AND SERVE

13 Preheat the oven to 180°C (356°F) fan-forced.

14 Bake for 30 minutes with the lid on. Remove the tin from the oven and tap the bottom of the tin firmly on the bench. Open the lid and remove the loaf immediately to prevent moisture build-up. Transfer the loaf to a wire cooling rack.

15 Once completely cooled, slice the shokupan to your preferred thickness (it's easier to slice thinly the day after baking).

STORE

16 Place the shokupan in an airtight container and keep at room temperature in a cool, dry place for 2–3 days. For longer storage, freeze individual slices, wrapped tightly in plastic wrap or foil (foil is preferred for faster freezing and better flavour retention), then place in a freezer-safe bag and seal. Toast directly from frozen (lightly misting the bread with water before toasting helps retain moisture) or thaw at room temperature and use in honey butter toast (see page 79), French toast (see page 86) or similar preparations.

NOTE

If kneading by hand, scale all ingredients by 15 per cent as you will lose approximately this amount of dough on your hands, mixing bowl and bench.

BLACK SUGAR SHOKUPAN

KOKUTO SHOKUPAN

黒糖食パン

Kokuto, also known as Okinawan black sugar, is a traditional unrefined sugar made from pure sugarcane juice. It has a deep molasses-like flavour, rich aroma and soft texture. Kokuto adds natural sweetness and complexity to baked goods, transforming everyday bread into something with a little extra character, much like the Okinawan Eisa folk dance. It's an easy way to step beyond the classic white shokupan into something more flavourful.

MAKES 1 STANDARD LOAF

YUDANE (MAKE AHEAD)

59 g (2.08 oz) bread flour	(20%)
6 g (0.21 oz) kokuto (black sugar)	(2%)
88 g (3.1 oz) boiling water	(30%)

FINAL DOUGH (ADDITIONS)

29 g (1.02 oz) cream (40% milkfat)	(10%)
147 g (5.19 oz) water	(50%)
235 g (8.29 oz) bread flour, plus extra for dusting	(80%)
18 g (0.63 oz) kokuto (black sugar)	(6%)
6 g (0.21 oz) fine sea salt	(2%)
4 g (0.14 oz) osmotolerant instant dry yeast	(1.2%)
24 g (0.85 oz) unsalted butter, softened	(8%)

(Values in parentheses indicate baker's percentages)

TIN DIMENSIONS WITH LID

196 × 106 × 110 mm
(7.72 × 4.17 × 4.33 in)

Day 1

MAKE THE YUDANE

1. Warm a bowl using hot water, then dry it thoroughly.
2. Place the flour and kokuto in the bowl and mix well. Add the boiling water in one swift motion, ensuring it evenly coats the flour.
3. While the bowl is still warm, mix the dough with a wooden spatula until it comes together into a cohesive lump.
4. Cover the bowl with plastic wrap, pressing it directly onto the surface of the yudane to prevent a crust forming. Once cooled to body temperature, refrigerate overnight to rest. (Yudane can be stored in the fridge for up to 3 days.)

Day 2

MIX THE FINAL DOUGH

5. Place the yudane, cream and water in the bowl of a stand mixer fitted with the dough hook, followed by the flour, kokuto, salt and yeast. Mix on speed 3 (low) for 5 minutes. Increase to speed 6 (medium–high) and mix for 20 minutes, or until the dough starts coming together. Gradually add the softened butter and continue mixing. In the final stage of mixing, the dough will come together into a lump and begin slapping against the bowl as it separates from the side. The finished dough should be glossy and pass a windowpane test (stretching it thin enough to let light through without tearing).

Desired final dough temperature: 26°C (79°F).

FIRST PROOF

6. Cover the bowl with a damp tea towel and proof the dough for 30 minutes. Perform a fold by stretching one side of the dough up out of the bowl and folding it down over the remaining dough in the bowl.

DIVIDE AND REST

7. Turn the dough out onto the bench and divide into two equal pieces. Round each piece gently by placing your palm over the dough and rolling it taut against the surface of the bench. Cover with the tea towel and rest on the bench for 20 minutes to relax the gluten.

↓ RECIPE CONTINUES

SHAPE

8 Lightly flour the bench and place the dough seam side up. Working with one piece of dough at a time, press down gently to release any air, then roll the dough into a rectangle about 30 cm (12 in) long (roughly three times the width of your loaf tin).

9 With a long edge facing you, fold the dough into thirds like a letter. The ends of the folded piece should be slightly narrower than the width of your tin (about 10 cm/4 in for the tin used in this book).

10 Press your palm along the length of the dough to help seal it, then roll it up into a log with moderate tension – not too tight and not too loose. The dough should feel springy but not stretched. Pinch the end to seal, then repeat with the remaining piece of dough.

11 Place both logs of dough seam side down and with the coils facing outwards in a greased 196 × 106 × 110 mm (7.72 × 4.17 × 4.33 in) Pullman loaf tin.

FINAL PROOF

12 Close the lid and proof at 30°C (86°F) for 60–90 minutes (see page 27), until the dough reaches about 8.5-tenths of the tin height.

BAKE AND SERVE

13 Preheat the oven to 180°C (356°F) fan-forced.

14 Bake for 30 minutes with the lid on. Remove the tin from the oven and tap the bottom of the tin firmly on the bench. Open the lid and remove the loaf immediately to prevent moisture build-up. Transfer the loaf to a wire cooling rack.

15 Once completely cooled, slice the shokupan to your preferred thickness (it's easier to slice thinly the day after baking). Enjoy fresh or toasted with butter, jam or anko (see page 80). It's also ideal for fruit sandwiches.

STORE

16 Place the shokupan in an airtight container and keep at room temperature in a cool, dry place for 2–3 days. For longer storage, freeze individual slices, wrapped tightly in plastic wrap or foil (foil is preferred for faster freezing and better flavour retention), then place in a freezer-safe bag and seal. Toast directly from frozen (lightly misting the bread with water before toasting helps retain moisture), or thaw at room temperature.

NOTE

If kneading by hand, scale all ingredients by 15 per cent as you will lose approximately this amount of dough on your hands, mixing bowl and bench.

BLACK SESAME AND HONEY SHOKUPAN

KUROGOMA HACHIMITSU SHOKUPAN

黒ごまハチミツ食パン

Black sesame and honey is a pairing with deep roots. The roasted bitterness of sesame has long been balanced with natural sweeteners in Japanese and Chinese confectionery, as well as in Middle Eastern tahini–honey traditions. Think goma-dare (sweet sesame sauce), kurogoma (black sesame) brittle made with syrup, or mochi, lightly sweetened. In this recipe, we use toasted black tahini paste for a richer, nuttier flavour than regular tahini, and leatherwood honey – but any honey you have on hand works beautifully.

MAKES 1 STANDARD LOAF

YUDANE (MAKE AHEAD)

59 g (2.08 oz) bread flour	(20%)
6 g (0.21 oz) raw (demerara) sugar	(2%)
88 g (3.1 oz) boiling water	(30%)

FINAL DOUGH (ADDITIONS)

29 g (1.02 oz) cream (40% milkfat)	(10%)
44 g (1.55 oz) honey	(15%)
29 g (1.02 oz) black tahini paste	(10%)
130 g (4.59 oz) water	(44%)
235 g (8.29 oz) bread flour, plus extra for dusting	(80%)
18 g (0.63 oz) raw (demerara) sugar	(6%)
6 g (0.21 oz) fine sea salt	(2%)
4 g (0.14 oz) osmotolerant instant dry yeast	(1.2%)
24 g (0.85 oz) unsalted butter, softened	(8%)
47 g (1.66 oz) black sesame seeds, toasted	(16%)

(Values in parentheses indicate baker's percentages)

TIN DIMENSIONS WITH LID

196 × 106 × 110 mm
(7.72 × 4.17 × 4.33 in)

Day 1

MAKE THE YUDANE

1 Warm a bowl using hot water, then dry it thoroughly.

2 Place the flour and raw sugar in the bowl and mix well. Add the boiling water in one swift motion, ensuring it evenly coats the flour.

3 While the bowl is still warm, mix the dough with a wooden spatula until it comes together into a cohesive lump.

4 Cover the bowl with plastic wrap, pressing it directly onto the surface of the yudane to prevent a crust forming. Once cooled to body temperature, refrigerate overnight to rest. (Yudane can be stored in the fridge for up to 3 days.)

Day 2

MIX THE FINAL DOUGH

5 Place the yudane, cream, honey, black tahini paste and water in the bowl of a stand mixer fitted with the dough hook, followed by the flour, sugar, salt and yeast. Mix on speed 3 (low) for 5 minutes. Increase to speed 6 (medium–high) and mix for 20 minutes, or until the dough starts coming together. Gradually add the softened butter and continue mixing. In the final stage of mixing, the dough will come together into a lump and begin slapping against the bowl as it separates from the side. Add the toasted black sesame seeds and mix on speed 2 (low) until they are dispersed throughout the dough. The finished dough should be glossy and pass a windowpane test (stretching it thin enough to let light through without tearing).

Desired final dough temperature: 26°C (79°F).

FIRST PROOF

6 Cover the bowl with a damp tea towel and proof the dough for 30 minutes. Perform a fold by stretching one side of the dough up out of the bowl and folding it down over the remaining dough in the bowl.

DIVIDE AND REST

7 Turn the dough out onto the bench and divide into two equal pieces. Round each piece gently by placing your palm over the dough and rolling it taut against the surface of the bench. Cover with the tea towel and rest on the bench for 20 minutes to relax the gluten.

SHAPE

8 Lightly flour the bench and place the dough seam side up. Working with one piece of dough at a time, press down gently to release any air, then roll the dough into a rectangle about 30 cm (12 in) long (roughly three times the width of your loaf tin).

↓ RECIPE CONTINUES

9 With a long edge facing you, fold the dough into thirds like a letter. The ends of the folded piece should be slightly narrower than the width of your tin (about 10 cm/4 in for the tin used in this book).

10 Press your palm along the length of the dough to help seal it, then roll it up into a log with moderate tension – not too tight and not too loose. The dough should feel springy but not stretched. Pinch the end to seal, then repeat with the remaining piece of dough.

11 Place both logs of dough seam side down and with the coils facing outwards in a greased 196 × 106 × 110 mm (7.72 × 4.17 × 4.33 in) Pullman loaf tin.

FINAL PROOF

12 Close the lid and proof at 30°C (86°F) for 60–90 minutes (see page 27), until the dough reaches about 8.5-tenths of the tin height.

BAKE AND SERVE

13 Preheat the oven to 180°C (356°F) fan-forced.

14 Bake for 30 minutes with the lid on. Remove the tin from the oven and tap the bottom of the tin firmly on the bench. Open the lid and remove the loaf immediately to prevent moisture build-up. Transfer the loaf to a wire cooling rack.

15 Once completely cooled, slice the shokupan to your preferred thickness (it's easier to slice thinly the day after baking). Enjoy fresh or toasted with butter and honey. It's also ideal for salad sandwiches.

STORE

16 Place the shokupan in an airtight container and keep at room temperature in a cool, dry place for 2–3 days. For longer storage, freeze individual slices, wrapped tightly in plastic wrap or foil (foil is preferred for faster freezing and better flavour retention), then place in a freezer-safe bag and seal. Toast directly from frozen (lightly misting the bread with water before toasting helps retain moisture), or thaw at room temperature.

NOTE

If kneading by hand, scale all ingredients by 15 per cent as you will lose approximately this amount of dough on your hands, mixing bowl and bench.

MATCHA SHOKUPAN

MATCHA SHOKUPAN

抹茶食パン

If red and white are the colours of Japan, then matcha is its green companion. Matcha pairs exceptionally well with dairy – butter, milk, condensed milk, even cream cheese – giving matcha shokupan a clean, nuanced flavour you can't get anywhere else. It's an easy way to bring Japanese tea culture into everyday baking, and visually, a good loaf looks like sliceable jade when you use high-quality, ceremonial-grade matcha powder.

And if you're like me, most of the time you'll end up using that half-forgotten matcha in the pantry – the one too old to drink but too expensive to throw away. It works perfectly in baked bread.

MAKES 1 STANDARD LOAF

YUDANE (MAKE AHEAD)

59 g (2.08 oz) bread flour	(20%)
6 g (0.21 oz) raw (demerara) sugar	(2%)
88 g (3.1 oz) boiling water	(30%)

FINAL DOUGH (ADDITIONS)

9 g (0.32 oz) ceremonial-grade matcha powder	(3%)
235 g (8.29 oz) bread flour, plus extra for dusting	(80%)
29 g (1.02 oz) cream (40% milkfat)	(10%)
171 g (6.03 oz) water	(58%)
18 g (0.63 oz) raw (demerara) sugar	(6%)
6 g (0.21 oz) fine sea salt	(2%)
4 g (0.14 oz) osmotolerant instant dry yeast	(1.2%)
24 g (0.85 oz) unsalted butter, softened	(8%)

(Values in parentheses indicate baker's percentages)

TIN DIMENSIONS WITH LID

196 × 106 × 110 mm
(7.72 × 4.17 × 4.33 in)

Day 1

MAKE THE YUDANE

1 Warm a bowl using hot water, then dry it thoroughly.

2 Place the flour and raw sugar in the bowl and mix well. Add the boiling water in one swift motion, ensuring it evenly coats the flour.

3 While the bowl is still warm, mix the dough with a wooden spatula until it comes together into a cohesive lump.

4 Cover the bowl with plastic wrap, pressing it directly onto the surface of the yudane to prevent a crust forming. Once cooled to body temperature, refrigerate overnight to rest. (Yudane can be stored in the fridge for up to 3 days.)

Day 2

MIX THE FINAL DOUGH

5 In a separate bowl, sift the matcha powder into the flour and mix thoroughly to ensure even distribution.

6 Place the yudane, cream and water in the bowl of a stand mixer fitted with the dough hook, followed by the matcha-flour mixture, sugar, salt and yeast. Mix on speed 3 (low) for 5 minutes. Increase to speed 6 (medium–high) and mix for 20 minutes, or until the dough starts coming together. Gradually add the softened butter and continue mixing. In the final stage of mixing, the dough will come together into a lump and begin slapping against the bowl as it separates from the side. The finished dough should be glossy and pass a windowpane test (stretching it thin enough to let light through without tearing).

Desired final dough temperature: 26°C (79°F).

FIRST PROOF

7 Cover the bowl with a damp tea towel and proof the dough for 30 minutes. Perform a fold by stretching one side of the dough up out of the bowl and folding it down over the remaining dough in the bowl.

DIVIDE AND REST

8 Turn the dough out onto the bench and divide into two equal pieces. Round each piece gently by placing your palm over the dough and rolling it taut against the surface of the bench. Cover with the tea towel and rest on the bench for 20 minutes to relax the gluten.

↓ RECIPE CONTINUES

SHAPE

9 Lightly flour the bench and place the dough seam side up. Working with one piece of dough at a time, press down gently to release any air, then roll the dough into a rectangle about 30 cm (12 in) long (roughly three times the width of your loaf tin).

10 With a long edge facing you, fold the dough into thirds like a letter. The ends of the folded piece should be slightly narrower than the width of your tin (about 10 cm/4 in for the tin used in this book).

11 Press your palm along the length of the dough to help seal it, then roll it up into a log with moderate tension – not too tight and not too loose. The dough should feel springy but not stretched. Pinch the end to seal, then repeat with the remaining piece of dough.

12 Place both logs of dough seam side down and with the coils facing outwards in a greased 196 × 106 × 110 mm (7.72 × 4.17 × 4.33 in) Pullman loaf tin.

FINAL PROOF

13 Close the lid and proof at 30°C (86°F) for 60–90 minutes (see page 27), until the dough reaches about 9-tenths of the tin height.

BAKE AND SERVE

14 Preheat the oven to 180°C (356°F) fan-forced.

15 Bake for 30 minutes with the lid on. Remove the tin from the oven and tap the bottom of the tin firmly on the bench. Open the lid and remove the loaf immediately to prevent moisture build-up. Transfer the loaf to a wire cooling rack.

16 Once completely cooled, slice the shokupan to your preferred thickness (it's easier to slice thinly the day after baking). Enjoy fresh or toasted with butter or jam. Spread with anko (see page 80) and whipped cream for serving with tea, or use to make fruit sandwiches.

STORE

17 Place the shokupan in an airtight container and keep at room temperature in a cool, dry place for 2–3 days. For longer storage, freeze individual slices, wrapped tightly in plastic wrap or foil (foil is preferred for faster freezing and better flavour retention), then place in a freezer-safe bag and seal. Toast directly from frozen (lightly misting the bread with water before toasting helps retain moisture), or thaw at room temperature.

NOTE

If kneading by hand, scale all ingredients by 15 per cent as you will lose approximately this amount of dough on your hands, mixing bowl and bench.

HOJICHA SHOKUPAN

HOJICHA SHOKUPAN

ほうじ茶食パン

If matcha is Kambei – the steady, noble main character in *Seven Samurai* – then hojicha is Kyuzo, the quiet master who lets everyone else talk while he simply gets things done. Where matcha is bright, grassy and upfront, hojicha is roasted, nutty and low-key comforting – more toasted rice than fresh meadow. It's also far more forgiving on the wallet. Using high-grade hojicha, especially first-flush leaves or stems, gives this loaf a deeper aroma and that calm, toasty warmth. Bake it once and you'll see why Kyuzo – and hojicha – steal the scene without ever raising their voice.

MAKES 1 STANDARD LOAF

YUDANE (MAKE AHEAD)

59 g (2.08 oz) bread flour	(20%)
6 g (0.21 oz) raw (demerara) sugar	(2%)
88 g (3.1 oz) boiling water	(30%)

FINAL DOUGH (ADDITIONS)

9 g (0.32 oz) hojicha powder	(3%)
235 g (8.29 oz) bread flour, plus extra for dusting	(80%)
29 g (1.02 oz) cream (40% milkfat)	(10%)
171 g (6.03 oz) water	(58%)
18 g (0.63 oz) raw (demerara) sugar	(6%)
6 g (0.21 oz) fine sea salt	(2%)
4 g (0.14 oz) osmotolerant instant dry yeast	(1.2%)
24 g (0.85 oz) unsalted butter, softened	(8%)

(Values in parentheses indicate baker's percentages)

TIN DIMENSIONS WITH LID

196 × 106 × 110 mm
(7.72 × 4.17 × 4.33 in)

Day 1

MAKE THE YUDANE

1 Warm a bowl using hot water, then dry it thoroughly.

2 Place the flour and raw sugar in the bowl and mix well. Add the boiling water in one swift motion, ensuring it evenly coats the flour.

3 While the bowl is still warm, mix the dough with a wooden spatula until it comes together into a cohesive lump.

4 Cover the bowl with plastic wrap, pressing it directly onto the surface of the yudane to prevent a crust forming. Once cooled to body temperature, refrigerate overnight to rest. (Yudane can be stored in the fridge for up to 3 days.)

Day 2

MIX THE FINAL DOUGH

5 In a separate bowl, sift the hojicha powder into the flour and mix thoroughly to ensure even distribution.

6 Place the yudane, cream and water in the bowl of a stand mixer fitted with the dough hook, followed by the hojicha–flour mixture, sugar, salt and yeast. Mix on speed 3 (low) for 5 minutes. Increase to speed 6 (medium–high) and mix for 20 minutes, or until the dough starts coming together. Gradually add the softened butter and continue mixing. In the final stage of mixing, the dough will come together into a lump and begin slapping against the bowl as it separates from the side. The finished dough should be glossy and pass a windowpane test (stretching it thin enough to let light through without tearing).

Desired final dough temperature: 26°C (79°F).

FIRST PROOF

7 Cover the bowl with a damp tea towel and proof the dough for 30 minutes. Perform a fold by stretching one side of the dough up out of the bowl and folding it down over the remaining dough in the bowl.

DIVIDE AND REST

8 Turn the dough out onto the bench and divide into two equal pieces. Round each piece gently by placing your palm over the dough and rolling it taut against the surface of the bench. Cover with the tea towel and rest on the bench for 20 minutes to relax the gluten.

↓ RECIPE CONTINUES

SHAPE

9 Lightly flour the bench and place the dough seam side up. Working with one piece of dough at a time, press down gently to release any air, then roll the dough into a rectangle about 30 cm (12 in) long (roughly three times the width of your loaf tin).

10 With a long edge facing you, fold the dough into thirds like a letter. The ends of the folded piece should be slightly narrower than the width of your tin (about 10 cm/4 in for the tin used in this book).

11 Press your palm along the length of the dough to help seal it, then roll it up into a log with moderate tension – not too tight and not too loose. The dough should feel springy but not stretched. Pinch the end to seal, then repeat with the remaining piece of dough.

12 Place both logs of dough seam side down and with the coils facing outwards in a greased 196 × 106 × 110 mm (7.72 × 4.17 × 4.33 in) Pullman loaf tin.

FINAL PROOF

13 Close the lid and proof at 30°C (86°F) for 60–90 minutes (see page 27), until the dough reaches about 9-tenths of the tin height.

BAKE AND SERVE

14 Preheat the oven to 180°C (356°F) fan-forced.

15 Bake for 30 minutes with the lid on. Remove the tin from the oven and tap the bottom of the tin firmly on the bench. Open the lid and remove the loaf immediately to prevent moisture build-up. Transfer the loaf to a wire cooling rack.

16 Once completely cooled, slice the shokupan to your preferred thickness (it's easier to slice thinly the day after baking). Enjoy without toasting to appreciate its gentle hojicha aroma, or spread with butter, anko (see page 80), whipped cream or honey.

STORE

17 Place the shokupan in an airtight container and keep at room temperature in a cool, dry place for 2–3 days. For longer storage, freeze individual slices, wrapped tightly in plastic wrap or foil (foil is preferred for faster freezing and better flavour retention), then place in a freezer-safe bag and seal. Toast directly from frozen (lightly misting the bread with water before toasting helps retain moisture), or thaw at room temperature.

NOTE

If kneading by hand, scale all ingredients by 15 per cent as you will lose approximately this amount of dough on your hands, mixing bowl and bench.

COFFEE SHOKUPAN

KOHI SHOKUPAN

コーヒー食パン

In Japan, coffee breads often rely on instant coffee, but in Melbourne – renowned for its specialty coffee culture – it felt natural to build this loaf on real espresso. At the bakery, we use single-origin coffee from Bench Coffee Co. because it's always within reach, but it's equally fine to use whatever you brew at home. The espresso gives the crumb a mellow roastiness without tipping into bitterness.

MAKES 1 STANDARD LOAF

YUDANE (MAKE AHEAD)

59 g (2.08 oz) bread flour	(20%)
6 g (0.21 oz) raw (demerara) sugar	(2%)
88 g (3.1 oz) boiling water	(30%)

FINAL DOUGH (ADDITIONS)

59 g (2.08 oz) espresso	(20%)
59 g (2.08 oz) cream (40% milkfat)	(20%)
80 g (2.82 oz) water	(27%)
235 g (8.29 oz) bread flour, plus extra for dusting	(80%)
18 g (0.63 oz) raw (demerara) sugar	(6%)
6 g (0.21 oz) fine sea salt	(2%)
4 g (0.14 oz) osmotolerant instant dry yeast	(1.2%)
24 g (0.85 oz) unsalted butter, softened	(8%)

(Values in parentheses indicate baker's percentages)

TIN DIMENSIONS WITH LID

196 × 106 × 110 mm
(7.72 × 4.17 × 4.33 in)

Day 1

MAKE THE YUDANE

1 Warm a bowl using hot water, then dry it thoroughly.

2 Place the flour and raw sugar in the bowl and mix well. Add the boiling water in one swift motion, ensuring it evenly coats the flour.

3 While the bowl is still warm, mix the dough with a wooden spatula until it comes together into a cohesive lump.

4 Cover the bowl with plastic wrap, pressing it directly onto the surface of the yudane to prevent a crust forming. Once cooled to body temperature, refrigerate overnight to rest. (Yudane can be stored in the fridge for up to 3 days.)

Day 2

5 Make the espresso and let it cool to room temperature.

MIX THE FINAL DOUGH

6 Place the yudane, cream, espresso and water in the bowl of a stand mixer fitted with the dough hook, followed by the flour, sugar, salt and yeast. Mix on speed 3 (low) for 5 minutes. Increase to speed 6 (medium–high) and mix for 20 minutes, or until the dough starts coming together. Gradually add the softened butter and continue mixing. In the final stage of mixing, the dough will come together into a lump and begin slapping against the bowl as it separates from the side. The finished dough should be glossy and pass a windowpane test (stretching it thin enough to let light through without tearing).

Desired final dough temperature: 26°C (79°F).

FIRST PROOF

7 Cover the bowl with a damp tea towel and proof the dough for 30 minutes. Perform a fold by stretching one side of the dough up out of the bowl and folding it down over the remaining dough in the bowl.

DIVIDE AND REST

8 Turn the dough out onto the bench and divide into two equal pieces. Round each piece gently by placing your palm over the dough and rolling it taut against the surface of the bench. Cover with the tea towel and rest on the bench for 20 minutes to relax the gluten.

↓ RECIPE CONTINUES

SHAPE

9 Lightly flour the bench and place the dough seam side up. Working with one piece of dough at a time, press down gently to release any air, then roll the dough into a rectangle about 30 cm (12 in) long (roughly three times the width of your loaf tin).

10 With a long edge facing you, fold the dough into thirds like a letter. The ends of the folded piece should be slightly narrower than the width of your tin (about 10 cm/4 in for the tin used in this book).

11 Press your palm along the length of the dough to help seal it, then roll it up into a log with moderate tension – not too tight and not too loose. The dough should feel springy but not stretched. Pinch the end to seal, then repeat with the remaining piece of dough.

12 Place both logs of dough seam side down and with the coils facing outwards in a greased 196 × 106 × 110 mm (7.72 × 4.17 × 4.33 in) Pullman loaf tin.

FINAL PROOF

13 Close the lid and proof at 30°C (86°F) for 60–90 minutes (see page 27), until the dough reaches about 9-tenths of the tin height.

BAKE AND SERVE

14 Preheat the oven to 180°C (356°F) fan-forced.

15 Bake for 30 minutes with the lid on. Remove the tin from the oven and tap the bottom of the tin firmly on the bench. Open the lid and remove the loaf immediately to prevent moisture build-up. Transfer the loaf to a wire cooling rack.

16 Once completely cooled, slice the shokupan to your preferred thickness (it's easier to slice thinly the day after baking). Enjoy fresh or toast and spread with butter, then sprinkle with cinnamon sugar for an extra treat.

STORE

17 Place the shokupan in an airtight container and keep at room temperature in a cool, dry place for 2–3 days. For longer storage, freeze individual slices, wrapped tightly in plastic wrap or foil (foil is preferred for faster freezing and better flavour retention), then place in a freezer-safe bag and seal. Toast directly from frozen (lightly misting the bread with water before toasting helps retain moisture), or thaw at room temperature.

NOTE

If kneading by hand, scale all ingredients by 15 per cent as you will lose approximately this amount of dough on your hands, mixing bowl and bench.

'NAMA CHOCOLATE' SHOKUPAN

NAMA CHOKORETO SHOKUPAN

生チョコレート食パン

Nama chocolate is one of Japan's most beloved edible souvenirs – the kind you see stacked in refrigerated airport displays, packed in neat square boxes and carted home in insulated bags like treasure. Silky, truffle-like and slightly boozy, it delivers a depth of chocolate flavour that regular bars can't match. Folding that richness into shokupan creates a loaf that feels simultaneously indulgent and playful: a cloud-soft crumb streaked with pockets of melting nama chocolate.

MAKES 1 STANDARD LOAF

YUDANE (MAKE AHEAD)

59 g (2.08 oz) bread flour	(20%)
6 g (0.21 oz) raw (demerara) sugar	(2%)
88 g (3.1 oz) boiling water	(30%)

NAMA CHOCOLATE

60 g (2.12 oz) cream (40% milkfat)	(25%)
100 g (3.53 oz) dark chocolate (55% cocoa solids), finely chopped	(40%)

FINAL DOUGH (ADDITIONS)

29 g (1.02 oz) full-cream (whole) milk	(10%)
112 g (3.95 oz) water	(38%)
235 g (8.29 oz) bread flour, plus extra for dusting	(80%)
18 g (0.63 oz) raw (demerara) sugar	(6%)
6 g (0.21 oz) salt	(2%)
4 g (0.14 oz) osmotolerant instant dry yeast	(1.2%)
24 g (0.85 oz) unsalted butter, softened	(8%)

(Values in parentheses indicate baker's percentages)

TIN DIMENSIONS WITH LID

196 × 106 × 110 mm (7.72 × 4.17 × 4.33 in)

Day 1

MAKE THE YUDANE

1 Warm a bowl using hot water, then dry it thoroughly.

2 Place the flour and raw sugar in the bowl and mix well. Add the boiling water in one swift motion, ensuring it evenly coats the flour.

3 While the bowl is still warm, mix the dough with a wooden spatula until it comes together into a cohesive lump.

4 Cover the bowl with plastic wrap, pressing it directly onto the surface of the yudane to prevent a crust forming. Once cooled to body temperature, refrigerate overnight to rest. (Yudane can be stored in the fridge for up to 3 days.)

Day 2

MAKE THE NAMA CHOCOLATE

5 Heat the cream in a saucepan over medium–low heat until just before boiling.

6 Place the dark chocolate in a heatproof bowl, then gradually pour in the cream. Whisk to melt and combine, then set aside to cool.

MIX THE FINAL DOUGH

7 Place the yudane, milk, water and one-third of the nama chocolate into the bowl of a stand mixer fitted with a dough hook, followed by the flour, sugar, salt and yeast. Mix on speed 3 (low) for 5 minutes. Increase to speed 6 (medium–high) and mix for 20 minutes, or until the dough starts coming together. Gradually add the softened butter and continue mixing. In the final stage of mixing, the dough will come together into a lump and begin slapping against the bowl as it separates from the side. The finished dough should be glossy and pass a windowpane test (stretching it thin enough to let light through without tearing).

Desired final dough temperature: 26°C (79°F).

FIRST PROOF

8 Cover the bowl with a damp tea towel and proof the dough for 30 minutes. Perform a fold by stretching one side of the dough up out of the bowl and folding it down over the remaining dough in the bowl.

DIVIDE AND REST

9 Turn the dough out onto the bench and divide into two equal pieces. Round each piece gently by placing your palm over the dough and rolling it taut against the surface of the bench. Cover with the tea towel and rest on the bench for 20 minutes to relax the gluten.

↓ RECIPE CONTINUES

SHAPE

10 Lightly flour the bench and place the dough seam side up. Working with one piece of dough at a time, press down gently to release any air, then roll the dough into a long oval about 30 cm (12 in) long (roughly three times the width of your loaf tin).

11 Use an offset spatula to spread half of the remaining nama chocolate down the length of the dough, keeping the chocolate in the middle. Repeat with the remaining dough and chocolate.

12 With a long edge facing you, fold the dough into thirds like a letter. The ends of the folded piece should be slightly narrower than the width of your tin (about 10 cm/4 in for the tin used in this book).

13 Press your palm along the length of the dough to help seal it, then roll it up into a log with moderate tension – not too tight and not too loose. The dough should feel springy but not stretched. Pinch the end to seal, then repeat with the remaining piece of dough.

14 Place both logs of dough seam side down and with the coils facing outwards in a greased 196 × 106 × 110 mm (7.72 × 4.17 × 4.33 in) Pullman loaf tin.

FINAL PROOF

15 Close the lid and proof at 30°C (86°F) for 60–90 minutes (see page 27), until the dough reaches about 9-tenths of the tin height.

BAKE AND SERVE

16 Preheat the oven to 180°C (356°F) fan-forced.

17 Bake for 30 minutes with the lid on. Remove the tin from the oven and tap the bottom of the tin firmly on the bench. Open the lid and remove the loaf immediately to prevent moisture build-up. Transfer the loaf to a wire cooling rack.

18 Once completely cooled, slice the shokupan to your preferred thickness (it's easier to slice thinly the day after baking). Enjoy fresh or toast and slather generously with butter for an indulgent dessert.

STORE

19 Place the shokupan in an airtight container and keep at room temperature in a cool, dry place for 2–3 days. For longer storage, freeze individual slices, wrapped tightly in plastic wrap or foil (foil is preferred for faster freezing and better flavour retention), then place in a freezer-safe bag and seal. Toast directly from frozen (lightly misting the bread with water before toasting helps retain moisture), or thaw at room temperature.

WHAT'S IN A NAMA?

'Nama' (生) literally means 'raw' in Japanese, but if something is labelled nama, consumers expect it to be fresher, moister, softer – almost melt-in-the-mouth. It taps into a preference for delicacy and immediacy, which is why you'll find 'nama everything': nama beer, nama pasta, nama caramel, nama ham, nama tea ... even a whole nama shokupan boom not long ago.

Nama chocolate, however, is legally defined. Since the 1980s, to call something 'nama chocolate' in Japan, it must meet the Fair Trade Commission's criteria:

- Chocolate base: at least 60 per cent of total weight
- Fresh cream: at least 10 per cent
- Water content: at least 10 per cent
- Must be dusted with cocoa/matcha/icing (confectioners') sugar or coated in chocolate with a filling that meets the above rules
- Within that, the chocolate base alone must account for 40 per cent of the total weight.

Which is why, in truth, our nama chocolate shokupan is more nama-style than legally 'nama chocolate'. But the spirit – soft, rich, melt-on-the-tongue – is what matters most.

NOTE

If kneading by hand, scale all ingredients by 15 per cent as you will lose approximately this amount of dough on your hands, mixing bowl and bench.

RAISIN SHOKUPAN

REZUN SHOKUPAN

レーズン食パン

Raisin bread has always been a divisive loaf in Japan. For many people, their first encounter was the dry, hard-crumb school-lunch version, leaving a lasting trauma. I think one in three – or maybe even one in two – people have memories of picking the raisins out of raisin bread when they were kids. I was definitely one of them. But as I get older, I've changed my mind. Toasted and spread with a good amount of butter, raisin bread becomes something unforgettable.

For me, the key is preparing the fruit properly. Instead of soaking the raisins in warm water, I steam them. It keeps their shape, enhances their aroma and gives a cleaner sweetness. When mixed into the dough, they stay plump without leaking moisture.

MAKES 1 STANDARD LOAF

YUDANE (MAKE AHEAD)

59 g (2.08 oz) bread flour	(20%)
6 g (0.21 oz) raw (demerara) sugar	(2%)
88 g (3.1 oz) boiling water	(30%)

FINAL DOUGH (ADDITIONS)

147 g (5.19 oz) raisins	(50%)
29 g (1.02 oz) cream (40% milkfat)	(10%)
147 g (5.19 oz) water	(50%)
235 g (8.29 oz) bread flour, plus extra for dusting	(80%)
18 g (0.63 oz) raw (demerara) sugar	(6%)
6 g (0.21 oz) fine sea salt	(2%)
4 g (0.14 oz) osmotolerant instant dry yeast	(1.2%)
24 g (0.85 oz) unsalted butter, softened	(8%)

(Values in parentheses indicate baker's percentages)

TIN DIMENSIONS WITH LID

196 × 106 × 110 mm
(7.72 × 4.17 × 4.33 in)

Day 1

MAKE THE YUDANE

1. Warm a bowl using hot water, then dry it thoroughly.
2. Place the flour and raw sugar in the bowl and mix well. Add the boiling water in one swift motion, ensuring it evenly coats the flour.
3. While the bowl is still warm, mix the dough with a wooden spatula until it comes together into a big lump.
4. Cover the bowl with plastic wrap, pressing it directly onto the surface of the yudane to prevent a crust forming. Once cooled to body temperature, refrigerate overnight to rest. (Yudane can be stored in the fridge for up to 3 days.)

Day 2

STEAM THE RAISINS

5. Fill the base of a saucepan with 5 cm (2 in) water and bring to the boil. Place the raisins in a single layer in a steamer basket and place the basket over the saucepan. Cover and steam for 15 minutes.
6. Spread the raisins on a tray without overlapping and set aside to cool.

MIX THE FINAL DOUGH

7. Place the yudane, cream and water into the bowl of a stand mixer fitted with a dough hook, followed by the flour, sugar, salt and yeast. Mix on speed 3 (low) for 5 minutes. Increase to speed 6 (medium–high) and mix for 20 minutes, or until the dough starts coming together. Gradually add the softened butter and continue mixing. In the final stage of mixing, the dough will come together into a lump and begin slapping against the bowl as it separates from the side. Add the raisins and mix on speed 2 (low) until they are dispersed throughout the dough. The finished dough should be glossy and pass a windowpane test (stretching it thin enough to let light through without tearing).

Desired final dough temperature: 26°C (79°F).

FIRST PROOF

8. Cover the bowl with a damp tea towel and proof the dough for 30 minutes. Perform a fold by stretching one side of the dough up out of the bowl and folding it down over the remaining dough in the bowl.

DIVIDE AND REST

9. Turn the dough out onto the bench and divide into two equal pieces. Round each piece gently by placing your palm over the dough and rolling it taut against the surface of the bench. Cover with the tea towel and rest on the bench for 20 minutes to relax the gluten.

↓ RECIPE CONTINUES

SHAPE

10 Lightly flour the bench and place the dough seam side up. Working with one piece of dough at a time, press down gently to release any air, then roll the dough into a rectangle about 30 cm (12 in) long (roughly three times the width of your loaf tin).

11 With a long edge facing you, fold the dough into thirds like a letter. The ends of the folded piece should be slightly narrower than the width of your tin (about 10 cm/4 in for the tin used in this book).

12 Press your palm along the length of the dough to help seal it, then roll it up into a log with moderate tension – not too tight and not too loose. The dough should feel springy but not stretched. Pinch the end to seal, then repeat with the remaining piece of dough.

13 Place both logs of dough seam side down and with the coils facing outwards in a greased 196 × 106 × 110 mm (7.72 × 4.17 × 4.33 in) Pullman loaf tin.

FINAL PROOF

14 Close the lid and proof at 30°C (86°F) for 60–90 minutes (see page 27), until the dough reaches about 8.5-tenths of the tin height.

BAKE AND SERVE

15 Preheat the oven to 180°C (356°F) fan-forced.

16 Bake for 30 minutes with the lid on. Remove the tin from the oven and tap the bottom of the tin firmly on the bench. Open the lid and remove the loaf immediately to prevent moisture build-up. Transfer the loaf to a wire cooling rack.

17 Once completely cooled, slice the shokupan to your preferred thickness (it's easier to slice thinly the day after baking). Enjoy fresh or toast and serve with butter. Raisin shokupan is ideal for everyday breakfasts and lunchboxes.

STORE

18 Place the shokupan in an airtight container and keep at room temperature in a cool, dry place for 2–3 days. For longer storage, freeze individual slices, wrapped tightly in plastic wrap or foil (foil is preferred for faster freezing and better flavour retention), then place in a freezer-safe bag and seal. Toast directly from frozen (lightly misting the bread with water before toasting helps retain moisture), or thaw at room temperature.

RAISIN D'ÊTRE

Raisins' true breakthrough in Japan came after World War II. As part of the national school-lunch program, raisins were mixed into dry coppepan to boost calories and iron. For an entire generation, this was their first encounter with dried fruit.

From there, Japan did what it does best: refine. Bakers learnt to wash, blanch, steam and balance raisins like a craft ingredient, often blending varieties for depth, brightness and acidity. This refinement reached its peak in Ginza where Centre The Bakery's 60 per cent raisin shokupan regularly draws queues that extend around the block, while shops like Kimuraya and the depachika counters of Mitsukoshi and Matsuya department stores turn raisin loaves and raisin sandwiches into limited-edition commodities.

This evolution also intersects with Japan's modern gut-katsu (腸活) movement – an interest in digestive health that has boosted demand for dried fruits, nuts and natural sweetness over artificial. Raisins, rich in fibre and minerals, now fit naturally into that trend: nutrient-dense, satisfying and easy to integrate into daily eating.

NOTE

If kneading by hand, scale all ingredients by 15 per cent as you will lose approximately this amount of dough on your hands, mixing bowl and bench.

FRUIT SHOKUPAN

FURUTSU SHOKUPAN

フルーツ食パン

In Japan, fruit is something we treat with a bit of respect. Even when dried, it still carries the feeling of the season. In this shokupan, we infuse the bright aroma of Japanese yuzu to go with figs and apricots. Each slice will taste slightly different, and that variation is part of the pleasure. For me, this bread is about balancing the soft dough and subtle fruit, something you can enjoy any time of the day. Instead of soaking the fruit in warm water, we steam it. This keeps the pieces plump and aromatic without leaching flavour or diluting the dough.

MAKES 1 STANDARD LOAF

YUDANE (MAKE AHEAD)

59 g (2.08 oz) bread flour	(20%)
6 g (0.21 oz) raw (demerara) sugar	(2%)
88 g (3.1 oz) boiling water	(30%)

FINAL DOUGH (ADDITIONS)

50 g (1.76 oz) dried yuzu peel	(17%)
50 g (1.76 oz) dried figs	(17%)
50 g (1.76 oz) dried apricots	(17%)
29 g (1.02 oz) cream (40% milkfat)	(10%)
147 g (5.19 oz) water	(50%)
235 g (8.29 oz) bread flour, plus extra for dusting	(80%)
18 g (0.63 oz) raw (demerara) sugar	(6%)
6 g (0.21 oz) fine sea salt	(2%)
1 g (0.04 oz) ground cinnamon	(0.35%)
4 g (0.14 oz) osmotolerant instant dry yeast	(1.2%)
24 g (0.85 oz) unsalted butter, softened	(8%)

(Values in parentheses indicate baker's percentages)

TIN DIMENSIONS WITH LID

196 × 106 × 110 mm
(7.72 × 4.17 × 4.33 in)

Day 1

MAKE THE YUDANE

1. Warm a bowl using hot water, then dry it thoroughly.
2. Place the flour and raw sugar in the bowl and mix well. Add the boiling water in one swift motion, ensuring it evenly coats the flour.
3. While the bowl is still warm, mix the dough with a wooden spatula until it comes together into a big lump.
4. Cover the bowl with plastic wrap, pressing it directly onto the surface of the yudane to prevent a crust forming. Once cooled to body temperature, refrigerate overnight to rest. (Yudane can be stored in the fridge for up to 3 days.)

Day 2

CUT AND STEAM THE DRIED FRUIT

5. Chop the dried yuzu peel, figs and apricots into your preferred size.
6. Fill the base of a saucepan with 5 cm (2 in) water and bring to the boil. Place the dried fruit in a single layer in a steamer basket and place the basket over the saucepan. Cover and steam for 15 minutes.
7. Spread the fruit on a tray without overlapping and set aside to cool.

MIX THE FINAL DOUGH

8. Place the yudane, cream and water into the bowl of a stand mixer fitted with a dough hook, followed by the flour, sugar, salt, cinnamon and yeast. Mix on speed 3 (low) for 5 minutes. Increase to speed 6 (medium–high) and mix for 20 minutes, or until the dough starts coming together. Gradually add the softened butter and continue mixing. In the final stage of mixing, the dough will come together into a lump and begin slapping against the bowl as it separates from the side. Add the steamed fruit and mix on speed 2 (low), until it is dispersed throughout the dough. The finished dough should be glossy and pass a windowpane test (stretching it thin enough to let light through without tearing).

   Desired final dough temperature: 26°C (79°F).

FIRST PROOF

9. Cover the bowl with a damp tea towel and proof the dough for 30 minutes. Perform a fold by stretching one side of the dough up out of the bowl and folding it down over the remaining dough in the bowl.

DIVIDE AND REST

10. Turn the dough out onto the bench and divide into two equal pieces. Round each piece gently by placing your palm over the dough and rolling it taut against the surface of the bench. Cover with the tea towel and rest on the bench for 20 minutes to relax the gluten.

↓ RECIPE CONTINUES

SHAPE

11 Lightly flour the bench and place the dough seam side up. Working with one piece of dough at a time, press down gently to release any air, then roll the dough into a rectangle about 30 cm (12 in) long (roughly three times the width of your loaf tin).

12 With a long edge facing you, fold the dough into thirds like a letter. The ends of the folded piece should be slightly narrower than the width of your tin (about 10 cm/4 in for the tin used in this book).

13 Press your palm along the length of the dough to help seal it, then roll it up into a log with moderate tension – not too tight and not too loose. The dough should feel springy but not stretched. Pinch the end to seal, then repeat with the remaining piece of dough.

14 Place both logs of dough seam side down and with the coils facing outwards in a greased 196 × 106 × 110 mm (7.72 × 4.17 × 4.33 in) Pullman loaf tin.

FINAL PROOF

15 Close the lid and proof at 30°C (86°F) for 60–90 minutes (see page 27), until the dough reaches about 9-tenths of the tin height.

BAKE AND SERVE

16 Preheat the oven to 180°C (356°F) fan-forced.

17 Bake for 30 minutes with the lid on. Remove the tin from the oven and tap the bottom of the tin firmly on the bench. Open the lid and remove the loaf immediately to prevent moisture build-up. Transfer the loaf to a wire cooling rack.

18 Once completely cooled, slice the shokupan to your preferred thickness (it's easier to slice thinly the day after baking). Enjoy fresh with whipped cream or your favourite jam, or toast and serve with butter. It also pairs well with cheese as an accompaniment to wine.

STORE

19 Place the shokupan in an airtight container and keep at room temperature in a cool, dry place for 2–3 days. For longer storage, freeze individual slices, wrapped tightly in plastic wrap or foil (foil is preferred for faster freezing and better flavour retention), then place in a freezer-safe bag and seal. Toast directly from frozen (lightly misting the bread with water before toasting helps retain moisture), or thaw at room temperature.

NOTE

If kneading by hand, scale all ingredients by 15 per cent as you will lose approximately this amount of dough on your hands, mixing bowl and bench.

WHOLEMEAL SHOKUPAN

HORUMIRU SHOKUPAN

ホールミール食パン

In Japan's household spending survey conducted by the Ministry of Internal Affairs and Communications, bread purchases surpassed rice for the first time in 2011. In recent years, advances in baking techniques have led to a wave of high-quality breads made with Japanese-grown wheat, as well as delicious whole-grain loaves that cater to a more health-conscious crowd.

When I moved to Australia, I was amazed to discover just how many types of flour there are – and how many different styles and methods of bread-making exist. But wholemeal shokupan has always felt familiar to me as the healthy-ish bread I grew up with.

This loaf is baked without a lid.

MAKES 1 STANDARD LOAF

YUDANE (MAKE AHEAD)

65 g (2.29 oz) bread flour	(20%)
98 g (3.46 oz) boiling water	(30%)

FINAL DOUGH (ADDITIONS)

10 g (0.35 oz) diastatic malt extract	(3%)
65 g (2.29 oz) buttermilk	(20%)
114 g (4.02 oz) water	(35%)
195 g (6.88 oz) bread flour, plus extra for dusting	(60%)
65 g (2.29 oz) wholemeal (whole-wheat) flour	(20%)
6 g (0.21 oz) fine sea salt	(1.8%)
4 g (0.14 oz) instant dry yeast	(1.2%)
13 g (0.46 oz) unsalted butter, softened	(4%)

(Values in parentheses indicate baker's percentages)

TIN DIMENSIONS WITH LID

196 × 106 × 110 mm
(7.72 × 4.17 × 4.33 in)

Day 1

MAKE THE YUDANE

1 Warm a bowl using hot water, then dry it thoroughly.

2 Place the flour in the bowl and add the boiling water in one swift motion, ensuring it evenly coats the flour.

3 While the bowl is still warm, mix the dough with a wooden spatula until it comes together into a big lump.

4 Cover the bowl with plastic wrap, pressing it directly onto the surface of the yudane to prevent a crust forming. Once cooled to body temperature, refrigerate overnight to rest. (Yudane can be stored in the fridge for up to 3 days.)

Day 2

MIX THE FINAL DOUGH

5 Place the yudane, diastatic malt extract, buttermilk and water into the bowl of a stand mixer fitted with a dough hook, followed by the flours, salt and yeast. Mix on speed 3 (low) for 5 minutes. Increase to speed 6 (medium–high) and mix for 20 minutes, or until the dough starts coming together. Gradually add the softened butter and continue mixing. In the final stage of mixing, the dough will come together into a lump and begin slapping against the bowl as it separates from the side. The finished dough should be glossy and pass a windowpane test (stretching it thin enough to let light through without tearing).

Desired final dough temperature: 26°C (79°F).

FIRST PROOF

6 Cover the bowl with a damp tea towel and proof the dough for 30 minutes. Perform a fold by stretching one side of the dough up out of the bowl and folding it down over the remaining dough in the bowl.

DIVIDE AND REST

7 Turn the dough out onto the bench and divide into three equal pieces. Round each piece gently by placing your palm over the dough and rolling it taut against the surface of the bench. Cover with the tea towel and rest on the bench for 20 minutes to relax the gluten.

↓ RECIPE CONTINUES

SHAPE

8. Lightly flour the bench and place the dough seam side up. Working with one piece of dough at a time, press down gently to release any air, then roll the dough into a rectangle about 20 cm (8 in) long (roughly twice the width of your loaf tin).
9. With a long edge facing you, fold the dough into thirds like a letter. The ends of the folded piece should be slightly narrower than the width of your tin (about 10 cm/4 in for the tin used in this book).
10. Press your palm along the length of the dough to help seal it, then roll it up into a log with moderate tension – not too tight and not too loose. The dough should feel springy but not stretched. Pinch the end to seal, then repeat with the remaining two pieces of dough.
11. Place the logs of dough seam side down and with the coils facing outwards in a greased 196 × 106 × 110 mm (7.72 × 4.17 × 4.33 in) Pullman loaf tin.

FINAL PROOF

12. Close the lid and proof at 30°C (86°F) for 60–90 minutes (see page 27), until the dough reaches about 9.5-tenths of the tin height.

BAKE AND SERVE

13. Preheat the oven to 180°C (356°F) fan-forced.
14. Remove the lid and spray water over the surface of the dough.
15. Bake for 30 minutes with the lid off. Remove the tin from the oven and tap the bottom of the tin firmly on the bench. Remove the loaf immediately to prevent moisture build-up. Transfer the loaf to a wire cooling rack.
16. Once completely cooled, sliced to your preferred thickness (it's easier to slice thinly the day after baking). Enjoy fresh or toasted, use to make sandwiches or serve alongside meals.

STORE

17. Place the shokupan in an airtight container and keep at room temperature in a cool, dry place for 2–3 days. For longer storage, freeze individual slices, wrapped tightly in plastic wrap or foil (foil is preferred for faster freezing and better flavour retention), then place in a freezer-safe bag and seal. Toast directly from frozen (lightly misting the bread with water before toasting helps retain moisture), or thaw at room temperature.

NOTE

If kneading by hand, scale all ingredients by 15 per cent as you will lose approximately this amount of dough on your hands, mixing bowl and bench.

ENGLISH SHOKUPAN

IGIRISU SHOKUPAN

イギリス食パン

English shokupan is also baked without a lid, which allows the dough to rise freely and gives it a rounded top. It contains no sugar and very little fat, resulting in a light texture with a clean wheat flavour. The crust is thin and crisp, making it a versatile bread that toasts beautifully and works well for everyday sandwiches. Personally, I find it perfect for making toast. Don't forget to slice it thinly!

MAKES 1 STANDARD LOAF

YUDANE (MAKE AHEAD)

65 g (2.29 oz) bread flour	(20%)
98 g (3.46 oz) boiling water	(30%)

FINAL DOUGH (ADDITIONS)

10 g (0.35 oz) diastatic malt extract	(3%)
65 g (2.29 oz) buttermilk	(20%)
147 g (5.19 oz) water	(45%)
260 g (9.17 oz) bread flour, plus extra for dusting	(80%)
6 g (0.21 oz) fine sea salt	(2%)
4 g (0.14 oz) instant dry yeast	(1.2%)
13 g (0.46 oz) unsalted butter, softened	(4%)

(Values in parentheses indicate baker's percentages)

TIN DIMENSIONS WITH LID

196 × 106 × 110 mm
(7.72 × 4.17 × 4.33 in)

Day 1

MAKE THE YUDANE

1 Warm a bowl using hot water, then dry it thoroughly.

2 Place the flour in the bowl and add the boiling water in one swift motion, ensuring it evenly coats the flour.

3 While the bowl is still warm, mix the dough with a wooden spatula until it comes together into a big lump.

4 Cover the bowl with plastic wrap, pressing it directly onto the surface of the yudane to prevent a crust forming. Once cooled to body temperature, refrigerate overnight to rest. (Yudane can be stored in the fridge for up to 3 days.)

Day 2

MIX THE FINAL DOUGH

5 Place the yudane, diastatic malt extract, buttermilk and water into the bowl of a stand mixer fitted with a dough hook, followed by the flour, salt and yeast. Mix on speed 3 (low) for 5 minutes. Increase to speed 6 (medium–high) and mix for 20 minutes, or until the dough starts coming together. Gradually add the softened butter and continue mixing. In the final stage of mixing, the dough will come together into a lump and begin slapping against the bowl as it separates from the side. The finished dough should be glossy and pass a windowpane test (stretching it thin enough to let light through without tearing).

Desired final dough temperature: 26°C (79°F).

FIRST PROOF

6 Cover the bowl with a damp tea towel and proof the dough for 30 minutes. Perform a fold by stretching one side of the dough up out of the bowl and folding it down over the remaining dough in the bowl.

DIVIDE AND REST

7 Turn the dough out onto the bench and divide into three equal pieces. Round each piece gently by placing your palm over the dough and rolling it taut against the surface of the bench. Cover with the tea towel and rest on the bench for 20 minutes to relax the gluten.

↓ RECIPE CONTINUES

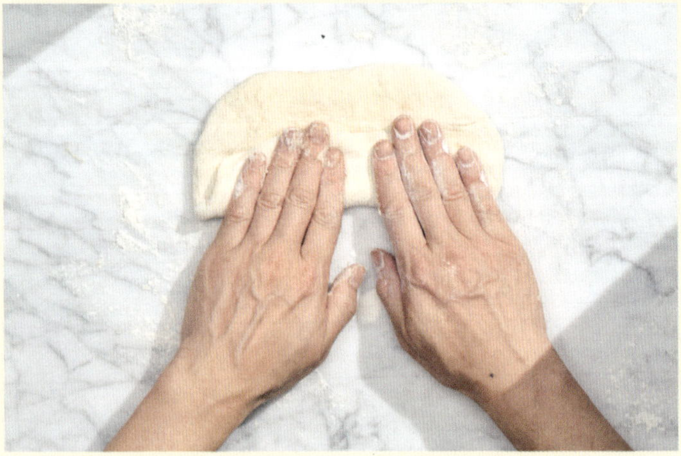

SHAPE

8 Lightly flour the bench and place the dough seam side up. Working with one piece of dough at a time, press down gently to release any air, then roll the dough into a rectangle about 20 cm (8 in) long (roughly twice the width of your loaf tin).

9 With a long edge facing you, fold the dough into thirds like a letter. The ends of the folded piece should be slightly narrower than the width of your tin (about 10 cm/4 in for the tin used in this book).

10 Press your palm along the length of the dough to help seal it, then roll it up into a log with moderate tension – not too tight and not too loose. The dough should feel springy but not stretched. Pinch the end to seal, then repeat with the remaining two pieces of dough.

11 Place the logs of dough seam side down and with the coils facing outwards in a greased 196 × 106 × 110 mm (7.72 × 4.17 × 4.33 in) Pullman loaf tin.

FINAL PROOF

12 Close the lid and proof at 30°C (86°F) for 60–90 minutes (see page 27), until the dough reaches about 9.5-tenths of the tin height.

BAKE AND SERVE

13 Preheat the oven to 180°C (356°F) fan-forced.

14 Remove the lid and spray water over the surface of the dough.

15 Bake for 30 minutes with the lid off. Remove the tin from the oven and tap the bottom of the tin firmly on the bench. Remove the loaf immediately to prevent moisture build-up. Transfer the loaf to a wire cooling rack.

16 Once completely cooled, slice the shokupan thinly (it's easier to do this the day after baking). This British-style bread is best toasted and spread with butter, and it also makes excellent toasted sandwiches.

STORE

17 Place the shokupan in an airtight container and keep at room temperature in a cool, dry place for 2–3 days. For longer storage, freeze individual slices, wrapped tightly in plastic wrap or foil (foil is preferred for faster freezing and better flavour retention), then place in a freezer-safe bag and seal. Toast directly from frozen (lightly misting the bread with water before toasting helps retain moisture), or thaw at room temperature.

NOTE

If kneading by hand, scale all ingredients by 15 per cent as you will lose approximately this amount of dough on your hands, mixing bowl and bench.

CHEESE SHOKUPAN

CHIZU SHOKUPAN

チーズ食パン

Cheese has long felt like a small luxury – something a bit richer, a bit special. If you want a little extra コク (koku, richness) or 旨味 (umami, flavour) in your bread, fold chunks of cheese into the shokupan dough to create pockets of melted goodness. It's perfect as a snack for kids, can be enjoyed for breakfast in various ways, or used as bread for sandwiches – a versatile and convenient loaf.

We recommend using several types of cheese, cut into fairly large pieces. Adjust the types and sizes to your liking; the recipe is forgiving and easy to personalise. Why not experiment and create your own original combination?

MAKES 1 STANDARD LOAF

YUDANE (MAKE AHEAD)

65 g (2.29 oz) bread flour	(20%)
98 g (3.46 oz) boiling water	(30%)

FINAL DOUGH (ADDITIONS)

10 g (0.35 oz) diastatic malt extract	(3%)
65 g (2.29 oz) buttermilk	(20%)
147 g (5.19 oz) water	(45%)
260 g (9.17 oz) bread flour, plus extra for dusting	(80%)
3 g (0.11 oz) fine sea salt	(1%)
4 g (0.14 oz) osmotolerant instant dry yeast	(1.2%)
13 g (0.46 oz) unsalted butter, softened	(4%)
176 g (6.21 oz) chunky cubed cheese (such as cheddar, gruyere, emmental or a mix)	(50 %)

(Values in parentheses indicate baker's percentages)

TIN DIMENSIONS WITH LID

196 × 106 × 110 mm
(7.72 × 4.17 × 4.33 in)

Day 1

MAKE THE YUDANE

1 Warm a bowl using hot water, then dry it thoroughly.

2 Place the flour in the bowl and add the boiling water in one swift motion, ensuring it evenly coats the flour.

3 While the bowl is still warm, mix the dough with a wooden spatula until it comes together into a big lump.

4 Cover the bowl with plastic wrap, pressing it directly onto the surface of the yudane to prevent a crust forming. Once cooled to body temperature, refrigerate overnight to rest. (Yudane can be stored in the fridge for up to 3 days.)

Day 2

MIX THE FINAL DOUGH

5 Place the yudane, diastatic malt extract, buttermilk and water into the bowl of a stand mixer fitted with a dough hook, followed by the flour, salt and yeast. Mix on speed 3 (low) for 5 minutes. Increase to speed 6 (medium–high) and mix for 20 minutes, or until the dough starts coming together. Gradually add the softened butter and continue mixing. In the final stage of mixing, the dough will come together into a lump and begin slapping against the bowl as it separates from the side. The finished dough should be glossy and pass a windowpane test (stretching it thin enough to let light through without tearing).

Desired final dough temperature: 26°C (79°F).

FIRST PROOF

6 Cover the bowl with a damp tea towel and proof the dough for 30 minutes. Perform a fold by stretching one side of the dough up out of the bowl and folding it down over the remaining dough in the bowl.

DIVIDE AND REST

7 Turn the dough out onto the bench and divide into three equal pieces. Round each piece gently by placing your palm over the dough and rolling it taut against the surface of the bench. Cover with the tea towel and rest on the bench for 20 minutes to relax the gluten.

SHAPE

8 Lightly flour the bench and place the dough seam side up. Working with one piece of dough at a time, press down gently to release any air, then roll the dough into an oval about 20 cm (8 in) long (roughly twice the width of your loaf tin).

↓ RECIPE CONTINUES

9 Dot one-third of the cheese over the dough, then fold the dough into thirds like a letter. The ends of the folded piece should be slightly narrower than the width of your tin (about 10 cm/4 in for the tin used in this book).

10 Press your palm along the length of the dough to help seal it, then roll it up into a log with moderate tension – not too tight and not too loose. The dough should feel springy but not stretched. Pinch the end to seal, then repeat with the remaining two pieces of dough and the cheese.

11 Place the logs of dough seam side down and with the coils facing outwards in a greased 196 × 106 × 110 mm (7.72 × 4.17 × 4.33 in) Pullman loaf tin.

FINAL PROOF

12 Close the lid and proof at 30°C (86°F) for 60–90 minutes (see page 27), until the dough reaches about 9.5-tenths of the tin height.

BAKE AND SERVE

13 Preheat the oven to 180°C (356°F) fan-forced.

14 Remove the lid and spray water over the surface of the dough.

15 Bake for 30 minutes with the lid off. Remove the tin from the oven and tap the bottom of the tin firmly on the bench. Remove the loaf immediately to prevent moisture build-up. Transfer the loaf to a wire cooling rack.

16 Once completely cooled, slice to your preferred thickness (it's easier to slice thinly the day after baking). Enjoy the cheesy shokupan on its own, or serve alongside a meal.

STORE

17 Place the shokupan in an airtight container and keep at room temperature in a cool, dry place for 2–3 days. For longer storage, freeze individual slices, wrapped tightly in plastic wrap or foil (foil is preferred for faster freezing and better flavour retention), then place in a freezer-safe bag and seal. Toast directly from frozen (lightly misting the bread with water before toasting helps retain moisture), or thaw at room temperature.

NOTE

If kneading by hand, scale all ingredients by 15 per cent as you will lose approximately this amount of dough on your hands, mixing bowl and bench.

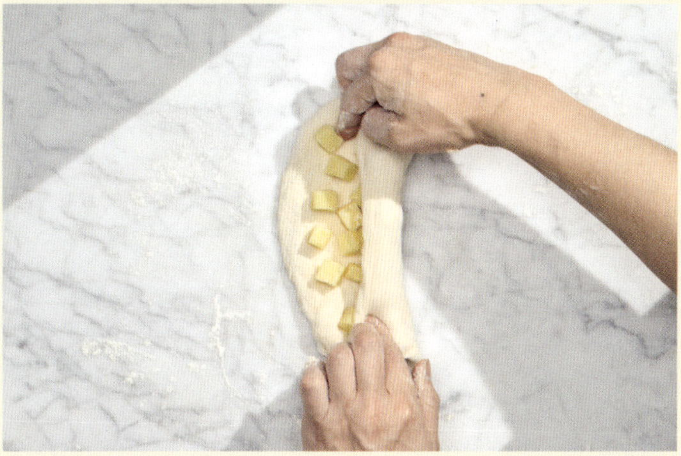

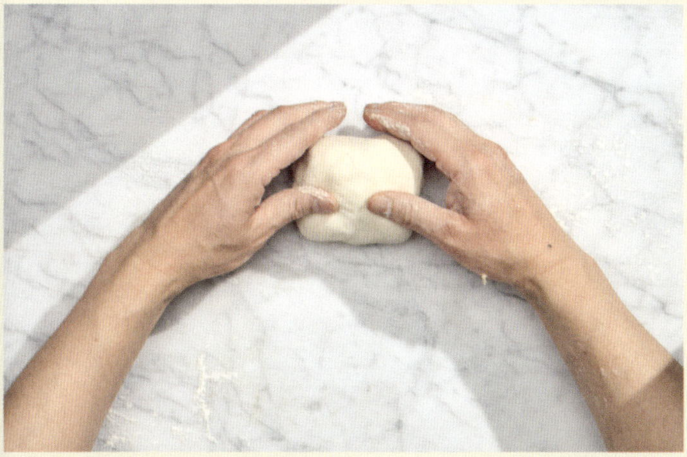

CHAPTER TWO

TOSUTO

TO RASUKU

CHAPTER TWO

TOSUTO TO RASUKU

トーストとラスク

In the dim-lit, jazz-filled corners of a traditional kissaten (coffee shop), the morning service is king. Here, a slice of tosuto (toast) is a physical sculpture of ritual, to go with the dark roasted coffee. Sliced thick – often 4 cm (1½ in) or more – and scored deeply in a diamond pattern so the butter on top can slowly melt its way inwards, the goal is a study in contrasts: brown 'shatter' on the outside that gives way to a steaming, cloud-soft centre.

Whether topped with a simple pat of salted butter, a thick layer of sweet anko (red bean paste) or given a 'pizza' treatment, Japanese toast is the best canvas to demonstrate our collective yearning for heat, browning and texture.

Then there is the rasuku (rusk). While the world might see a rusk as mere twice-baked bread, the Japanese panyasan (bakery) treats it as a confection. Shokupan is sliced, cubed, drenched in melted butter, tossed in granulated sugar and baked low and slow until every drop of moisture is replaced by a crisp, caramelised snap. What began as a practical way to extend shelf life – to demonstrate mottainai (waste not) – has become its own kind of snack: something you buy boxed as a gift, or eat absent-mindedly with tea, the way you might eat biscuits.

The following recipes are about these afterlives: a perfect loaf of shokupan is never really finished; it's waiting for its next form.

HONEY BUTTER TOAST

HANI BATA TOSUTO

ハニーバタートースト

Honey butter toast is one of the longest-running items on our menu. When we first started Little Cardigan, we wanted to create something people unfamiliar with shokupan could enjoy. We soak a thick slice of shokupan in an unreasonable amount of honey and butter, then bake it until the outside turns into a crisp, golden shell. The inside stays soft, soaking up all the flavours and creating contrast. The organic Tasmanian leatherwood honey, with its floral aroma, cuts through the richness, while the pink flaky salt added at the end brings everything together. You can swap the type of honey, butter or salt, but at Little Cardigan, we believe the fewer the ingredients, the higher their quality must be.

MAKES 5

- 150 g (5.29 oz) leatherwood honey
- 150 g (5.29 oz) cultured unsalted butter
- 5 thick slices Shokupan (page 34)
- 45 g (1.59 oz) raw (demerara) sugar, for coating
- pink flaky salt

1. Preheat the oven to 170°C (338°F) fan-forced. Line a baking tray with baking paper.
2. Melt the honey and butter together in a large heatproof bowl set over a saucepan of simmering water (or use short bursts in the microwave), stirring until smooth and combined.
3. Dip each slice of shokupan into the melted honey–butter mixture, coating evenly. Let any excess drip off.
4. Coat one side of each slice with raw sugar, then place the slices sugared side down on the prepared tray.
5. Bake for 10 minutes, then flip and bake for another 8–10 minutes, until the surface is golden and caramelised.
6. Cool on a wire rack to crisp up, sprinkle with pink flaky salt and enjoy.

TOAST WITH SWEET RED BEAN PASTE AND BUTTER

AN BATA TOSUTO

あんバタートースト

Few dishes explain Japan's kissaten culture better than a thick slice of toast crowned with anko (red bean paste) and butter.

According to local cafe lore, the story starts in 1921 at 満つ葉 (Matsuba), a coffeehouse in Sakae, Nagoya. The owner noticed students dipping their buttered toast into zenzai (a sweet red bean soup) and decided to combine the two. The result was ogura toast – a crisp slice of shokupan spread with adzuki bean paste, served with coffee. Matsuba became a local institution, closing in 2002, but then reopening in 2023 under its descendant 喫茶まつば (Kissa Matsuba) – a sister shop that continues the tradition and keeps the ritual alive in Nagoya's morning-service cafes.

'An butter toast' – its richer, butter-forward cousin – spread far beyond Nagoya. Every cafe and convenience store now has a version: thick or thin slices, chunky or smooth red bean paste (tsubu-an or koshi-an), butter melting into sweetness. It's breakfast that tastes like dessert, or maybe the other way around.

MAKES 2

- 2 slices Shokupan (page 34), toasted
- butter of your choice, for spreading and topping

ANKO (SWEET RED BEAN PASTE)

- 200 g (7.05 oz) adzuki beans
- 160 g (5.64 oz) raw (demerara) sugar
- 2 g (0.07 oz) fine sea salt

ANKO YIELD

≈600 g (21.16 oz)

MAKE THE ANKO

1. Wash the beans well and place in a saucepan with enough water to cover (about double the amount of water to beans). There's no need to soak the beans before cooking; just rinse them.
2. Bring the beans to the boil, uncovered, then reduce the heat to low and simmer for 10 minutes. Turn off the heat, cover with a lid and let sit for 30 minutes to steam the beans. (Steaming the beans smooths out their wrinkles and makes them evenly soft.)
3. Drain, then return the beans to the saucepan and add fresh water to cover again.
4. Place the saucepan over high heat and bring to the boil. Reduce the heat to low and gently simmer, uncovered, so that the beans just jiggle slightly while cooking. If the beans start to rise above the water, add a little hot water each time and skim off any foam as needed.
5. Cook until the beans can be squashed easily between your fingers. (The cooking time will vary depending on the freshness of the beans. If the beans are very fresh, they may take only 20 minutes to cook; older beans may take up to an hour. Rather than relying only on a set amount of time, it's most reliable to judge by the look and feel of the beans.)
6. Turn off the heat. Allow the beans to rest for at least 30 minutes, but preferably overnight.
7. Gently mix the sugar into the beans with a spatula, being careful not to crush them.
8. Simmer the beans over medium–low heat, stirring often, for 15–30 minutes, until the mixture thickens to form a paste (use both time and texture as a guide). The anko is ready when it clumps together for a moment after stirring, then slowly loosens again. The anko will firm up further as it cools, so the key is to turn off the heat while it is still slightly loose. Remove from the heat, add the salt and set aside to cool slightly.
9. Store the anko in an airtight container in the fridge for 2–3 days. For longer storage, freeze in portions for up to 2 months.

ASSEMBLE

10. Spread the toasted shokupan evenly with butter, then add a generous spoon of anko. Top with thick sliced butter and serve.

KAYA TOAST WITH SOFT-BOILED EGG

KAYA TOSUTO

カヤトースト

Before I came to Australia, I had never tried kaya – the coconut custard jam made from coconut cream, sugar, egg and pandan juice. But for my business partner Frankie and our team members from Southeast Asia, charcoal-toasted bread with kaya and butter is the taste of childhood. They dip it into soft-boiled eggs seasoned with soy sauce and white pepper. I wanted them to feel at home, so I learnt to make kaya and added it to our menu. Maybe it will help create new childhood memories for the kids growing up in Brunswick.

This recipe makes enough kaya to fill two 250 g (8.82 oz) jars. You can scale it down, but making the full batch is easier, and it tends to disappear quickly anyway – on toast, between crackers, or shared with friends.

The method uses a stick blender to turn fresh pandan leaves into pandan juice. If you can't find fresh pandan, you can try the bottled version, or just make the kaya without it; the flavour will be different, but the spirit of kaya toast still comes through.

SERVES 1

KAYA JAM

- 13 g (0.46 oz) pandan leaf
- 50 g (1.76 oz) water
- 250 g (8.82 oz) raw (demerara) sugar
- 250 g (8.82 oz) coconut cream
- 100 g (3.53 oz) egg yolk (from approx. 5 eggs)
- 2 g (0.07 oz) salt

KAYA TOAST SET

- 1 egg
- soy sauce, to taste
- white pepper, to taste (use Sarawak white pepper, if available)
- salted butter, for spreading
- 2 slices Shokupan (page 34), toasted

KAYA JAM YIELD

≈500 g (17.64 oz)

MAKE THE KAYA JAM

1. Blend the pandan leaf and water in a small bowl using a stick blender until very finely chopped. Strain the mixture through muslin (cheesecloth) to extract the pandan essence.
2. Clean the stick blender, then blend the sugar and coconut cream in a separate bowl until the sugar is dissolved. Add the egg yolks and blend until just combined. Avoid overmixing.
3. Use a sieve to strain the egg mixture into a saucepan. Add the pandan essence and warm the mixture over medium heat for 5 minutes, stirring constantly with a spatula to avoid the mixture sticking to the base of the pan.
4. Reduce the heat to medium–low and cook for 8 minutes, stirring gently. Reduce the heat to low. At this stage, the mixture should be hot, with white foamy swirls on the surface. Continue stirring slowly, scraping the base of the pan as you go (see Note). When the white swirls disappear and the mixture looks glossy, you're almost done. Keep stirring until the kaya thickens enough to leave a faint trail when you draw the spatula across the base of the pan. Lift the spatula – the kaya should fall in a slow, steady drip. Add the salt and stir.
5. Transfer the kaya jam to clean jars and refrigerate for up to 2 weeks.

PREPARE THE EGG AND ASSEMBLE

6. Cook the egg using a sous vide at 62°C (144°F) for 45 minutes. Alternatively, bring a small saucepan of water to the boil. Turn off the heat, add the egg to the pan and leave, uncovered, for 12–15 minutes.
7. Crack the egg gently into a small ramekin or similar dish. Add soy sauce and white pepper, to taste.
8. Spread the butter and kaya jam onto the toasted shokupan. Enjoy the kaya toast and egg separately, or you can dip the kaya toast into the egg.

NOTE It's important to cook the kaya gently over low heat. High heat will scramble the yolks and make the kaya grainy. The times above are just a guideline, so be guided by the look and feel of the kaya.

'PIZZA' TOAST

PIZA TOSUTO

ピザトースト

It might sound outrageous to Italians, but when we were children, our first pizza was pizza toast. It is deeply rooted in everyday home life, not only as a quick breakfast option on busy mornings, but also as a regular snack for children. As long as there's ketchup and cheese in the fridge, even kids can easily make a tasty pizza toast by themselves. And if you add sliced onions, bell pepper, ham or salami, it becomes an even more satisfying, 'almost authentic' pizza-style toast.

MAKES 3

- 3 slices Shokupan (page 34), lightly toasted
- 45 g (1.59 oz) onion, thinly sliced
- 60 g (2.12 oz) green bell pepper (capsicum), sliced into 5 mm (¼ in) thick rings
- 75 g (2.65 oz) ham, bacon, salami or Frankfurt sausages, thinly sliced
- 75 g (2.65 oz) shredded mozzarella or pizza cheese blend

PIZZA-TOAST SAUCE

- 3 tablespoons tomato ketchup
- 1 tablespoon olive oil
- 1 teaspoon Worcestershire sauce

1. Preheat the oven to 200°C (392°F) fan-forced.
2. Combine the ingredients for the pizza-toast sauce. (Olive oil enhances the flavour of the sauce and helps prevent the vegetables' moisture from soaking into the bread.)
3. Spread the pizza-toast sauce evenly on the toasted shokupan and top with the onion, bell pepper, meat and cheese.
4. Place the topped shokupan on a baking tray. Bake for about 10 minutes, until the cheese is melted and the top is lightly golden brown.
5. Remove from the oven and serve.

THE ORIGINAL PIZZA TOAST

In Tokyo, just one minute's walk from Yurakucho Tokyo station, sandwiched between a jewellery store and a lottery retail shop, is Benisica; a kissaten that oozes old-school cool.

At the shop front, you'll see a faded photo of Keanu Reeves surrounded by the staff when he stopped by. Next to it is another sign that reads 元祖ピザトースト (the original pizza toast).

Back in the 1960s, believe it or not, pizza was an exotic luxury, the sort of thing you'd queue up and get on a waiting list for. The owner of Benisica was smitten with the Italian dish and improvised with something readily available. Thick slices of shokupan stood in for dough; tomato ketchup, cheese and toppings were added, then baked until golden and bubbling.

By the time the 1964 Olympics rolled around, pizza toast had become a national obsession, gracing cafe counters from Ginza to Osaka.

More than half a century later, many bakeries have their own rendition and interpretation of what constitutes a pizza toast.

FRENCH TOAST

FURENCHI TOSUTO

フレンチトースト

In France, pain perdu (French toast) was a way to save stale bread – soaked in egg and cream or milk, pan-fried in butter, brought back to life. In Japan, what was once a poor man's food turned into a hotel breakfast luxury. Thick-cut shokupan, soft to the core, like pudding with a crispy golden crust, topped with fruit, syrup or even ice cream. In Hong Kong (China), there's a louder cousin – deep-fried, dripping with condensed milk and peanut butter. Both are chasing the small, rewarding moments of our everyday lives.

When it comes to French toast, I can't help but think of the film *Kramer vs. Kramer* (1979). People around my age – or serious movie lovers – are probably the last ones who still make that connection. There's that scene where Dustin Hoffman, playing a father in the middle of a divorce, clumsily makes French toast for his son for the first time. Later in the film, once he's grown into the role of a parent, he cooks it smoothly and effortlessly. Because I saw that film when I was young, every time I make French toast, I still feel the urge to sit on the kitchen bench like the son does. In the movie, French toast serves as a symbol of the father's efforts to rebuild his relationship with his son and the love he pours into caring for him.

MAKES 3

- 60 g (2.12 oz) egg yolk (from approx. 3 eggs)
- 110 g (3.88 oz) raw (demerara) sugar
- 300 g (10.58 oz) cream (40% milkfat)
- 300 g (10.58 oz) full-cream (whole) milk
- 1 vanilla bean, split lengthways and seeds scraped
- 3 thick slices Shokupan (page 34)
- butter, for cooking
- icing (confectioners') sugar, for dusting (optional)
- maple syrup / agave syrup / honey, to serve

PREPARE THE EGG MIXTURE

1. Place the egg yolk and raw sugar in a bowl and whisk until well combined.
2. Place the cream, milk and vanilla bean pod and seeds in a saucepan and warm over low heat for about 5 minutes, until it reaches body temperature.
3. Pour the warm cream–milk mixture into the egg–sugar mixture and stir to combine. Discard the vanilla bean.
4. Pour the mixture into an airtight container, then submerge the shokupan. Seal and refrigerate for 30 minutes.

BAKE AND SERVE

5. Preheat the oven to 200°C (392°F) fan-forced.
6. Melt a little butter in a large ovenproof frying pan over medium heat. Remove the pan from the heat, add the soaked slices of shokupan, then transfer to the oven and bake for 10–12 minutes, until the shokupan is golden. Flip the shokupan slices and bake for a further 10 minutes, or until both sides are golden brown.
7. Transfer the French toast to a plate, dust with icing sugar, if desired, and serve with maple syrup or your choice of topping.

SUGAR RUSK

SHUGA RASUKU

シュガーラスク

Too good to waste!

Unlike me, many children around me didn't like bread crusts. Since bakeries often trimmed them off for sandwiches, I suppose that's how the idea of using the leftovers came about. Stale shokupan, too, found new life in recipes such as rusks, showing how nothing went to waste.

It's so good you won't stop – you might even start saving the crusts for sugar rusk!

MAKES 150 G (5.29 OZ)

- 3 slices Shokupan (about 150 g/5.29 oz; see page 34)
- 50 g (1.76 oz) cultured unsalted butter, melted
- 50 g (1.76 oz) raw (demerara) sugar

1. Preheat the oven to 150°C (302°F) fan-forced. Line a baking tray with baking paper.
2. Cut the shokupan into sticks or bite-sized cubes, about 1–2 cm (½–¾ in) thick.
3. Place the bread pieces in a large bowl. Pour the melted butter over the bread and toss until evenly coated.
4. Sprinkle the raw sugar over the buttered bread, then toss again until the sugar adheres evenly to all sides.
5. Spread the coated bread pieces on the prepared tray in a single layer. Bake for 40–50 minutes, until crisp and lightly golden.
6. Transfer to a wire rack to cool completely. The rusks will become crunchy as they cool. Enjoy as a sweet snack.
7. Store leftover rusks in an airtight container at room temperature for up to 1 week.

CINNAMON SUGAR RUSK

SHINAMON SHUGA RASUKU

シナモンシュガーラスク

You can start with a simple sugar rusk and customise it with your favourite flavours. Here, we're making cinnamon rusk, but cocoa or kinako (roasted soybean flour) would work just as well!

MAKES 150 G (5.29 OZ)

- 3 slices Shokupan crusts (about 150 g/5.29 oz; see page 34)
- 50 g (1.76 oz) cultured unsalted butter, melted
- 50 g (1.76 oz) raw (demerara) sugar
- 5 g (0.18 oz) ground cinnamon

1. Preheat the oven to 150°C (302°F) fan-forced. Line a baking tray with baking paper.
2. Cut the shokupan crusts into 1 cm (½ in) thick sticks or any bite-sized shape of your choice.
3. In a small bowl, combine the melted butter, sugar and cinnamon.
4. Lightly spread the cinnamon butter onto the soft side of each bread piece.
5. Spread the coated bread pieces on the prepared tray in a single layer. Bake for 40–50 minutes, until crisp and lightly golden.
6. Transfer to a wire rack to cool completely. The rusks will become crunchy as they cool. Enjoy with tea or coffee.
7. Store leftover rusks in an airtight container at room temperature for up to 1 week.

GARLIC RUSK

GARIKKU RASUKU

ガーリックラスク

Nowadays, some bakeries in Japan bake bread specifically for rusk, but it originally began as a clever way for bakers to make use of leftover crusts, unsold baguettes, or pieces of country bread by slicing them thin and baking them in the residual heat of the oven.

This garlic rusk is a perfect snack to enjoy with beer or wine. I can already imagine it creating a high demand for shokupan crusts!

MAKES 150 G (5.29 OZ)

- 3 slices Shokupan crusts (about 150 g/5.29 oz; see page 34)
- 50 g (1.76 oz) cultured unsalted butter, melted
- 2–3 garlic cloves (about 10 g/0.35 oz), finely minced
- 5 g (0.18 oz) parsley, finely chopped
- 3 g (0.11 oz) fine sea salt

1. Preheat the oven to 150°C (302°F) fan-forced. Line a baking tray with baking paper.
2. Cut the shokupan crusts into sticks or bite-sized cubes, about 1–2 cm (½–¾ in) thick.
3. In a large bowl, combine the melted butter, minced garlic, chopped parsley and salt. Mix well.
4. Add the bread pieces and toss until evenly coated with the garlic butter.
5. Spread the coated bread pieces on the prepared tray in a single layer. Bake for 40–50 minutes, until crisp and lightly golden.
6. Transfer to a wire rack to cool completely. The rusks will become crunchy as they cool. Enjoy with a cold beer or a glass of wine.
7. Store leftover rusks in an airtight container at room temperature for up to 1 week.

CHAPTER THREE

KASHIPAN

CHAPTER THREE

KASHIPAN

菓子パン

If shokupan is the steady, rhythmic heartbeat that keeps the lights on in every Japanese bakery, then the soul – the creative, chaotic and playful side of the operation, the reason you get into this business in the first place – is, without question, kashipan.

Written as 菓子パン, the simple translation of 'sweet bread' or 'candy bread' doesn't quite do it justice. That colourful line-up behind the glass triggers a primal sense of desire in anyone with a few coins in their pocket.

When bread first arrived in Japan during the Meiji Restoration, it wasn't exactly a hit. The hard crusts and savoury loaves of the West were alien to a palate raised on rice. It took a former samurai, Yasubei Kimura, to crack the code. In 1874, Kimura created the anpan: a soft, slightly sweet bun filled with the familiar comfort of anko (sweet red bean paste). It was a reverseTrojan Horse, smuggling in the foreign concept of bread by wrapping it around something deeply, undeniably Japanese. Getting it in front of Emperor Meiji a year later wasn't just an honour – it was a stroke of marketing genius that cemented anpan's place in the national consciousness.

Anpan proved that bread didn't have to be a foreign affair; it could be a canvas for an entire ecosystem of buns, both sweet and savoury.

There's the kurimupan, a bun filled with thick, sturdy custard. There's the nonsensical melonpan – a sweet bun wearing a crisp cookie for a hat, which has absolutely nothing to do with melons. And on the other side of the aisle, someone decided to wrap thick curry in dough and deep-fry it like a doughnut to make karepan. Every attempt was made to take a foreign idea, pull it apart and rebuild it into something better – or at the very least, something more interesting.

As a baker, you can spend days chasing the perfect, uniform crumb of a shokupan loaf. But kashipan is where the real fun is.

I remember the transactional power of my first hundred-yen coin, slapped on a bakery counter in exchange for an anpan. That first bite – the soft dough giving way to the sweet, earthy paste – is a memory hardwired into my brain.

So this chapter is about getting your hands dirty and making something fun and portable. We'll dive into the classics that have fuelled Japan for over a century, before exploring more contemporary flavours.

Let's have some fun.

RED BEAN PASTE BUN

ANPAN

あんパン

If the Japanese bakery has an origin story, this is it.

あんぱん (anpan) – a soft, round roll filled with sweet red bean paste – was first baked in 1874 by Kimuraya, a bakery founded by Yasubei Kimura, a former samurai turned baker. At the time, bread was still foreign, dense and salty, suited for Western palates. Kimura softened the dough with milk and sakadane (a natural yeast starter used in sake brewing) and filled it with something familiar: anko – sweet adzuki bean paste. From that moment, bread became something Japan could call its own.

The story goes that Emperor Meiji was presented with anpan filled with gyuhi (a soft mochi) and salted sakura blossoms, sparking a national craze. Soon every bakery was making its own version.

Even today, Japanese customers judge a bakery by its anpan. Every Japanese person I know has a very specific preference: koshi-an (smooth red bean paste without skin) or tsubu-an (red bean paste with a coarse texture); the ratio of red bean filling to bun; whether the topping is salt-pickled sakura blossom or black sesame; the texture of the bun; the list goes on.

In 1980s detective dramas, whenever the detectives were doing stake-outs in their cars, their go-to meal was always anpan and a canned coffee.

MAKES 8

SPONGE DOUGH (MAKE AHEAD)

125 g (4.41 oz) bread flour	(50%)
8 g (0.28 oz) raw (demerara) sugar	(3%)
3 g (0.11 oz) osmotolerant instant dry yeast	(1.2%)
100 g (3.53 oz) full-cream (whole) milk, lukewarm	(40%)

FINAL DOUGH (ADDITIONS)

20 g (0.71 oz) cream (40% milkfat)	(8%)
40 g (1.41 oz) egg (from approx. 1 egg)	(16%)
15 g (0.53 oz) water	(6%)
125 g (4.41 oz) bread flour, plus extra for dusting	(50%)
5 g (0.18 oz) fine sea salt	(2%)
43 g (1.52 oz) raw (demerara) sugar	(17%)
25 g (0.88 oz) unsalted butter, softened	(10%

(Values in parentheses indicate baker's percentages)

↓ MORE INGREDIENTS

Day 1

MAKE THE SPONGE DOUGH

1 Combine the flour, sugar and yeast in a bowl. Add the lukewarm milk and mix until no dry flour remains. Cover and proof at room temperature until doubled in size, about 1 hour. Refrigerate overnight (up to 16 hours).

Desired final sponge dough temperature before refrigeration: 26°C (79°F).

Day 2

MIX THE FINAL DOUGH

2 Place the cream, egg and water into the bowl of a stand mixer fitted with a dough hook, followed by the flour and salt. Tear the sponge dough into pieces and add to the bowl. Mix on speed 3 (low) for 5 minutes. Increase to speed 6 (medium–high) and mix for 10 minutes. Add the sugar and mix on speed 6 for a further 10 minutes, or until the dough starts coming together. Gradually add the softened butter and continue mixing. In the final stage of mixing, the dough will come together into a lump and begin slapping against the bowl as it separates from the side. The finished dough should be glossy and pass a windowpane test (stretching it thin enough to let light through without tearing).

Desired final dough temperature: 26°C (79°F).

FIRST PROOF

3 Cover the bowl with a damp tea towel and proof the dough for 30 minutes. Perform a fold by stretching one side of the dough up out of the bowl and folding it down over the remaining dough in the bowl.

DIVIDE AND REST

4 Turn the dough out onto the bench and divide into 8 × 60 g (2.12 oz) portions. Round each piece gently by placing your palm over the dough and rolling it taut against the surface of the bench. Cover with the tea towel and rest on the bench for 20 minutes to relax the gluten.

↓ RECIPE CONTINUES

TO ASSEMBLE

- 440 g (15.52 oz) Anko (see page 80)
- black sesame seeds, to garnish

EGG WASH

- 50 g (1.76 oz) egg (from approx. 1 egg)
- 15 g (0.53 oz) water or full-cream (whole) milk

SHAPE

5 Lightly flour the bench and place the dough seam side up. Flatten the dough pieces into 8–10 cm (3¼–4 in) discs, keeping the edges thinner and the centre slightly thicker to prevent the filling from breaking through the dough.

6 Scoop a portion of anko (around 55 g/1.94 oz) onto the centre of one dough disc. Lift the edge of the dough up and around the filling, pleating and pinching firmly to seal completely. Make sure no bean paste is exposed. Turn the dough seam side down and gently round the dough between your palms until smooth and dome-shaped. Place on a baking tray lined with baking paper. Repeat with the remaining dough and filling.

FINAL PROOF

7 Proof at 30°C (86°F) for 45 minutes (see page 27) or until the dough looks puffy and light.

BAKE AND SERVE

8 Preheat the oven to 180°C (356°F) fan-forced.

9 Whisk the egg wash ingredients together in a small bowl, then strain the mixture through a sieve. Brush the surface of the buns with the egg wash.

10 Place a tablespoon of black sesame seeds in a small dish. Wet your forefinger, dip it into the seeds, then gently press to adhere them to the top of a bun. Repeat for all the buns.

11 Bake for 9 minutes, or until evenly golden brown. Cool on a wire rack.

12 Enjoy fresh with coffee, tea, green tea or milk. In Japan, anpan is eaten throughout the day – for breakfast, lunch, dessert or as a quick snack. When you're short on time, it's easy to eat on the go without getting your hands dirty. It's also comforting to tuck one into your bag, much like a snack bar.

STORE

13 Once completely cool, store the anpan, wrapped tightly in plastic wrap and in an airtight container for up to 1 day. For longer storage, freeze for up to 2 weeks. Thaw at room temperature for 2–3 hours, or toast directly from frozen for a crisp exterior and soft interior. As these buns contain no preservatives, they are best enjoyed as soon as possible.

THE HERO WITH THE SWEET BEAN FACE

If anpan gave Japan its first bread, Anpanman is Japan's Mickey Mouse.

Created in 1973 by author Takashi Yanase, Anpanman is a superhero whose head is literally made of anpan. When someone is hungry, he offers a piece of himself – a simple act of kindness that became one of Japan's most enduring moral lessons.

Anpanman also has his own anime series, which began airing in 1988 and now counts over 1500 episodes, making it one of the longest-running series in the world. Its cast of pastry heroes (Karepan Man, Shokupan Man, Melonpanna) turned the humble bakery shelf into a mythic universe, where food wasn't just sustenance but community.

For many children, Anpanman is one of their very first words – right after mama and papa. He is also their first introduction to bread, and generosity. His message will remain timeless: 'It's okay to give a part of yourself to help someone else.'

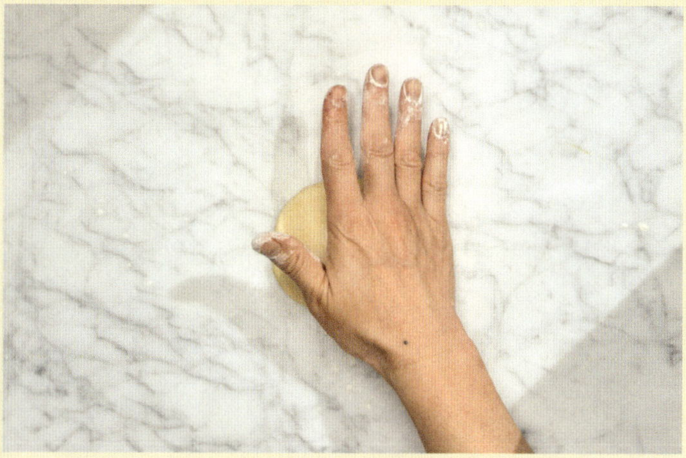

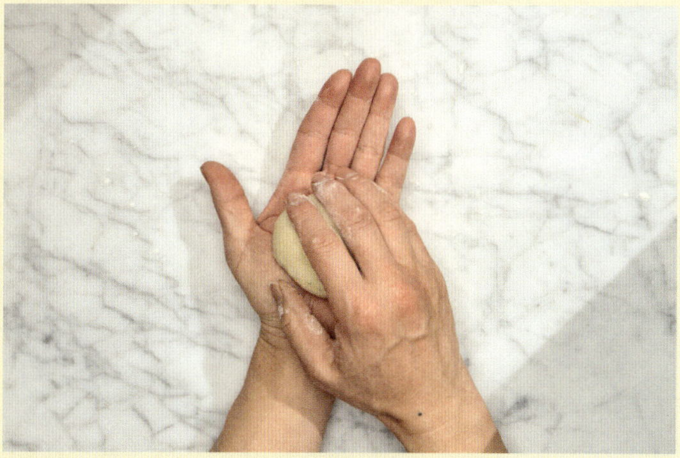

JAM BUN

JAMUPAN

ジャムパン

Jam has a longer history in Japan than most people realise. It first arrived in the Meiji era as a Western luxury, spread through naval rations in the early 20th century, and became truly national in the 1950s when the school-lunch program paired coppepan with strawberry or apricot jam to elevate an otherwise simple meal. As Japan's fruit-growing regions boomed, jam evolved into something distinctly local – Tochiotome strawberries, Yamanashi peaches, Kochi yuzu marmalade.

But for anyone who grew up in Japan, especially in the 1970s and 80s, 'jam' meant one thing and one thing only: strawberry jam. It was the first commercialised flavour that shaped the industry, the one every bakery relied on. Sure, there are other varieties such as blueberry, apricot and orange, but when you see anything labelled with 'jam' in Japan – even the mass-produced, plastic-wrapped 'jam bread' in supermarkets – it will proudly carry a bright red strawberry jam centre.

Whether children these days will immediately picture a strawberry when they hear 'jam' is anyone's guess, but for this bun, strawberry jam remains the perfect choice. So let's say it loud and clear – we're making a jam bun!

You can use store-bought jam, of course, but since we're here, let's make jam buns with homemade strawberry jam.

MAKES 8

SPONGE DOUGH (MAKE AHEAD)

125 g (4.41 oz) bread flour	(50%)
8 g (0.28 oz) raw (demerara) sugar	(3%)
3 g (0.11 oz) osmotolerant instant dry yeast	(1.2%)
100 g (3.53 oz) full-cream (whole) milk, lukewarm	(40%)

STRAWBERRY JAM (JELLY)

500 g (17.64 oz) strawberries, hulled and trimmed
about 200 g (7.05 oz) raw (demerara) sugar (see Notes)
about 10 g (0.35 oz) lemon juice (see Notes)

STRAWBERRY JAM YIELD

450 g (1 lb)

Day 1

MAKE THE SPONGE DOUGH

1 Combine the flour, sugar and yeast in a bowl. Add the lukewarm milk and mix until no dry flour remains. Cover and proof at room temperature until doubled in size, about 1 hour. Refrigerate overnight (up to 16 hours).

Desired final sponge dough temperature before refrigeration: 26°C (79°F).

Day 2

MAKE THE STRAWBERRY JAM

2 Wash the strawberries, then cut them into halves or quarters, depending on their size. Weigh the trimmed strawberries and prepare the sugar and lemon juice (see Notes).

3 Place the strawberries in a bowl, sprinkle over the sugar and add the lemon juice. Mix well and let sit for 30–60 minutes to draw out the juices.

4 Transfer the strawberries and their juice to a large saucepan. Warm over medium heat, stirring occasionally, until the sugar dissolves.

5 Bring to a gentle boil over high heat, then reduce the heat to medium–high and simmer, stirring constantly to prevent sticking and burning. Skim any foam from the surface and continue to cook for 20–30 minutes, until thickened and the jam reaches 103–105°C (217–221°F).

6 To test if the jam is ready, dip a cool spoon into the boiling jam and lift it out. Early on, the jam will drip easily. As it cooks, the drops will thicken. When two drops merge and fall in a slow ribbon or 'sheet', the jam is ready. Remove from the heat and allow to cool completely.

NOTES

Measure the sugar and lemon juice based on the weight of the strawberries after trimming (38–40 per cent sugar and 2 per cent lemon juice). This creates a lighter, fresher-tasting jam.

Good jam cooks quickly at relatively high heat – never leave the saucepan unattended.

The sugar isn't just for sweetness; it draws moisture out of the fruit and concentrates its flavour, allowing the jam to cook down without adding extra water.

For filling the buns, it's best to use a slightly thicker jam. Cook it down until it reaches a custard-like thickness.

FINAL DOUGH (ADDITIONS)

20 g (0.71 oz) cream (40% milkfat)	(8%)
40 g (1.41 oz) egg (from approx. 1 egg)	(16%)
15 g (0.53 oz) water	(6%)
125 g (4.41 oz) bread flour, plus extra for dusting	(50%)
5 g (0.18 oz) fine sea salt	(2%)
43 g (1.52 oz) raw (demerara) sugar	(17%)
25 g (0.88 oz) unsalted butter, softened	(10%)

(Values in parentheses indicate baker's percentages)

EGG WASH

50 g (1.76 oz) egg (from approx. 1 egg)
15 g (0.53 oz) water or full-cream (whole) milk

TO GARNISH

flaked almonds

MIX THE FINAL DOUGH

7 Place the cream, egg and water into the bowl of a stand mixer fitted with a dough hook, followed by the flour and salt. Tear the sponge dough into pieces and add to the bowl. Mix on speed 3 (low) for 5 minutes. Increase to speed 6 (medium–high) and mix for 10 minutes. Add the sugar and mix on speed 6 for a further 10 minutes, or until the dough starts coming together. Gradually add the softened butter and continue mixing. In the final stage of mixing, the dough will come together into a lump and begin slapping against the bowl as it separates from the side. The finished dough should be glossy and pass a windowpane test (stretching it thin enough to let light through without tearing).

Desired final dough temperature: 26°C (79°F).

FIRST PROOF

8 Cover the bowl with a damp tea towel and proof the dough for 30 minutes. Perform a fold by stretching one side of the dough up out of the bowl and folding it down over the remaining dough in the bowl.

DIVIDE AND REST

9 Turn the dough out onto the bench and divide into 8 × 60 g (2.12 oz) portions. Round each piece gently by placing your palm over the dough and rolling it taut against the surface of the bench. Cover with the tea towel and rest on the bench for 20 minutes to relax the gluten.

SHAPE

10 Lightly flour the bench and place the dough seam side up. Flatten the dough pieces into 8–10 cm (3¼–4 in) discs, keeping the edges thinner and the centre slightly thicker to prevent the filling from breaking through the dough.

11 Scoop a portion of jam (around 55 g/1.94 oz) onto the centre of one dough disc. Lift the edge of the dough up and around the jam, pleating and pinching firmly to seal completely. Make sure no jam is exposed. Turn the dough seam side down and gently round the bun between your palms until smooth and dome-shaped. Place on a baking tray lined with baking paper. Repeat with the remaining dough and jam.

FINAL PROOF

12 Proof at 30°C (86°F) for 45 minutes (see page 27) or until the dough looks puffy and light.

BAKE AND SERVE

13 Preheat the oven to 180°C (356°F) fan-forced.

14 Whisk the egg wash ingredients together in a small bowl, then strain the mixture through a sieve. Brush the surface of the buns with the egg wash and place a flaked almond on top.

15 Bake for 9 minutes, or until evenly golden brown. Cool on a wire rack.

16 Jam buns make the perfect afternoon snack and are equally good for breakfast. They also pair beautifully with tea or milk tea. Take care when eating, as the jam filling can be very hot when freshly baked.

STORE

17 Once completely cool, store the buns in a zip-lock bag to prevent drying for up to 1 day. As jam-filled breads spoil quickly, especially in warm weather, they should not be left out for extended periods. Avoid refrigeration, as this can dry out the bread. For longer storage, freeze individual buns, wrapped tightly in plastic wrap and placed in a freezer-safe bag, for up to 2 weeks. Thaw at room temperature for about 3 hours, then lightly toast to restore the freshly baked flavour.

CUSTARD CREAM BUN

KURIMUPAN

クリームパン

First baked at Nakamuraya in Tokyo in 1904, the custard cream bun was Japan's answer to choux à la crème. The three signature slits along its curved edge aren't just for decoration; they let steam escape so the custard doesn't burst through the dough.

It's a piece of functional beauty; a shape carried from a collective childhood into the bakery's identity. Just hearing the name 'custard cream bun' ignites a small, steady pleasure – simple, familiar and loved at any age.

However, custard is careful work: when you heat up egg yolks, the proteins unfold and start to bond with each other, trapping the milk and sugar into a delicate network. If the temperature is too hot, the custard will curdle.

My custard uses a blend of cornflour (cornstarch) and plain (all-purpose) flour, which provides a safety net. The starch thickens first, shielding the eggs from overheating, so you can cook them a little harder without splitting. The moment the custard suddenly loosens and turns glossy – that's the sweet spot.

Rapid cooling matters, too. Spreading the custard flat and covering the surface stops steam from creating condensation, which would turn your custard watery. Into the freezer it goes – 30 minutes of cold shock locks in that shine and texture.

MAKES 8

SPONGE DOUGH (MAKE AHEAD)

125 g (4.41 oz) bread flour	(50%)
8 g (0.28 oz) raw (demerara) sugar	(3%)
3 g (0.11 oz) osmotolerant instant dry yeast	(1.2%)
100 g (3.53 oz) full-cream (whole) milk, lukewarm	(40%)

CUSTARD CREAM

- 25 g (0.88 oz) cornflour (cornstarch)
- 10 g (0.35 oz) plain (all-purpose) flour
- 300 g (10.58 oz) full-cream (whole) milk
- 60 g (2.12 oz) raw (demerara) sugar
- ½ vanilla bean, split lengthways and seeds scraped
- 60 g (2.12 oz) egg yolk (from approx. 3 eggs)
- 25 g (0.88 oz) unsalted butter

CUSTARD CREAM YIELD

480 g (16.93 oz)

↓ MORE INGREDIENTS

Day 1

MAKE THE SPONGE DOUGH

1. Combine the flour, sugar and yeast in a bowl. Add the lukewarm milk and mix until no dry flour remains. Cover and proof at room temperature until doubled in size, about 1 hour. Refrigerate overnight (up to 16 hours).

   Desired final sponge dough temperature before refrigeration: 26°C (79°F).

Day 2

MAKE THE CUSTARD CREAM

2. Sift the cornflour and plain flour together and set aside.
3. In a saucepan, combine the milk, 20 g (0.71 oz) of the sugar and the vanilla bean pod and seeds. Heat until just simmering.
4. In a heatproof bowl, whisk the egg yolk and the remaining 40 g (1.41 oz) sugar until pale and thick.
5. Slowly pour the hot milk into the egg-yolk mixture, whisking constantly to avoid curdling. Strain the mixture back into the saucepan through a fine-mesh sieve.
6. Set the pan over medium–high heat, stirring the mixture constantly with a rubber spatula and scraping the base of the pan to prevent burning. As the custard thickens and begins to bubble, continue stirring until it suddenly loosens and becomes smooth and glossy.
7. Remove from the heat, add the butter and stir until fully incorporated. Discard the vanilla bean pod.
8. Spread the custard onto a tray, press plastic wrap directly onto the surface and chill in the freezer for 30 minutes.
9. Gently whisk until smooth and creamy before moving the custard to the fridge.

↓ RECIPE CONTINUES

FINAL DOUGH (ADDITIONS)

20 g (0.71 oz) cream (40% milkfat)	(8%)
40 g (1.41 oz) egg (from approx. 1 egg)	(16%)
15 g (0.53 oz) water	(6%)
125 g (4.41 oz) bread flour, plus extra for dusting	(50%)
5 g (0.18 oz) fine sea salt	(2%)
43 g (1.52 oz) raw (demerara) sugar	(20%)
25 g (0.88 oz) unsalted cultured butter, softened	(10%)

(Values in parentheses indicate baker's percentages)

EGG WASH

50 g (1.76 oz) egg (from approx. 1 egg)
15 g (0.53 oz) water or full-cream (whole) milk

MIX THE FINAL DOUGH

10 Place the cream, egg and water into the bowl of a stand mixer fitted with a dough hook, followed by the flour and salt. Tear the sponge dough into pieces and add to the bowl. Mix on speed 3 (low) for 5 minutes. Increase to speed 6 (medium–high) and mix for 10 minutes. Add the sugar and mix on speed 6 for a further 10 minutes, or until the dough starts coming together. Gradually add the softened butter and continue mixing. In the final stage of mixing, the dough will come together into a lump and begin slapping against the bowl as it separates from the side. The finished dough should be glossy and pass a windowpane test (stretching it thin enough to let light through without tearing).

Desired final dough temperature: 26°C (79°F).

FIRST PROOF

11 Cover the bowl with a damp tea towel and proof the dough for 30 minutes. Perform a fold by stretching one side of the dough up out of the bowl and folding it down over the remaining dough in the bowl.

DIVIDE AND REST

12 Turn the dough out onto the bench and divide into 8 × 60 g (2.12 oz) portions. Round each piece gently by placing your palm over the dough and rolling it taut against the surface of the bench. Cover with the tea towel and rest on the bench for 20 minutes to relax the gluten.

SHAPE

13 Lightly flour the bench and place the dough seam side up. Flatten each piece into a 1 cm (½ in) thick oval. Place 50 g (1.76 oz) chilled custard in the centre, then fold the dough in half to enclose the filling. Press the edges firmly to seal. Using a dough scraper, make three slits along the curved edge. Place on a baking tray lined with baking paper and repeat with the remaining dough and custard.

FINAL PROOF

14 Proof at 30°C (86°F) for 45 minutes (see page 27) or until the dough looks puffy and light.

BAKE AND SERVE

15 Preheat the oven to 180°C (356°F) fan-forced.

16 Whisk the egg wash ingredients together in a small bowl, then strain the mixture through a sieve. Brush the surface of the buns with the egg wash.

17 Bake for 9 minutes, or until golden brown. Cool on a wire rack.

18 Like jam buns (see page 102), custard cream buns are perfect for a boost of energy to get you through the day and make a great small snack to quell an afternoon slump. They can be lightly warmed in a toaster, or eaten slightly chilled, as long as they haven't dried out.

STORE

19 Once completely cool, store the buns in a zip-lock bag to prevent drying for up to 1 day. As custard-filled breads spoil quickly, especially in warm weather, they should not be left out for extended periods. Avoid refrigeration, as this can dry out the buns. For longer storage, freeze individual buns, wrapped tightly in plastic wrap and placed in a freezer-safe bag, for up to 2 weeks. Thaw at room temperature for about 3 hours, then lightly toast to restore the freshly baked flavour.

ABOUT CUSTARD POWDER

If making custard cream feels like too much science before breakfast, there's always the shortcut: custard powder. Invented in 1837 by Alfred Bird for his egg-allergic wife, it's basically cornflour (cornstarch) flavoured with vanilla and coloured yellow – a starch-thickened imitation of the real thing.

Custard powder has its place: quick, stable and nostalgic in that school-dinner way. But in custard cream buns, where you taste every layer of bread and custard, it's worth taking the long route.

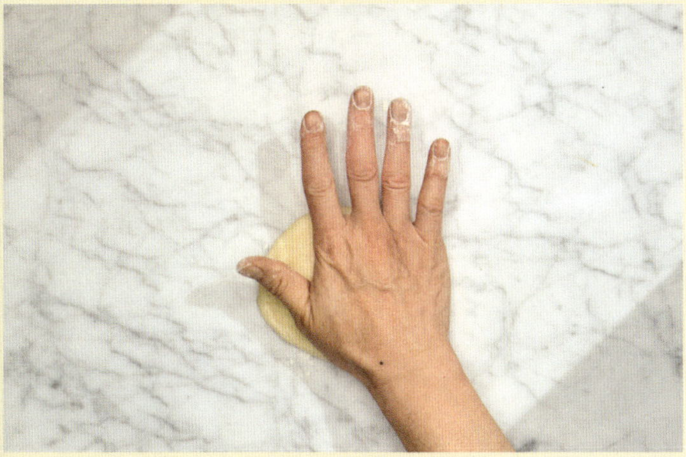

BUSH WARBLER BUN

UGUISUPAN

ウグイスパン

Uguisupan is named after the Japanese bush warbler – a small, shy bird you rarely see, but instantly recognised by its clear spring call, 'ho-hokekyo'. In Japan, the uguisu is a symbol of early spring, so much so that anything soft green is affectionately called 'uguisu-colour', even though the bird itself is brown. That's where this bread gets its name: from the gentle green of its edamame filling. Uguisupan has a gentle, almost grassy, pea-like sweetness that sets it apart from richer bean-paste buns.

MAKES 8

SPONGE DOUGH (MAKE AHEAD)

125 g (4.41 oz) bread flour	(50%)
8 g (0.28 oz) raw (demerara) sugar	(3%)
3 g (0.11 oz) osmotolerant instant dry yeast	(1.2%)
100 g (3.53 oz) full-cream (whole) milk, lukewarm	(40%)

UGUISUAN (EDAMAME BEAN PASTE)

250 g (8.82 oz) shelled edamame (fresh or frozen)
100–120 g (3.53–4.23 oz) water
150 g (5.29 oz) raw (demerara) sugar
pinch of fine sea salt

UGUISUAN (EDAMAME BEAN PASTE)

400 g (14.11 oz)

Day 1

MAKE THE SPONGE DOUGH

1 Combine the flour, sugar and yeast in a bowl. Add the lukewarm milk and mix until no dry flour remains. Cover and proof at room temperature until doubled in size, about 1 hour. Refrigerate overnight (up to 16 hours).

Desired final sponge dough temperature before refrigeration: 26°C (79°F).

Day 2

MAKE THE UGUISUAN

2 If using fresh edamame, boil them in salted water for 4–5 minutes. Drain and shock in cold water to stop the cooking process. Remove the thin outer skins carefully. If using frozen edamame, thaw and peel after blanching briefly.

3 Combine the peeled edamame with 100 g (3.53 oz) of the water in a blender or food processor. Blend until smooth, adding the remaining water gradually and only as needed. The texture should be thick yet pourable.

4 Transfer the blended paste to a saucepan over medium–low heat. Add the sugar in three stages, stirring constantly. Cook until the paste thickens and you can see the base of the saucepan when scraping a spatula across. Season with a pinch of salt.

5 Cool completely before using. The uguisuan can be refrigerated for 3–4 days or frozen for up to 1 month.

MIX THE FINAL DOUGH

6 Place the cream, egg and water into the bowl of a stand mixer fitted with a dough hook, followed by the flour and salt. Tear the sponge dough into pieces and add to the bowl. Mix on speed 3 (low) for 5 minutes. Increase to speed 6 (medium–high) and mix for 10 minutes. Add the sugar and mix on speed 6 for a further 10 minutes, or until the dough starts coming together. Gradually add the softened butter and continue mixing. In the final stage of mixing, the dough will come together into a lump and begin slapping against the bowl as it separates from the side. The finished dough should be glossy and pass a windowpane test (stretching it thin enough to let light through without tearing).

Desired final dough temperature: 26°C (79°F).

FIRST PROOF

7 Cover the bowl with a damp tea towel and proof the dough for 30 minutes. Perform a fold by stretching one side of the dough up out of the bowl and folding it down over the remaining dough in the bowl.

FINAL DOUGH (ADDITIONS)

20 g (0.71 oz) cream (40% milkfat)	(8%)
40 g (1.41 oz) egg (from approx. 1 egg)	(16%)
15 g (0.53 oz) water	(6%)
125 g (4.41 oz) bread flour, plus extra for dusting	(50%)
5 g (0.18 oz) fine sea salt	(2%)
43 g (1.52 oz) raw (demerara) sugar	(17%)
25 g (0.88 oz) unsalted butter, softened	(10%)

(Values in parentheses indicate baker's percentages)

EGG WASH (OPTIONAL)

50 g (1.76 oz) egg (from approx. 1 egg)
15 g (0.53 oz) water or full-cream (whole) milk

DIVIDE AND REST

8 Turn the dough out onto the bench and divide into 8 × 60 g (2.12 oz) portions. Round each piece gently by placing your palm over the dough and rolling it taut against the surface of the bench. Cover with the tea towel and rest on the bench for 20 minutes to relax the gluten.

SHAPE

9 Lightly flour the bench and place the dough seam side up. Flatten the dough pieces into 8–10 cm (3¼–4 in) discs, keeping the edges thinner and the centre slightly thicker to prevent the filling from breaking through the dough.

10 Scoop a portion of uguisuan (around 50 g/1.76 oz) onto the centre of one dough disc. Lift the edge of the dough up and around the filling and pinch to seal. Turn the dough seam side down and gently round the bun between your palms until smooth. Place on a baking tray lined with baking paper. Repeat with the remaining dough and filling.

FINAL PROOF

11 Proof at 30°C (86°F) for 45 minutes (see page 27) or until the dough looks puffy and light.

BAKE AND SERVE

12 Preheat the oven to 180°C (356°F) fan-forced.

13 Score two parallel slits across the top of each bun.

14 If using the egg wash, whisk the ingredients together in a small bowl, then strain the mixture through a sieve. Brush the surface of the buns with the egg wash.

15 Bake for 9 minutes, or until pale golden and just set. Cool on a wire rack.

16 Bush warbler buns are filling and satisfying, making them perfect for any time of day – morning, afternoon or evening – whenever you're hungry. They pair beautifully with refreshing cold drinks such as chilled green tea or iced coffee.

STORE

17 Once completely cool, store the buns in a zip-lock bag to prevent drying for up to 1 day. As bean-filled breads spoil quickly, especially in warm weather, they should not be left out for extended periods. Avoid refrigeration, as this can dry out the buns. For longer storage, freeze individual buns, wrapped tightly in plastic wrap and placed in a freezer-safe bag, for up to 2 weeks. Thaw at room temperature for about 3 hours, then lightly toast to restore the freshly baked flavour.

MELON BUN

MERONPAN

メロンパン

If the melon bun were a costume, it would be the one everyone wants to try on: round, golden, dressed in a crisscross cookie crust. It's a treat of contrasts – crunchy shell, gentle core, the best of both bakery worlds.

Despite its name, melon bun rarely tastes of melon. Its moniker comes from its appearance – the cracked, grid-like cookie crust that resembles melon rind.

Today, melon buns come in every size and variation: filled with custard, swirled with chocolate, matched with matcha, or reinvented with seasonal fruits.

Making melon buns means balancing two doughs: one soft, rising bread; the other a cookie dough, lightly sweet and gently cracked.

MAKES 8

COOKIE CRUST/'MELON SKIN' (MAKE AHEAD)

68 g (2.40 oz) cultured unsalted butter, softened	
1 vanilla bean, split lengthways and seeds scraped (or 1 teaspoon vanilla paste)	
78 g (2.75 oz) raw (demerara) sugar, plus extra for coating	
53 g (1.87 oz) egg (from approx. 1 egg), beaten	
141 g (4.97 oz) plain (all-purpose) flour	
15 g (0.53 oz) almond meal (ground almonds)	
2 g (0.07 oz) baking powder	

SPONGE DOUGH (MAKE AHEAD)

125 g (4.41 oz) bread flour	(50%)
8 g (0.28 oz) raw (demerara) sugar	(3%)
3 g (0.11 oz) osmotolerant instant dry yeast	(1.2%)
100 g (3.53 oz) full-cream (whole) milk, lukewarm	(40%)

↓ MORE INGREDIENTS

Day 1

MAKE THE COOKIE CRUST DOUGH

1 Place the softened butter, vanilla seeds or paste and sugar in a bowl. Mix until creamy but not aerated.

2 Add the egg in 3–4 stages, mixing thoroughly after each addition so the mixture emulsifies smoothly.

3 Add the plain flour, almond meal and baking powder, then mix gently with a spatula until combined.

4 Divide the dough into 8 × 40 g (1.41 oz) portions and roll into balls. Wrap each piece separately in plastic wrap, then flatten slightly and refrigerate overnight. (Alternatively, you can chill the dough as a whole slab and divide it the next day.)

MAKE THE SPONGE DOUGH

5 Combine the bread flour, sugar and yeast in a bowl. Add the lukewarm milk and mix until no dry flour remains. Cover and proof at room temperature until doubled in size, about 1 hour. Refrigerate overnight (up to 16 hours).

Desired final sponge dough temperature before refrigeration: 26°C (79°F).

Day 2

MIX THE FINAL DOUGH

6 Place the cream, egg and water into the bowl of a stand mixer fitted with a dough hook, followed by the bread flour and salt. Tear the sponge dough into pieces and add to the bowl. Mix on speed 3 (low) for 5 minutes. Increase to speed 6 (medium–high) and mix for 10 minutes. Add the sugar and mix on speed 6 for a further 10 minutes, or until the dough starts coming together. Gradually add the softened butter and continue mixing. In the final stage of mixing, the dough will come together into a lump and begin slapping against the bowl as it separates from the side. The finished dough should be glossy and pass a windowpane test (stretching it thin enough to let light through without tearing).

Desired final dough temperature: 26°C (79°F).

↓ RECIPE CONTINUES

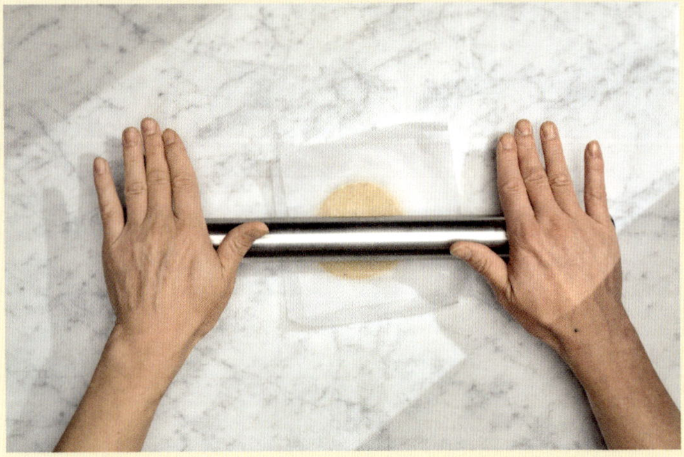

FINAL DOUGH (ADDITIONS)

20 g (0.71 oz) cream (40% milkfat)	(8%)
40 g (1.41 oz) egg (from approx. 1 egg)	(16%)
15 g (0.53 oz) water	(6%)
125 g (4.41 oz) bread flour	(50%)
5 g (0.18 oz) fine sea salt	(2%)
43 g (1.52 oz) raw (demerara) sugar	(20%)
25 g (0.88 oz) unsalted cultured butter, softened	(10%)

(Values in parentheses indicate baker's percentages)

FIRST PROOF

7 Cover the bowl with a damp tea towel and proof the dough for 30 minutes. Perform a fold by stretching one side of the dough up out of the bowl and folding it down over the remaining dough in the bowl.

DIVIDE AND REST

8 Turn the dough out onto the bench and divide into 8 × 60 g (2.12 oz) portions. Round each piece gently by placing your palm over the dough and rolling it taut against the surface of the bench. Cover and refrigerate for 20–30 minutes.

SHAPE

9 Take one 40 g (1.41 oz) cookie dough piece from the fridge. Place it between two sheets of baking paper and roll it into a thin disc slightly larger than a dough ball. Peel off the top layer of baking paper.

10 Prepare a small bowl of raw sugar. Carefully place the disc, dough side down, onto the sugar and peel away the baking paper. Press gently to adhere the sugar to the dough.

11 Place a dough ball, seam side up, next to the sugar bowl. Lift the sugared disc out of the bowl and drape it, sugared side up, over the dough ball, tucking in the edges to seal. Repeat with the remaining cookie crust pieces and dough.

FINAL PROOF

12 Place the shaped buns on a baking tray lined with baking paper. Proof at 30°C (86°F) for 45 minutes (see page 27) or until slightly puffy but not doubled in size (an overproofed melon bun will collapse).

BAKE AND SERVE

13 Preheat the oven to 180°C (356°F) fan-forced.

14 Bake for 9 minutes, or until the cookie crust is set and lightly golden at the edges. Cool on a wire rack.

15 Melon buns are perfect for an afternoon treat. As a child, they were often bought instead of packaged snacks or boxed sweets, and even now, when I'm craving something just a little sweet, I still find myself stopping by a bakery for one. They're also delicious when filled generously with whipped cream or custard.

STORE

16 Enjoy as soon as possible, as the cookie crust gradually absorbs moisture and loses its crispness. If not eating straight away, allow to cool completely, then wrap each bun tightly in plastic wrap and freeze to preserve the texture. Store frozen buns for up to 2 weeks. Thaw at room temperature for 2–3 hours, then warm in the oven to restore crispness before serving.

EVERY BITE A LEGEND

The origin of the melon bun is contested. One theory credits Hovhannes 'Ivan' Sagoyan, an Armenian baker brought to Tokyo by Okura Kihachiro, and associates him with early versions of the bread at the Imperial Hotel. Another story points to a Kobe bakery, Kinseido, which called its version 'sunrise' (サンライズ) in the 1930s, inspired by the naval flag and wartime motifs. Still, neither of these accounts is conclusive – melon buns' true birth remains part legend, part bakery lore.

CHOCO CHIP MELON BUN

CHOKO CHIPPU MERONPAN

チョコチップメロンパン

The chocolate chip melon bun was probably the first 'remix' encounter of the melon bun we knew as kids. It has become a true classic – a must-have item that everyone knows and loves. These days, it's common to see 'evolved' versions, such as chocolate-infused dough or chocolate cookie crusts loaded with extra chips.

Here, I've chosen to share a simple, timeless recipe for the classic chocolate chip melonpan. Once you master the original, why not let your imagination run wild and create your own signature version?

MAKES 8

CHOCOLATE CHIP COOKIE CRUST/ 'MELON SKIN' (MAKE AHEAD)

48 g (1.69 oz) cultured unsalted butter, softened	
1 vanilla bean, split lengthways and seeds scraped (or 1 teaspoon vanilla paste)	
78 g (2.75 oz) raw (demerara) sugar, plus extra for coating	
53 g (1.87 oz) egg (from approx. 1 egg), beaten	
141 g (4.97 oz) plain (all-purpose) flour	
15 g (0.53 oz) almond meal (ground almonds)	
2 g (0.07 oz) baking powder	
40 g (1.41 oz) dark chocolate chips	

SPONGE DOUGH (MAKE AHEAD)

125 g (4.41 oz) bread flour	(50%)
8 g (0.28 oz) raw (demerara) sugar	(3%)
3 g (0.11 oz) osmotolerant instant dry yeast	(1.2%)
100 g (3.53 oz) full-cream (whole) milk, lukewarm	(40%)

Day 1

MAKE THE CHOCOLATE CHIP COOKIE CRUST DOUGH

1 Place the softened butter, vanilla seeds or paste and sugar in a bowl. Mix until creamy but not aerated.

2 Add the egg in 3–4 stages, mixing thoroughly after each addition so the mixture emulsifies smoothly.

3 Add the plain flour, almond meal and baking powder, then gently mix with a spatula until combined.

4 Add the dark chocolate chips and mix until they are evenly incorporated into the dough.

5 Divide the dough into 8 × 45 g (1.59 oz) portions and roll into balls. Wrap each piece separately in plastic wrap, then flatten slightly and refrigerate overnight. (Alternatively, you can chill the dough as a whole slab and divide it the next day.)

MAKE THE SPONGE DOUGH

6 Combine the bread flour, sugar and yeast in a bowl. Add the lukewarm milk and mix until no dry flour remains. Cover and proof at room temperature until doubled in size, about 1 hour. Refrigerate overnight (up to 16 hours).

Desired final sponge dough temperature before refrigeration: 26°C (79°F).

Day 2

MIX THE FINAL DOUGH

7 Place the cream, egg and water into the bowl of a stand mixer fitted with a dough hook, followed by the bread flour and salt. Tear the sponge dough into pieces and add to the bowl. Mix on speed 3 (low) for 5 minutes. Increase to speed 6 (medium-high) and mix for 10 minutes. Add the sugar and mix on speed 6 for a further 10 minutes, or until the dough starts coming together. Gradually add the softened butter and continue mixing. In the final stage of mixing, the dough will come together into a lump and begin slapping against the bowl as it separates from the side. The finished dough should be glossy and pass a windowpane test (stretching it thin enough to let light through without tearing).

Desired final dough temperature: 26°C (79°F).

FIRST PROOF

8 Cover the bowl with a damp tea towel and proof the dough for 30 minutes. Perform a fold by stretching one side of the dough up out of the bowl and folding it down over the remaining dough in the bowl.

FINAL DOUGH (ADDITIONS)

20 g (0.71 oz) cream (40% milkfat)	(8%)
40 g (1.41 oz) egg (from approx. 1 egg)	(16%)
15 g (0.53 oz) water	(6%)
125 g (4.41 oz) bread flour	(50%)
5 g (0.18 oz) fine sea salt	(2%)
43 g (1.52 oz) raw (demerara) sugar	(20%)
25 g (0.88 oz) unsalted cultured butter, softened	(10%)

(Values in parentheses indicate baker's percentages)

DIVIDE AND REST

9 Turn the dough out onto the bench and divide into 8 × 60 g (2.12 oz) portions. Round each piece gently by placing your palm over the dough and rolling it taut against the surface of the bench. Cover and refrigerate for 20–30 minutes.

SHAPE

10 Take one 45 g (1.59 oz) cookie dough piece from the fridge. Place it between two sheets of baking paper and roll it into a thin disc slightly larger than a dough ball. Peel off the top layer of baking paper.

11 Prepare a small bowl of raw sugar. Carefully place the disc, dough side down, onto the sugar and peel away the baking paper. Press gently to adhere the sugar to the dough.

12 Place a dough ball, seam side up, next to the sugar bowl. Lift the sugared disc out of the bowl and drape it, sugared side up, over the dough ball, tucking in the edges to seal. Repeat with the remaining cookie crust pieces and dough.

FINAL PROOF

13 Place the shaped buns on a baking tray lined with baking paper. Proof at 30°C (86°F) for 45 minutes (see page 27) or until slightly puffy but not doubled in size (an overproofed melon bun will collapse).

BAKE AND SERVE

14 Preheat the oven to 180°C (356°F) fan-forced.

15 Bake for 9 minutes, or until the cookie crust is set and lightly golden at the edges. Cool on a wire rack.

16 Like melon buns, this is a sweet treat – perfect when you need a quick sugar boost or when you're craving something sweet. The chocolate chips make it especially satisfying with coffee or tea.

STORE

17 Enjoy as soon as possible, as the cookie crust gradually absorbs moisture and loses its crispness. If not eating straight away, allow to cool completely, then wrap each bun tightly in plastic wrap and freeze to preserve the texture. Store frozen buns for up to 2 weeks. Thaw at room temperature for 2–3 hours, then warm in the oven to restore crispness before serving.

MATCHA MELON BUN

MATCHA MERONPAN

抹茶メロンパン

Matcha melon bun is our take on the classic: melon bun topped with a roasted green matcha cookie crust. It has a different personality from the original – gentler, aromatic and distinctly Japanese in its aftertaste.

For this recipe, we recommend using ceremonial-grade matcha if possible. The difference shows up immediately: the green stays vivid after baking, and the flavour is clearer. It's one of those cases where a better-quality ingredient makes all the difference.

MAKES 8

MATCHA COOKIE CRUST/ 'MELON SKIN' (MAKE AHEAD)

68 g (2.40 oz) cultured unsalted butter, softened	
1 vanilla bean, split lengthways and seeds scraped (or 1 teaspoon vanilla paste)	
78 g (2.75 oz) raw (demerara) sugar, plus extra for coating	
53 g (1.87 oz) egg (from approx. 1 egg), beaten	
134 g (4.73 oz) plain (all-purpose) flour	
15 g (0.53 oz) almond meal (ground almonds)	
2 g (0.07 oz) baking powder	
7 g (0.25 oz) ceremonial-grade matcha powder, plus extra for dusting	

SPONGE DOUGH (MAKE AHEAD)

125 g (4.41 oz) bread flour	(50%)
8 g (0.28 oz) raw (demerara) sugar	(3%)
3 g (0.11 oz) osmotolerant instant dry yeast	(1.2%)
100 g (3.53 oz) full-cream (whole) milk, lukewarm	(40%)

Day 1

MAKE THE MATCHA COOKIE CRUST DOUGH

1. Place the softened butter, vanilla seeds or paste and sugar in a bowl. Mix until creamy but not aerated.
2. Add the egg in 3–4 stages, mixing thoroughly after each one so the mixture emulsifies smoothly.
3. Mix the plain flour, almond meal, baking powder and matcha thoroughly in a bowl.
4. Add the flour–matcha mixture to the batter and mix gently with a spatula until combined.
5. Divide the dough into 8 × 40 g (1.41 oz) portions and roll into balls. Wrap each piece separately in plastic wrap, then flatten slightly and refrigerate overnight. (Alternatively, you can chill the dough as a whole slab and divide it the next day.)

MAKE THE SPONGE DOUGH

6. Combine the bread flour, sugar and yeast in a bowl. Add the lukewarm milk and mix until no dry flour remains. Cover and proof at room temperature until doubled in size, about 1 hour. Refrigerate overnight (up to 16 hours).

Desired final sponge dough temperature before refrigeration: 26°C (79°F).

Day 2

MIX THE FINAL DOUGH

7. Place the cream, egg and water into the bowl of a stand mixer fitted with a dough hook, followed by the bread flour and salt. Tear the sponge dough into pieces and add to the bowl. Mix on speed 3 (low) for 5 minutes. Increase to speed 6 (medium–high) and mix for 10 minutes. Add the sugar and mix on speed 6 for a further 10 minutes, or until the dough starts coming together. Gradually add the softened butter and continue mixing. In the final stage of mixing, the dough will come together into a lump and begin slapping against the bowl as it separates from the side. The finished dough should be glossy and pass a windowpane test (stretching it thin enough to let light through without tearing).

Desired final dough temperature: 26°C (79°F).

FIRST PROOF

8. Cover the bowl with a damp tea towel and proof the dough for 30 minutes. Perform a fold by stretching one side of the dough up out of the bowl and folding it down over the remaining dough in the bowl.

FINAL DOUGH (ADDITIONS)

20 g (0.71 oz) cream (40% milkfat)	(8%)
40 g (1.41 oz) egg (from approx. 1 egg)	(16%)
15 g (0.53 oz) water	(6%)
125 g (4.41 oz) bread flour	(50%)
5 g (0.18 oz) fine sea salt	(2%)
43 g (1.52 oz) raw (demerara) sugar	(20%)
25 g (0.88 oz) unsalted cultured butter, softened	(10%)

(Values in parentheses indicate baker's percentages)

DIVIDE AND REST

9 Turn the dough out onto the bench and divide into 8 × 60 g (2.12 oz) portions. Round each piece gently by placing your palm over the dough and rolling it taut against the surface of the bench. Cover and refrigerate for 20–30 minutes.

SHAPE

10 Take one 40 g (1.41 oz) cookie dough piece from the fridge. Place it between two sheets of baking paper and roll into a thin disc slightly larger than a dough ball. Peel off the top layer of baking paper.

11 Prepare a small bowl of raw sugar. Carefully place the disc, dough side down, onto the sugar and peel away the baking paper. Press gently to adhere the sugar to the dough.

12 Place a dough ball, seam side up, next to the sugar bowl. Lift the sugared disc out of the bowl and drape it, sugared side up, over the dough ball, tucking in the edges to seal. Repeat with the remaining cookie crust pieces and dough.

FINAL PROOF

13 Place the shaped buns on a baking tray lined with baking paper. Proof at 30°C (86°F) for 45 minutes (see page 27) or until slightly puffy but not doubled in size (an overproofed melon bun will collapse).

BAKE AND SERVE

14 Preheat the oven to 180°C (356°F) fan-forced.

15 Bake for 9 minutes, or until the cookie crust is set and lightly golden at the edges. Cool on a wire rack. As a final touch, dust a light coating of matcha powder over each bun, to taste.

16 Serve with green tea or black tea to complement the matcha flavour. Matcha melon buns are also delicious filled with whipped cream or anko (see page 80). A refined sweet treat – they are perfect for a relaxed afternoon with friends.

STORE

17 Enjoy as soon as possible, as the cookie crust gradually absorbs moisture and loses its crispness. If not eating straight away, allow to cool completely, then wrap each bun tightly in plastic wrap and freeze to preserve the texture. Store frozen buns for up to 2 weeks. Thaw at room temperature for 2–3 hours, then warm in the oven to restore crispness before serving.

HOJICHA MELON BUN

HOJICHA MERONPAN

ほうじ茶メロンパン

Hojicha melon bun is made by topping a simple kashipan dough with a hojicha cookie crust. The goal is straightforward: the roasted aroma of the tea should come through with every bite. We bake the crust a little firmer for a clear crunch, and keep the sweetness modest so the hojicha flavour stands out.

At the bakery in Melbourne, our hojicha melon bun is a bit more technical – a brioche base with hojicha cookie crust and hojicha milk jam (jelly) inside. For this book, I've pared it back to a cleaner version that's easier to make at home while still capturing that deep roasted fragrance of the hojicha.

MAKES 8

HOJICHA COOKIE CRUST/'MELON SKIN' (MAKE AHEAD)

68 g (2.40 oz) cultured unsalted butter, softened	
1 vanilla bean, split lengthways and seeds scraped (or 1 teaspoon vanilla paste)	
78 g (2.75 oz) raw (demerara) sugar, plus extra for coating	
68 g (2.40 oz) egg (from approx. 1 large egg), beaten	
131 g (4.62 oz) plain (all-purpose) flour	
15 g (0.53 oz) almond meal (ground almonds)	
2 g (0.07 oz) baking powder	
10 g (0.35 oz) hojicha powder, plus extra for dusting	

SPONGE DOUGH (MAKE AHEAD)

125 g (4.41 oz) bread flour	(50%)
8 g (0.28 oz) raw (demerara) sugar	(3%)
3 g (0.11 oz) osmotolerant instant dry yeast	(1.2%)
100 g (3.53 oz) full-cream (whole) milk, lukewarm	(40%)

Day 1

MAKE THE HOJICHA COOKIE CRUST DOUGH

1 Place the softened butter, vanilla seeds or paste and sugar in a bowl. Mix until creamy but not aerated.

2 Add the egg in 3–4 stages, mixing thoroughly after each addition so the mixture emulsifies smoothly.

3 Mix the plain flour, almond meal, baking powder and hojicha thoroughly in a bowl.

4 Add the flour–hojicha mixture to the batter and mix gently with a spatula until combined.

5 Divide the dough into 8 × 40 g (1.41 oz) portions and roll into balls. Wrap each piece separately in plastic wrap, then flatten slightly and refrigerate overnight. (Alternatively, you can chill the dough as a whole slab and divide it the next day.)

MAKE THE SPONGE DOUGH

6 Combine the bread flour, sugar and yeast in a bowl. Add the lukewarm milk and mix until no dry flour remains. Cover and proof at room temperature until doubled in size, about 1 hour. Refrigerate overnight (up to 16 hours).

Desired final sponge dough temperature before refrigeration: 26°C (79°F).

Day 2

MIX THE FINAL DOUGH

7 Place the cream, egg and water into the bowl of a stand mixer fitted with a dough hook, followed by the bread flour and salt. Tear the sponge dough into pieces and add to the bowl. Mix on speed 3 (low) for 5 minutes. Increase to speed 6 (medium–high) and mix for 10 minutes. Add the sugar and mix on speed 6 for a further 10 minutes, or until the dough starts coming together. Gradually add the softened butter and continue mixing. In the final stage of mixing, the dough will come together into a lump and begin slapping against the bowl as it separates from the side. The finished dough should be glossy and pass a windowpane test (stretching it thin enough to let light through without tearing).

Desired final dough temperature: 26°C (79°F).

FIRST PROOF

8 Cover the bowl with a damp tea towel and proof the dough for 30 minutes. Perform a fold by stretching one side of the dough up out of the bowl and folding it down over the remaining dough in the bowl.

FINAL DOUGH (ADDITIONS)

20 g (0.71 oz) cream (40% milkfat)	(8%)
40 g (1.41 oz) egg (from approx. 1 egg)	(16%)
15 g (0.53 oz) water	(6%)
125 g (4.41 oz) bread flour	(50%)
5 g (0.18 oz) fine sea salt	(2%)
43 g (1.52 oz) raw (demerara) sugar	(20%)
25 g (0.88 oz) unsalted cultured butter, softened	(10%)

(Values in parentheses indicate baker's percentages)

DIVIDE AND REST

9 Turn the dough out onto the bench and divide into 8 × 60 g (2.12 oz) portions. Round each piece gently by placing your palm over the dough and rolling it taut against the surface of the bench. Cover and refrigerate for 20–30 minutes.

SHAPE

10 Take one 40 g (1.41 oz) cookie dough piece from the fridge. Place it between two sheets of baking paper and roll into a thin disc slightly larger than a dough ball. Peel off the top layer of baking paper.

11 Prepare a small bowl of raw sugar. Carefully place the disc, dough side down, onto the sugar and peel away the baking paper. Press gently to adhere the sugar to the dough.

12 Place a dough ball, seam side up, next to the sugar bowl. Lift the sugared disc out of the bowl and drape it, sugared side up, over the dough ball, tucking in the edges to seal. Repeat with the remaining cookie crust pieces and dough.

FINAL PROOF

13 Place the shaped buns on a baking tray lined with baking paper. Proof at 30°C (86°F) for 45 minutes (see page 27) or until slightly puffy but not doubled in size (an overproofed melon bun will collapse).

BAKE AND SERVE

14 Preheat the oven to 180°C (356°F) fan-forced.

15 Bake for 9 minutes, or until the cookie crust is set and lightly golden at the edges. Cool on a wire rack. As a final touch, dust a light coating of hojicha powder over each bun, to taste.

16 Serve with tea to complement the hojicha flavour. It's also delicious filled with whipped cream.

STORE

17 Enjoy as soon as possible, as the cookie crust gradually absorbs moisture and loses its crispness. If not eating straight away, allow to cool completely, then wrap each bun tightly in plastic wrap and freeze to preserve the texture. Store frozen buns for up to 2 weeks. Thaw at room temperature for 2–3 hours, then warm in the oven to restore crispness before serving.

CHOCO CORNET

CHOKO KORONE

チョココロネ

Here's an icebreaker: ask your Japanese friend how they eat their cornet. From the head or from the tail – it's a question every Japanese kid has faced at least once.

The cornet is a soft, coiled bun shaped like a seashell, filled with chocolate or custard cream. It sits at that sweet intersection between bread and dessert, designed for small hands and easy joy. The name comes from the metal mould it's baked around – a coronet – the same tool once used in Europe to make puff pastry horns. But the idea of filling that hollow after baking is a Japanese touch.

The cornet's appeal isn't nostalgia so much as rhythm – the familiar spiral, the clean break of the tip, the way it fits perfectly into a paper bag or a school lunchbox. Some foods survive because they're comforting; the cornet survives because it's complete.

MAKES 8

SPONGE DOUGH (MAKE AHEAD)

125 g (4.41 oz) bread flour	(50%)
8 g (0.28 oz) raw (demerara) sugar	(3%)
3 g (0.11 oz) osmotolerant instant dry yeast	(1.2%)
100 g (3.53 oz) full-cream (whole) milk, lukewarm	(40%)

CHOCOLATE CUSTARD CREAM

- 25 g (0.88 oz) cornflour (cornstarch)
- 10 g (0.35 oz) plain (all-purpose) flour
- 300 g (10.58 oz) full-cream (whole) milk
- 60 g (2.12 oz) raw (demerara) sugar
- ½ vanilla bean, split lengthways and seeds scraped
- 60 g (2.12 oz) egg yolk (from approx. 3 eggs)
- 25 g (0.88 oz) cultured unsalted butter
- 75 g (2.65 oz) dark chocolate (55% cocoa solids), roughly chopped

CHOCOLATE CUSTARD CREAM YIELD

555 g (19.57 oz)

Day 1

MAKE THE SPONGE DOUGH

1. Combine the bread flour, sugar and yeast in a bowl. Add the lukewarm milk and mix until no dry flour remains. Cover and proof at room temperature until doubled in size, about 1 hour. Refrigerate overnight (up to 16 hours).

   Desired final sponge dough temperature before refrigeration: 26°C (79°F).

Day 2

MAKE THE CHOCOLATE CUSTARD

2. Sift the cornflour and plain flour together and set aside.
3. In a saucepan, combine the milk, 20 g (0.71 oz) of the sugar and the vanilla bean pod and seeds. Heat until just simmering.
4. In a heatproof bowl, whisk the egg yolk and the remaining 40 g (1.41 oz) sugar until pale and thick.
5. Slowly pour the hot milk into the egg-yolk mixture, whisking constantly to avoid curdling. Strain the mixture back into the saucepan through a fine-mesh sieve.
6. Set the pan over medium–high heat, stirring the mixture constantly with a rubber spatula and scraping the base of the pan to prevent burning. As the custard thickens and begins to bubble, continue stirring until it suddenly loosens and becomes smooth and glossy.
7. Remove from the heat, add the butter and dark chocolate and mix until fully incorporated. Discard the vanilla bean pod.
8. Spread the custard onto a tray, press plastic wrap directly onto the surface and chill in the freezer for 30–60 minutes.
9. Gently whisk until smooth and creamy before moving the custard to the fridge.

MIX THE FINAL DOUGH

10. Place the cream, egg and water into the bowl of a stand mixer fitted with a dough hook, followed by the bread flour and salt. Tear the sponge dough into pieces and add to the bowl. Mix on speed 3 (low) for 5 minutes. Increase to speed 6 (medium–high) and mix for 10 minutes. Add the raw sugar and mix on speed 6 for a further 10 minutes or until the dough starts coming together. Gradually add the softened butter and continue mixing. In the final stage of mixing, the dough will come together into a lump and begin slapping against the bowl as it separates from the side. The finished dough should be glossy and pass a windowpane test (stretching it thin enough to let light through without tearing).

    Desired final dough temperature: 26°C (79°F).

FIRST PROOF

11. Cover the bowl with a damp tea towel and proof the dough for 30 minutes. Perform a fold by stretching one side of the dough up out of the bowl and folding it down over the remaining dough in the bowl.

THE GREAT CHOCO CORNET DEBATE

'Do you eat the choco cornet from the head or the tail?'

The question exploded in 2007 after appearing in the anime *Lucky☆Star*, where the characters spend a full scene discussing which end to start from – the pointed tip or the open, bready top. The exchange was so memorable that it sparked real-life polls and online arguments across Japan.

Yamazaki Baking even ran a campaign referencing the debate, and convenience stores briefly printed playful diagrams showing 'Team Head' vs. 'Team Tail'.

Surveys typically show a split: about 60 per cent start from the head for the chocolate hit, while 40 per cent begin at the tail to save the best for last.

FINAL DOUGH (ADDITIONS)

20 g (0.71 oz) cream (40% milkfat)	(8%)
40 g (1.41 oz) egg (from approx. 1 egg)	(16%)
15 g (0.53 oz) water	(6%)
125 g (4.41 oz) bread flour, plus extra for dusting	(50%)
5 g (0.18 oz) fine sea salt	(2%)
43 g (1.52 oz) raw (demerara) sugar	(20%)
25 g (0.88 oz) unsalted cultured butter, softened	(10%)

(Values in parentheses indicate baker's percentages)

EGG WASH (OPTIONAL)

50 g (1.76 oz) egg (from approx. 1 egg)
15 g (0.53 oz) water or full-cream (whole) milk

DIVIDE AND REST

12 Turn the dough out onto the bench and divide into 8 × 60 g (2.12 oz) portions. Round each piece into an oval by gently placing your palm over the dough and rolling it taut against the surface of the bench. Cover with the tea towel and rest on the bench for 20 minutes to relax the gluten.

SHAPE

13 Lightly flour the bench, then flatten each piece of dough into an oval. Working with one piece of dough at a time, with a long edge facing you, fold the dough into thirds by bringing the top and bottom edges into the middle, then fold it in half. Pinch the seam tightly to seal, then roll the dough gently back and forth until it stretches to about 30 cm (12 in) in length.

14 Lightly coat eight cream horn moulds with oil spray. Wrap the rolled dough strips around the moulds, starting from the wide end and working towards the narrow end. Press the end gently to seal, then place on a baking tray lined with baking paper.

FINAL PROOF

15 Proof at 30°C (86°F) for 45 minutes (see page 27) or until the dough looks puffy and light.

BAKE

16 Preheat the oven to 180°C (356°F) fan-forced.

17 If using the egg wash, whisk the ingredients together in a small bowl, then strain the mixture through a sieve. Brush the surface of the cornets with the egg wash.

18 Bake for 9 minutes, or until golden brown. Carefully remove the cornets from the moulds and transfer to a wire rack to cool.

FINISH

19 Whip the chocolate custard cream lightly to soften it, then transfer to a piping bag fitted with your desired nozzle. Once the cornets are completely cooled, pipe 65 g (2.29 oz) of the chocolate custard cream into the open end of each cornet.

SERVE

20 Serve as an afternoon treat. The smooth, sweet chocolate custard makes it feel extra special.

STORE

21 The cornets are best enjoyed on the day they are made or within 24 hours, as the custard cream will make the cornets soggy. For longer storage, freeze individual unfilled cornets, wrapped tightly in plastic wrap and placed in a freezer-safe bag, for up to 2 weeks. For the custard cream, spread it thinly and evenly on a sheet of plastic wrap, then wrap carefully with more plastic wrap and freeze it flat. Do not pipe the custard cream before freezing. Thaw the shells and the custard cream at room temperature. Lightly warm the shells in the oven, if desired. Transfer the custard cream to a bowl and whisk gently, then spoon into a piping bag and pipe the custard cream into the cornets just before serving.

CUSTARD CORNET

KURIMU KORONE

クリームコロネ

Some kids never choose chocolate. And some days, even chocolate-lovers want something gentler. That's where the custard cornet steps in – the same soft, coiled seashell bun as its chocolate cousin, but filled with a cool, silky custard cream that tastes like sunshine and milk.

Japan is famous for creating variations that meet every imaginable preference, and the custard cornet feels like a product of that mindset: if there's a black spiral, there should be a white one; if there's chocolate, there must be cream. It's all about maintaining harmony.

MAKES 8

SPONGE DOUGH (MAKE AHEAD)

125 g (4.41 oz) bread flour	(50%)
8 g (0.28 oz) raw (demerara) sugar	(3%)
3 g (0.11 oz) osmotolerant instant dry yeast	(1.2%)
100 g (3.53 oz) full-cream (whole) milk, lukewarm	(40%)

CUSTARD CREAM

- 25 g (0.88 oz) cornflour (cornstarch)
- 10 g (0.35 oz) plain (all-purpose) flour
- 300 g (10.58 oz) full-cream (whole) milk
- 60 g (2.12 oz) raw (demerara) sugar
- ½ vanilla bean, split lengthways and seeds scraped
- 60 g (2.12 oz) egg yolk (from approx. 3 eggs)
- 25 g (0.88 oz) cultured unsalted butter

CUSTARD CREAM YIELD

480 g (17.0 oz)

↓ MORE INGREDIENTS

Day 1

MAKE THE SPONGE DOUGH

1 Combine the bread flour, sugar and yeast in a bowl. Add the lukewarm milk and mix until no dry flour remains. Cover and proof at room temperature until doubled in size, about 1 hour. Refrigerate overnight (up to 16 hours).

Desired final sponge dough temperature before refrigeration: 26°C (79°F).

Day 2

MAKE THE CUSTARD CREAM

2 Sift the cornflour and plain flour together and set aside.

3 In a saucepan, combine the milk, 20 g (0.71 oz) of the raw sugar and the vanilla bean pod and seeds. Heat until just simmering.

4 In a heatproof bowl, whisk the egg yolk and the remaining 40 g (1.41 oz) sugar until pale and thick.

5 Slowly pour the hot milk into the egg-yolk mixture, whisking constantly to avoid curdling. Strain the mixture back into the saucepan through a fine-mesh sieve.

6 Set the pan over medium–high heat, stirring the mixture constantly with a rubber spatula and scraping the base of the pan to prevent burning. As the custard thickens and begins to bubble, continue stirring until it suddenly loosens and becomes smooth and glossy.

7 Remove from the heat, add the butter and mix until fully incorporated.

8 Spread the custard onto a tray, press plastic wrap directly onto the surface and chill in the freezer for 30–60 minutes.

9 Gently whisk until smooth and creamy before moving the custard to the fridge.

MIX THE FINAL DOUGH

10 Place the cream, egg and water into the bowl of a stand mixer fitted with a dough hook, followed by the bread flour and salt. Tear the sponge dough into pieces and add to the bowl. Mix on speed 3 (low) for 5 minutes. Increase to speed 6 (medium–high) and mix for 10 minutes. Add the raw sugar and mix on speed 6 for a further 10 minutes or until the dough starts coming together. Gradually add the softened butter and continue mixing. In the final stage of mixing, the dough will come together into a lump and begin slapping against the bowl as it separates from the side. The finished dough should be glossy and pass a windowpane test (stretching it thin enough to let light through without tearing).

Desired final dough temperature: 26°C (79°F).

FIRST PROOF

11 Cover the bowl with a damp tea towel and proof the dough for 30 minutes. Perform a fold by stretching one side of the dough up out of the bowl and folding it down over the remaining dough in the bowl.

↓ RECIPE CONTINUES

FINAL DOUGH (ADDITIONS)

20 g (0.71 oz) cream (40% milkfat)	(8%)
40 g (1.41 oz) egg (from approx. 1 egg)	(16%)
15 g (0.53 oz) water	(6%)
125 g (4.41 oz) bread flour, plus extra for dusing	(50%)
5 g (0.18 oz) fine sea salt	(2%)
43 g (1.52 oz) raw (demerara) sugar	(20%)
25 g (0.88 oz) unsalted cultured butter, softened	(10%)

(Values in parentheses indicate baker's percentages)

EGG WASH (OPTIONAL)

50 g (1.76 oz) egg (from approx. 1 egg)
15 g (0.53 oz) water or full-cream (whole) milk

DIVIDE AND REST

12 Turn the dough out onto the bench and divide into 8 × 60 g (2.12 oz) portions. Round each piece into an oval by gently placing your palm over the dough and rolling it taut against the surface of the bench. Cover with the tea towel and rest on the bench for 20 minutes to relax the gluten.

SHAPE

13 Lightly flour the bench, then flatten each piece of dough into an oval. Working with one piece of dough at a time, with a long edge facing you, fold the dough into thirds by bringing the top and bottom edges into the middle, then fold it in half. Pinch the seam tightly to seal, then roll the dough gently back and forth until it stretches to about 30 cm (12 in) in length.

14 Lightly coat eight cream horn moulds with oil spray. Wrap the rolled dough strips around the moulds, starting from the wide end and working towards the narrow end. Press the end gently to seal, then place on a baking tray lined with baking paper.

FINAL PROOF

15 Proof at 30°C (86°F) for 45 minutes (see page 27) or until the dough looks puffy and light.

BAKE

16 Preheat the oven to 180°C (356°F) fan-forced.

17 If using the egg wash, whisk the ingredients together in a small bowl, then strain the mixture through a sieve. Brush the surface of the cornets with the egg wash.

18 Bake for 9 minutes, or until golden brown. Carefully remove the cornets from the moulds and transfer to a wire rack to cool.

FINISH

19 Whip the custard cream lightly to soften it, then transfer to a piping bag fitted with your desired nozzle. Once the cornets are completely cooled, pipe 60 g (2.12 oz) of the custard cream into the open end of each cornet.

SERVE

20 Serve as an afternoon treat. As a child I remember the conundrum of choosing between cream buns and cream cornets. Sometimes it was about mood – whether to enjoy a bun with its filling hidden inside, or the playful fun of a cornet, twirling it in your hands and adjusting the cream as you eat.

STORE

21 The cornets are best enjoyed on the day they are made or within 24 hours, as the custard cream will make the cornets soggy. For longer storage, freeze individual unfilled cornets, wrapped tightly in plastic wrap and placed in a freezer-safe bag, for up to 2 weeks. For the custard cream, spread it thinly and evenly on a sheet of plastic wrap, then wrap carefully with more plastic wrap and freeze it flat. Do not pipe the custard cream before freezing. Thaw the shells and the custard cream at room temperature. Lightly warm the shells in the oven, if desired. Transfer the custard cream to a bowl and whisk gently, then spoon into a piping bag and pipe the custard cream into the cornets just before serving.

TRI-COLOUR BUN

SANSHOKUPAN

三色パン

Japanese bread culture, which began with anpan (see page 98), includes many breads with fillings. Most are small, single-serve portions. This approach may have been influenced by Chinese dumplings. In Japanese bakeries, there's even a term – 包あん (hoan), wrapping a filling inside dough – which closely echoes the Chinese 包 (bao); the same character and the same idea. The motion is identical to what dim sum chefs do when they tuck filling into dough using their hands and a small scraper.

Thanks to anpan, this wrapping technique became a standard skill in Japanese bakeries – and that's how I learnt it too.

Sanshokupan (three-flavour bread) is made from three small buns joined together, each with a different filling. You don't know which flavour is in which one bun until you tear it open, and that small reveal is part of the charm. It's fun to choose which piece to eat first, or who to share which one with. Getting three flavours in one go feels a little special.

You can fill these buns with anything you like, but here we use the classic trio: anko, custard cream and strawberry jam.

MAKES 5

SPONGE DOUGH (MAKE AHEAD)

125 g (4.41 oz) bread flour	(50%)
8 g (0.28 oz) raw (demerara) sugar	(3%)
3 g (0.11 oz) osmotolerant instant dry yeast	(1.2%)
100 g (3.53 oz) full-cream (whole) milk, lukewarm	(40%)

FINAL DOUGH (ADDITIONS)

20 g (0.71 oz) cream (40% milkfat)	(8%)
40 g (1.41 oz) egg (from approx. 1 egg)	(16%)
15 g (0.53 oz) water	(6%)
125 g (4.41 oz) bread flour, plus extra for dusting	(50%)
5 g (0.18 oz) fine sea salt	(2%)
43 g (1.52 oz) raw (demerara) sugar	(17%)
25 g (0.88 oz) unsalted butter, softened	(10%)

(Values in parentheses indicate baker's percentages)

Day 1

MAKE THE SPONGE DOUGH

1 Combine the flour, sugar and yeast in a bowl. Add the lukewarm milk and mix until no dry flour remains. Cover and proof at room temperature until doubled in size, about 1 hour. Refrigerate overnight (up to 16 hours).

Desired final sponge dough temperature before refrigeration: 26°C (79°F).

Day 2

MIX THE FINAL DOUGH

2 Place the cream, egg and water into the bowl of a stand mixer fitted with a dough hook, followed by the flour and salt. Tear the sponge dough into pieces and add to the bowl. Mix on speed 3 (low) for 5 minutes. Increase to speed 6 (medium–high) and mix for 10 minutes. Add the sugar and mix on speed 6 for a further 10 minutes, or until the dough starts coming together. Gradually add the softened butter and continue mixing. In the final stage of mixing, the dough will come together into a lump and begin slapping against the bowl as it separates from the side. The finished dough should be glossy and pass a windowpane test (stretching it thin enough to let light through without tearing).

Desired final dough temperature: 26°C (79°F).

FIRST PROOF

3 Cover the bowl with a damp tea towel and proof the dough for 30 minutes. Perform a fold by stretching one side of the dough up out of the bowl and folding it down over the remaining dough in the bowl.

DIVIDE AND REST

4 Turn the dough out onto the bench and divide into 5 sets of 3 × 30 g (1.06 oz) portions. Round each piece gently by placing your palm over the dough and rolling it taut against the surface of the bench. Cover with the tea towel and rest on the bench for 20 minutes to relax the gluten.

THE GREAT-GRANDDADDY OF JAPANESE SWEETS

Wagashi dates back over a thousand years, with early forms appearing in the Nara period (710–794 CE) when Japan first encountered Chinese confections. By the Heian period (794–1185 CE), aristocrats enjoyed simple sweets made from rice, nuts and fruit. More refined styles developed in the Edo era (1603–1868), when sugar became easier to obtain and tea culture shaped how sweets were designed and served.

Modern matcha culture leans towards lattes, cakes and soft serve, but ceremonial matcha is naturally astringent – clean, grassy, intentionally bitter. Wagashi was made to counterbalance that sharpness. In tea ceremony, the pairing is a way of tuning the palate to the seasons and paying attention to the small details of nature.

FILLINGS

100 g (3.53 oz) Anko (see page 80)
100 g (3.53 oz) Custard cream (see page 130)
100 g (3.53 oz) Strawberry jam (see page 102)

EGG WASH

50 g (1.76 oz) egg (from approx. 1 egg)
15 g (0.53 oz) water or full-cream (whole) milk

SHAPE

5 Lightly flour the bench and place the dough seam side up. Flatten the dough pieces into 6–8 cm (2½–3¼ in) discs, keeping the edges thinner and the centre slightly thicker to prevent the filling from breaking through the dough.

6 Scoop a portion of anko (around 20 g/0.71 oz) onto the centre of one dough disc. Lift the edge of the dough up and around the filling, pleating and pinching firmly to seal completely. Make sure no bean paste is exposed. Repeat to make five anko buns, then repeat the process for the custard and jam fillings and the remaining dough, making sure you remember which buns have which filling.

7 Turn the buns seam side down and gently round between your palms until smooth and dome-shaped.

8 Group the buns into five sets of three, so that each set has an anko, custard and jam bun. Transfer to a baking tray lined with baking paper, arranging each set of buns in a triangle just lightly touching.

FINAL PROOF

9 Proof at 30°C (86°F) for 45 minutes (see page 27) or until the dough looks puffy and light.

BAKE AND SERVE

10 Preheat the oven to 180°C (356°F) fan-forced.

11 Whisk the egg wash ingredients together in a small bowl, then strain the mixture through a sieve. Brush the surface of the buns with the egg wash.

12 Bake for 9 minutes, or until evenly golden brown. Cool on a wire rack.

13 Dive straight in! The real joy of tri-colour buns is deciding where to tear it first – it's a little like Russian roulette, as you never know which flavour you'll get. You can tear and taste each section separately, or take a generous bite and let the flavours mix together.

STORE

14 Once completely cool, store the tri-colour buns, wrapped tightly in plastic wrap and in an airtight container, for up to 1 day. For longer storage, freeze individual tri-colour buns, wrapped tightly in plastic wrap and placed in a freezer-safe bag, for up to 2 weeks. Thaw at room temperature for 2–3 hours before eating.

CHARACTER BUN

DOBUTSU PAN

動物パン

When I became a baker at a small neighbourhood bakery in Japan, no one was happier than my family. My wife and daughter had always loved *Karasu No Panyasan* (*Mr Crow's Bakery*), a picture book by Satoshi Kako. There's a spread in that book showing breads in every imaginable shape, filling both pages so completely that you almost hesitate to turn the page. It made me realise just how free and playful bread can be.

The bakery where I worked had a few breads shaped like familiar characters – ones that probably skirted copyright a little. A honey-loving bear, a smiling anpan face ...

Drawing those expressions with chocolate or icing was pure fun. Kids adored them, of course. And my wife and daughter could always pick out which ones I had made just by looking at their faces. (Apparently mine had the best smiles.)

The moments that make baking feel magical are when the dough is completely in your hands – when you can shape it however you like, and then watch it come out of the oven glowing golden brown, smelling warm and toasty, with a shiny, proud little expression of its own. And the fact that it's something you can actually eat – that's the best part.

I want more people, especially children, to feel that same joy. I spend my mornings covered in flour, racing against fermenting dough in the kitchen long before sunrise. But the instant I see kids wandering around the shop, nibbling on the bread I made, all that tiredness just disappears.

And if you're making these at home, draw any face or character you like – half the fun is seeing who appears once the oven door opens.

MAKES 7

SPONGE DOUGH (MAKE AHEAD)

125 g (4.41 oz) bread flour	(50%)
8 g (0.28 oz) raw (demerara) sugar	(3%)
3 g (0.11 oz) osmotolerant instant dry yeast	(1.2%)
100 g (3.53 oz) full-cream (whole) milk, lukewarm	(40%)

Day 1

MAKE THE SPONGE DOUGH

1 Combine the flour, sugar and yeast in a bowl. Add the lukewarm milk and mix until no dry flour remains. Cover and proof at room temperature until doubled in size, about 1 hour. Refrigerate overnight (up to 16 hours).

Desired final sponge dough temperature before refrigeration: 26°C (79°F).

Day 2

MIX THE FINAL DOUGH

2 Place the cream, egg and water into the bowl of a stand mixer fitted with a dough hook, followed by the flour and salt. Tear the sponge dough into pieces and add to the bowl. Mix on speed 3 (low) for 5 minutes. Increase to speed 6 (medium–high) and mix for 10 minutes. Add the sugar and mix on speed 6 for a further 10 minutes, or until the dough starts coming together. Gradually add the softened butter and continue mixing. In the final stage of mixing, the dough will come together into a lump and begin slapping against the bowl as it separates from the side. The finished dough should be glossy and pass a windowpane test (stretching it thin enough to let light through without tearing).

Desired final dough temperature: 26°C (79°F).

FIRST PROOF

3 Cover the bowl with a damp tea towel and proof the dough for 30 minutes. Perform a fold by stretching one side of the dough up out of the bowl and folding it down over the remaining dough in the bowl.

DIVIDE AND REST

4 Turn the dough out onto the bench and divide into 7 × 70 g (2.47 oz) portions. From each portion, cut off two 5 g (0.18 oz) pieces for the ears and one 2 g (0.07 oz) piece for the nose.

5 Round the main portions of dough by gently by placing your palm over the dough and rolling it taut against the surface of the bench. Cover with the tea towel and rest on the bench for 20 minutes to relax the gluten.

FINAL DOUGH (ADDITIONS)

20 g (0.71 oz) cream (40% milkfat)	(8%)
40 g (1.41 oz) egg (from approx. 1 egg)	(16%)
15 g (0.53 oz) water	(6%)
125 g (4.41 oz) bread flour, plus extra for dusting	(50%)
5 g (0.18 oz) fine sea salt	(2%)
43 g (1.52 oz) raw (demerara) sugar	(20%)
25 g (0.88 oz) unsalted cultured butter, softened	(10%)

(Values in parentheses indicate baker's percentages)

EGG WASH

50 g (1.76 oz) egg (from approx. 1 egg)
15 g (0.53 oz) water or full-cream (whole) milk

CHOCOLATE DETAILING

80 g (2.82 oz) dark chocolate chips
4 g (0.14 oz) coconut oil

SHAPE

6 Lightly flour the bench and place the dough seam side down. Flatten the dough pieces into 6–8 cm (2½–3¼ in) discs.

7 Roll the dough for the ears into rounds. Roll the dough very thinly for the noses, about the thickness of a gyoza wrapper. Spray a little water on the dough, then stick the ears and noses to each of the dough discs.

FINAL PROOF

8 Proof at 30°C (86°F) for 45 minutes (see page 27) or until the dough looks puffy and light.

MAKE THE EGG WASH

9 Whisk the egg wash ingredients together in a small bowl, then strain the mixture through a sieve.

MAKE THE CHOCOLATE DETAILING

10 Melt the chocolate in a heatproof bowl set over a saucepan of barely simmering water. When almost fully melted, add the coconut oil and stir to combine. Transfer the chocolate mixture to a piping bag (see page 145).

BAKE

11 Preheat the oven to 180°C (356°F) fan-forced.

12 Brush the surface of the buns lightly with egg wash.

13 Bake for 9 minutes, or until evenly golden brown. Cool on a wire rack.

FINISH

14 Pipe faces onto the bears, adding eyes and a mouth.

SERVE

15 Enjoy your creations as soon as possible after decorating, to enjoy both the appearance and texture at their best. These breads are all about fun – from shaping them to taking the first bite – and are perfect to make with friends or children.

STORE

16 The buns are best enjoyed on the day they are made or within 24 hours. For longer storage, freeze individual undecorated buns, wrapped tightly in plastic wrap and placed in a freezer-safe bag, for up to 2 weeks. Thaw at room temperature before decorating with fresh chocolate detailing.

CHOCOLATE DETAILING WITH A BAKING-PAPER PIPING BAG

YOU WILL NEED:

- Baking paper
- Sharp knife or scissors
- 1 × quantity Chocolate detailing (see page 143)

MAKE A BAKING-PAPER PIPING BAG

1 Cut a piece of baking paper into a 20 × 10 cm (8 × 4 in) rectangle.

2 With a long edge facing you, fold the paper from one corner upwards to create an offset triangle.

3 Using a sharp knife or a pair of scissors, cut along the fold line to create two triangles.

4 Place a triangle on the bench with the longest edge sitting on the left. Fold the bottom of the triangle up to the midway point, then unfold it.

5 Using the fold as a guide, roll the baking paper into a small cone from the bottom-left corner, keeping hold of the corner as you roll, as this will form the tip of the cone. Adjust the cone so the tip is tight and precise.

6 Fold the overlapping top edges inwards once or twice to secure the shape. This helps the piping bag hold its form and prevents it from opening while you work.

MELT THE CHOCOLATE AND FILL THE BAG

7 Follow the instructions on page 143 to make the chocolate detailing.

8 As chocolate cools quickly, it's best to work in small amounts. Spoon a small amount of the melted chocolate into the bag, filling it about two-thirds full.

9 Twist the top to push the chocolate down towards the tip.

TEST FLOW

10 Snip a tiny opening at the tip (about 1–2 mm/$\frac{1}{16}$ in to start). If the chocolate is difficult to pipe, cut a slightly larger hole – you can always cut a little bigger, but you can't make the opening smaller.

11 Pipe onto a plate or sheet of baking paper first to test the flow.

WRITE OR DECORATE

12 Hold the bag like a pen and gently squeeze.

13 Move smoothly and steadily to draw lines or patterns.

SET

14 Let the chocolate set at room temperature.

15 Do not refrigerate the buns once decorated, as this can affect the quality of the buns. If the chocolate in the bag begins to set before you finish, prepare a fresh bag. This step gets easier with practice.

MILK FRANCE

MIRUKU FURANSU

ミルクフランス

Whenever I return to Tokyo, there's one bread I always buy first at the airport convenience store: Yamazaki Baking's Nice Stick. Born in 1977, Nice Stick is Yamazaki's masterpiece – a 30 cm (12 in) bread roll that's become one of Japan's longest-running bestsellers, shifting more than 73 million sticks a year. It's a simple idea: a slender, soft roll filled from tip to tip with a line of milk cream, designed for easy eating and endless sharing.

If Yamazaki has the Nice Stick, then Milk France is the slender bread filled with sweet cream that you can find in bakeries all over Japan. Yes, due to trademark restrictions, we call it 'Milk France', but it's essentially the same kind of long, cream-filled bread. By the way, the reason it's called 'France' is that in Japan, baguettes are referred to as 'French bread', and since this bread is shaped like a long baguette, it became 'Milk France'.

When I opened my bakery in Melbourne, I decided to make Milk France simply because I wanted to eat it myself. I carefully crafted the sweetness and softness of the cream and the balance of the milky flavour, all while thinking fondly of that beloved long, cream-filled bread. I believe the beauty of handmade bread is that no matter how hard you try, you can't quite replicate the factory-made feel – and that's part of its charm.

MAKES 7

SPONGE DOUGH (MAKE AHEAD)

125 g (4.41 oz) bread flour	(50%)
8 g (0.28 oz) raw (demerara) sugar	(3%)
3 g (0.11 oz) osmotolerant instant dry yeast	(1.2%)
100 g (3.53 oz) full-cream (whole) milk, lukewarm	(40%)

MILK CREAM

200 g (7.05 oz) unsalted cultured butter, brought to room temperature
140 g (4.94 oz) icing (confectioners') sugar
3 g (0.11 oz) vanilla extract
40 g (1.41 oz) sweetened condensed milk
30 g (1.06 oz) cream (40% milkfat)

Day 1

MAKE THE SPONGE DOUGH

1 Combine the flour, sugar and yeast in a bowl. Add the lukewarm milk and mix until no dry flour remains. Cover and proof at room temperature until doubled in size, about 1 hour. Refrigerate overnight (up to 16 hours).

Desired final sponge dough temperature before refrigeration: 26°C (79°F).

Day 2

MAKE THE MILK CREAM

2 Place the butter in a bowl, then sift in the icing sugar. Mix roughly with a hand mixer until combined. Add the vanilla extract and condensed milk, then beat on high speed for 3–4 minutes, until the mixture becomes light and pale. Add the cream and mix on low speed until fully combined. Set aside in the fridge.

MIX THE FINAL DOUGH

3 Place the cream, egg and water into the bowl of a stand mixer fitted with a dough hook, followed by the flours and salt. Tear the sponge dough into pieces and add to the bowl. Mix on speed 3 (low) for 5 minutes. Increase to speed 6 (medium–high) and mix for 10 minutes. Add the sugar and mix on speed 6 for a further 10 minutes, or until the dough starts coming together. Gradually add the softened butter and continue mixing. In the final stage of mixing, the dough will come together into a lump and begin slapping against the bowl as it separates from the side. The finished dough should be glossy and pass a windowpane test (stretching it thin enough to let light through without tearing).

Desired final dough temperature: 26°C (79°F).

FIRST PROOF

4 Cover the bowl with a damp tea towel and proof the dough for 30 minutes. Perform a fold by stretching one side of the dough up out of the bowl and folding it down over the remaining dough in the bowl.

DIVIDE AND REST

5 Turn the dough out onto the bench and divide into 7 × 70 g (2.47 oz) portions. Round each piece into an oval by gently by placing your palm over the dough and rolling it taut against the surface of the bench. Cover with the tea towel and rest on the bench for 20 minutes to relax the gluten.

FINAL DOUGH (ADDITIONS)

20 g (0.71 oz) cream (40% milkfat)	(8%)
40 g (1.41 oz) egg (from approx. 1 egg)	(16%)
25 g (0.88 oz) water	(10%)
85 g (3.0 oz) bread flour, plus extra for dusting	(34%)
40 g (1.41 oz) plain (all-purpose) flour	(16%)
5 g (0.18 oz) fine sea salt	(2%)
35 g (1.23 oz) raw (demerara) sugar	(14%)
35 g (1.23 oz) unsalted butter, softened	(14%)

(Values in parentheses indicate baker's percentages)

EGG WASH

50 g (1.76 oz) egg (from approx. 1 egg)
15 g (0.53 oz) water or full-cream (whole) milk

SHAPE

6 Lightly flour the bench and place the dough seam side up. Flatten each piece of dough into a rectangle shape. Working with one piece of dough at a time, with a long edge facing you, fold the dough into thirds by bringing the top and bottom edges into the middle, then fold it in half. Pinch the seam tightly to seal, then roll the dough gently back and forth until it stretches to about 16 cm (6¼ in) in length. Arrange seam side down on a baking tray lined with baking paper.

7 Score the dough with a series of shallow, overlapping diagonal cuts.

FINAL PROOF

8 Proof at 30°C (86°F) for 45 minutes (see page 27) or until the dough looks puffy and light.

BAKE

9 Preheat the oven to 180°C (356°F) fan-forced.

10 Whisk the egg wash ingredients together in a small bowl, then strain the mixture through a sieve. Brush the surface of the dough with the egg wash.

11 Bake for 9 minutes, or until evenly browned. Cool on a wire rack.

FINISH

12 Remove the milk cream from the fridge and whisk well. Transfer the cream to a piping bag fitted with your chosen nozzle.

13 Make a cut along the length of each baguette and pipe in the milk cream.

SERVE

14 Enjoy as a light snack any time of day. It's easy to keep reaching for another, so enjoy in moderation and savour each piece.

STORE

15 Milk France are best eaten on the day they are made. If not eating straight away, store the cream in an airtight container in the fridge and consume within 24 hours. Wrap the baguettes individually in plastic wrap or store in an airtight container at room temperature for 2–3 days. For longer storage, freeze the bread only, wrapped tightly in plastic wrap and in a freezer-safe bag, for up to 2 weeks. Thaw at room temperature and fill with fresh milk cream just before serving.

AMASHOKU

AMASHOKU

アマショク

Amashoku is a nostalgic Showa-era bread: simple, lightly sweet, does the job.

When I was a kid, my dad used to eat this often. I didn't know its name back then – I just called it 'Mount Fuji bread' because of the way the top cracked open like a little peak of a mountain. I've always loved its flavour but find it a little dry, so this version uses a small amount of honey to soften the crumb and give it a gentle, moist finish.

MAKES 6

- 20 g (0.71 oz) unsalted butter
- 50 g (1.76 oz) egg (from approx. 1 egg), beaten
- 10 g (0.35 oz) full-cream (whole) milk
- 50 g (1.76 oz) raw (demerara) sugar
- 10 g (0.35 oz) honey (or glucose syrup)
- 100 g (3.53 oz) plain (all-purpose) flour
- 3 g (0.11 oz) baking powder
- 1.5 g (0.05 oz) baking soda

1. Before you begin, bring the butter, egg and milk to room temperature.
2. Preheat the oven to 180°C (356°F) fan-forced. Line a baking tray with baking paper.
3. Place the butter in a large bowl and beat it until smooth. Add the sugar and mix well until fully incorporated. Add the egg in three stages, mixing well after each addition.
4. Add the milk and honey and mix until smooth.
5. Sift the flour, baking powder and baking soda into the bowl, then mix gently with a rubber spatula until fully incorporated.
6. Spoon the batter into a piping bag fitted with a round nozzle.
7. Pipe one-sixth of the batter into a 5 cm (2 in) diameter domed cone shape on the prepared tray. Repeat with the remaining batter to make six amashoku, leaving space in between each one for spreading.
8. Lightly grease a knife with neutral oil and gently score a cross on the top of each amashoku.
9. Bake for 8 minutes, or until golden brown.
10. Transfer the amashoku to a wire rack to cool.

SERVE

11. Enjoy as a teatime treat. As a child, I remember my dad enjoying amashoku with his beer – an unusual pairing, looking back. As it's the kind of sweet that can dry your mouth, be sure to have a drink on hand as you enjoy it. With its soft, sponge-like texture, it's especially lovely served with tea or coffee.

STORE

12. Wrap each piece individually in plastic wrap or store in an airtight container and keep for 2–3 days at room temperature. For longer storage, freeze individually wrapped amashoku for up to 2 weeks. Thaw at room temperature, then warm lightly in the oven before serving.

CHAPTER FOUR

RORUPAN

CHAPTER FOUR

RORUPAN

ロールパン

In this chapter, we focus on breads that sit quietly at the centre of everyday life – simple rolls that slip easily into lunchboxes, adorn breakfast tables and support weeknight dinners.

One thing that sets Japanese bread culture apart from its Western counterpart is its emphasis on individual portions. That pattern took hold after World War II, when school lunches were introduced to improve children's nutrition, and the format naturally spread into households. During the high-growth era, neighbourhood bakeries expanded on this idea, creating small, ready-to-eat breads that suited busy families and became part of daily routines.

These breads don't have the showmanship of kashipan (sweet bread) or souzaipan (savoury filled bread), but their appeal is steady and reassuring. Once you bake them, you start to understand why they've stayed favourites for so long: they're modest, dependable and strangely addictive in their simplicity.

BUTTER ROLL

BATA RORU

バターロール

Butter rolls arrived in Japan with the introduction of Western baking, but unlike European dinner rolls, they were softened and sweetened to suit local tastes. The dough is enriched with milk, sugar and butter – not enough to be brioche, but just enough to give it a delicate sheen and tender crumb. Each roll is shaped into a small crescent, its smooth surface brushed with egg wash before baking.

Where shokupan was made to slice and coppepan to fill, the butter roll was designed to hold its own. It sits somewhere between bread and confectionery: rich enough to be eaten plain, yet also good company to any meal. This adaptability made it a permanent breakfast fixture in hotels and homes, and a steady presence in school lunches throughout the 1960s.

In the 1970s, the 'butter roll forming machine' was introduced, allowing bakeries across Japan to produce butter rolls with consistent quality. This technological innovation helped establish Japan's unique butter roll culture, making them easily available at convenience stores and supermarkets today. They are usually sold in packs of four or six rolls and, recently, versions filled with margarine have become popular.

Butter rolls are perfect for busy households: individually portioned, ready to eat without toasting and easy for kids to grab. They're convenient for lunchboxes and great as a sandwich base or served alongside a meal. Once you discover the deliciousness and convenience of butter rolls, chances are you'll find yourself making them almost every week.

MAKES 8

SPONGE DOUGH (MAKE AHEAD)

125 g (4.41 oz) bread flour	(50%)
8 g (0.28 oz) raw (demerara) sugar	(3%)
3 g (0.11 oz) osmotolerant instant dry yeast	(1.2%)
100 g (3.53 oz) full-cream (whole) milk, lukewarm	(40%)

FINAL DOUGH (ADDITIONS)

20 g (0.71 oz) cream (40% milkfat)	(8%)
40 g (1.41 oz) egg (from approx. 1 egg)	(16%)
15 g (0.53 oz) water	(6%)
85 g (3.0 oz) bread flour, plus extra for dusting	(34%)
40 g (1.41 oz) plain (all-purpose) flour	(16%)
5 g (0.18 oz) fine sea salt	(2%)
27 g (0.95 oz) raw (demerara) sugar	(11%)
35 g (1.23 oz) cultured unsalted butter, softened	(14%)

(Values in parentheses indicate baker's percentages)

↓ MORE INGREDIENTS

Day 1

MAKE THE SPONGE DOUGH

1 Combine the bread flour, sugar and yeast in a bowl. Add the lukewarm milk and mix until no dry flour remains. Cover and proof at room temperature until doubled in size, about 1 hour. Refrigerate overnight (up to 16 hours).

Desired final sponge dough temperature before refrigeration: 26°C (79°F).

Day 2

MIX THE FINAL DOUGH

2 Place the cream, egg and water into the bowl of a stand mixer fitted with a dough hook, followed by the flours and salt. Tear the sponge dough into pieces and add to the bowl. Mix on speed 3 (low) for 5 minutes. Increase to speed 6 (medium–high) and mix for 10 minutes. Add the sugar and mix on speed 6 for a further 10 minutes, or until the dough starts coming together. Gradually add the softened butter and continue mixing. In the final stage of mixing, the dough will come together into a lump and begin slapping against the bowl as it separates from the side. The finished dough should be glossy and pass a windowpane test (stretching it thin enough to let light through without tearing).

Desired final dough temperature: 26°C (79°F).

FIRST PROOF

3 Cover the bowl with a damp tea towel and proof the dough for 30 minutes. Perform a fold by stretching one side of the dough up out of the bowl and folding it down over the remaining dough in the bowl.

DIVIDE AND REST

4 Turn the dough out onto the bench and divide into 8 × 60 g (2.12 oz) portions. Round each piece gently by placing your palm over the dough and rolling it taut against the surface of the bench. Cover and rest in the fridge for 30 minutes to relax the gluten.

↓ RECIPE CONTINUES

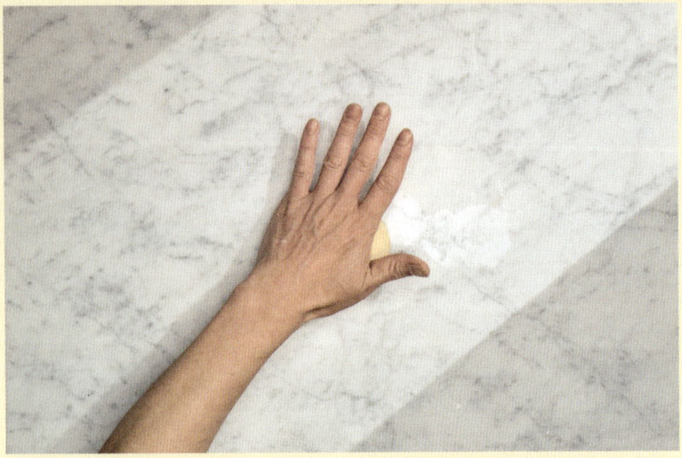

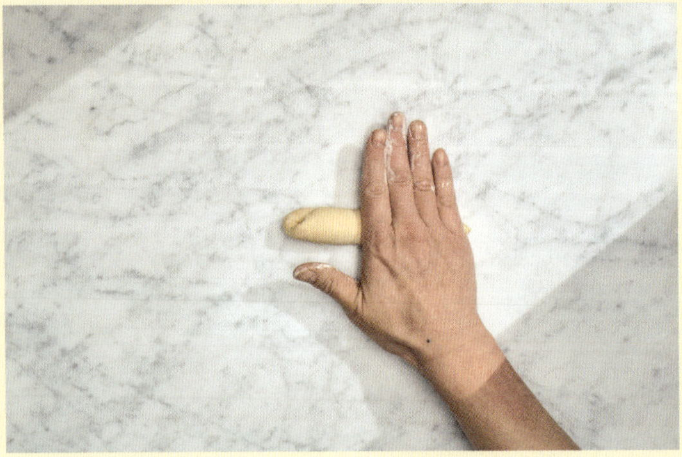

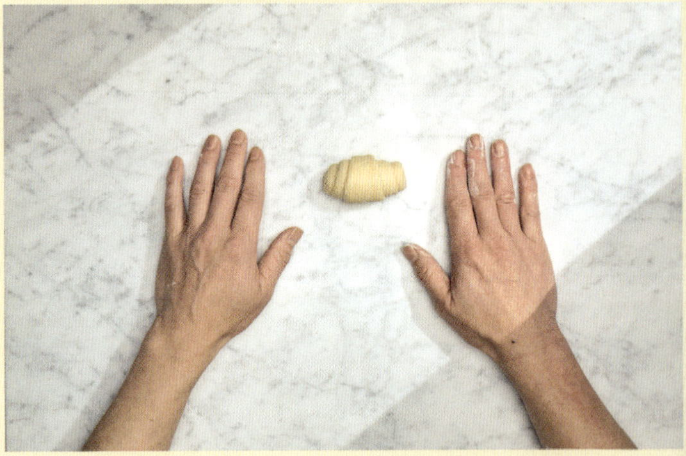

EGG WASH

50 g (1.76 oz) egg
(from approx. 1 egg)

15 g (0.53 oz) cream
or full-cream (whole) milk

SHAPE

5 Lightly flour the bench and place the dough seam side up. Working with one piece of dough at a time, flatten the dough, then fold it in half and gently roll to form a teardrop shape. Use a rolling pin to elongate the shape until it is 12–15 cm (4¾–6 in) long. Cover and rest again in the fridge for 15 minutes.

6 Flatten the dough once more (especially near the wide end), then roll tightly from the wide end towards the tip, tucking the tip underneath.

7 Arrange the dough, seam side down, on a baking tray lined with baking paper.

FINAL PROOF

8 Proof at 30°C (86°F) for 45 minutes (see page 27) or until the dough looks puffy and light.

BAKE AND SERVE

9 Preheat the oven to 185°C (365°F) fan-forced.

10 Whisk together the egg wash ingredients in a small bowl, then strain the mixture through a sieve. Brush the surface of the rolls lightly with the egg wash.

11 Bake for 9 minutes, or until the tops of the rolls are evenly golden brown. Cool on a wire rack.

12 Serve as part of a breakfast spread, as a side to meals or use to make sandwiches.

STORE

13 Wrap each roll individually in plastic wrap or store in an airtight container and keep at room temperature for up to 2 days. For longer storage, freeze individually wrapped rolls in a freezer-safe bag for up to 2 weeks. Thaw at room temperature, then warm in the oven before serving.

SALT BUN

SHIOPAN

塩パン

Where the butter roll behaves politely at breakfast, shiopan – literally 'salt bread' – crackles under your fingers and leaves a salty gloss on your lips. The hole in its middle is a feature: proof that butter once lived there.

Originating around 2003, the salt bun is now a standard product all over Japan. In recent years, it has also gained popularity in South Korea and Taiwan, China, and it seems that the trend has arrived in Melbourne as well. Honestly, I first learnt about shiopan after moving to Melbourne, and when I saw it for the first time, I thought, 'Isn't this just a regular butter roll?' Nowadays, it's become one of Little Cardigan's most popular items, and I often find myself reaching for one too.

The dough has a firmer texture than our shokupan, offering a slight chewiness without being too heavy. You can enjoy the delightful contrast between the crunchy bottom and the perfect balance of butter and salt that spreads in your mouth.

Remember, when the ingredients are simple, focus on using the best you can find. It makes all the difference.

MAKES 8

SPONGE DOUGH (MAKE AHEAD)

125 g (4.41 oz) bread flour	(50%)
8 g (0.28 oz) raw (demerara) sugar	(3%)
3 g (0.11 oz) osmotolerant instant dry yeast	(1.2%)
100 g (3.53 oz) full-cream (whole) milk, lukewarm	(40%)

FINAL DOUGH (ADDITIONS)

20 g (0.71 oz) cream (40% milkfat)	(8%)
40 g (1.41 oz) egg (from approx. 1 egg)	(16%)
15 g (0.53 oz) water	(6%)
85 g (3.0 oz) bread flour, plus extra for dusting	(34%)
40 g (1.41 oz) plain (all-purpose) flour	(16%)
5 g (0.18 oz) fine sea salt	(2%)
27 g (0.95 oz) raw (demerara) sugar	(11%)
35 g (1.23 oz) cultured unsalted butter, softened	(14%)

(Values in parentheses indicate baker's percentages)

↓ MORE INGREDIENTS

Day 1

MAKE THE SPONGE DOUGH

1 Combine the bread flour, sugar and yeast in a bowl. Add the lukewarm milk and mix until no dry flour remains. Cover and proof at room temperature until doubled in size, about 1 hour. Refrigerate overnight (up to 16 hours).

Desired final sponge dough temperature before refrigeration: 26°C (79°F).

Day 2

MIX THE FINAL DOUGH

2 Place the cream, egg and water into the bowl of a stand mixer fitted with a dough hook, followed by the flours and salt. Tear the sponge dough into pieces and add to the bowl. Mix on speed 3 (low) for 5 minutes. Increase to speed 6 (medium–high) and mix for 10 minutes. Add the sugar and mix on speed 6 for a further 10 minutes, or until the dough starts coming together. Gradually add the softened butter and continue mixing. In the final stage of mixing, the dough will come together into a lump and begin slapping against the bowl as it separates from the side. The finished dough should be glossy and pass a windowpane test (stretching it thin enough to let light through without tearing).

Desired final dough temperature: 26°C (79°F).

FIRST PROOF

3 Cover the bowl with a damp tea towel and proof the dough for 30 minutes. Perform a fold by stretching one side of the dough up out of the bowl and folding it down over the remaining dough in the bowl.

DIVIDE AND REST

4 Turn the dough out onto the bench and divide into 8 × 60 g (2.12 oz) portions. Round each piece gently by placing your palm over the dough and rolling it taut against the surface of the bench. Cover and rest in the fridge for 30 minutes to relax the gluten.

SHAPE

5 Lightly flour the bench and place the dough seam side up. Working with one piece of dough at a time, flatten the dough, then fold it in half and gently roll to form a teardrop shape. Use a rolling pin to elongate the shape until it is 12–15 cm (4¾–6 in) long. Cover and rest again in the fridge for 15 minutes.

↓ RECIPE CONTINUES

FOR SHAPING AND FINISHING

8 × 10 g (0.35 oz) salted butter logs
20 g (0.71 oz) salted butter, melted
pink flaky salt, to garnish

6 Flatten the dough once more (especially near the wide end). Place a 10 g (0.35 oz) salted butter log across the wide end, then roll the dough tightly towards the tip, tucking the tip underneath.

7 Arrange the dough, seam side down, on a baking tray lined with baking paper. Repeat with the remaining dough and butter.

FINAL PROOF

8 Proof at 28°C (82°F) for 1 hour (see page 27) or until the dough looks puffy and light.

BAKE

9 Preheat the oven to 185°C (365°F) fan-forced.

10 Lightly spray water over the surface of each bun. Bake for 9 minutes, or until the tops of the buns are evenly golden brown.

FINISH

11 While still hot, brush each roll generously with the melted salted butter, then sprinkle with pink flaky salt. Cool on a wire rack for 10 minutes before serving.

SERVE

12 Serve for breakfast, lunch or dinner, or enjoy as a quick snack. I love nibbling on them whenever I feel like something to eat. You can add your favourite jam or spread, but for me, the best way is to bite straight into one while it's still warm and just cool enough to hold.

STORE

13 Wrap each bun individually in plastic wrap or store in an airtight container and keep at room temperature for up to 2 days. For longer storage, freeze individually wrapped rolls in a freezer-safe bag for up to 2 weeks. Thaw at room temperature, then warm in the oven before serving.

SALT SAVES THE DAY

The story goes that in the early 2000s, sales dipped at Pan Maison, a small bakery in the quiet port town of Yawatahama, Ehime. Owner Mitoshi Hirata, inspired by Europe's salted breads, wondered if he could make something lighter, softer, more Japanese. He wrapped a pat of butter in dough, sprinkled salt on top, and baked it. The butter melted, crisping the bottom of the bread and perfuming the air. Customers came and returned. Then came the bloggers, the magazines, the imitators.

By the mid-2010s, shiopan had swept Japan – and now its Korean and Hong Kong (China) cousins are trending back towards Europe. It's not an exaggeration to call shiopan the croissant of Asia, but with a saltier attitude.

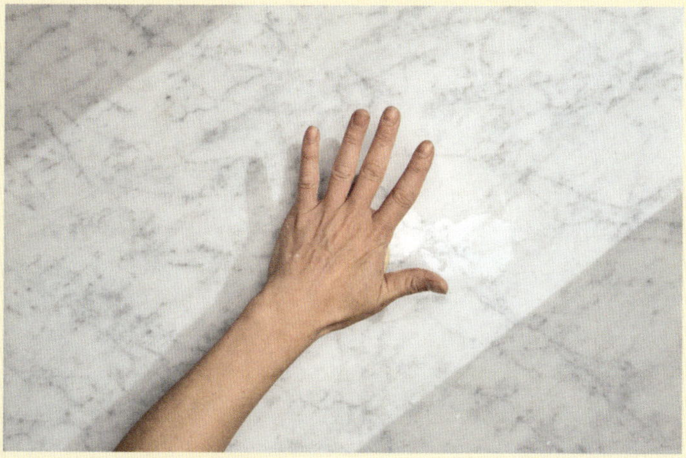
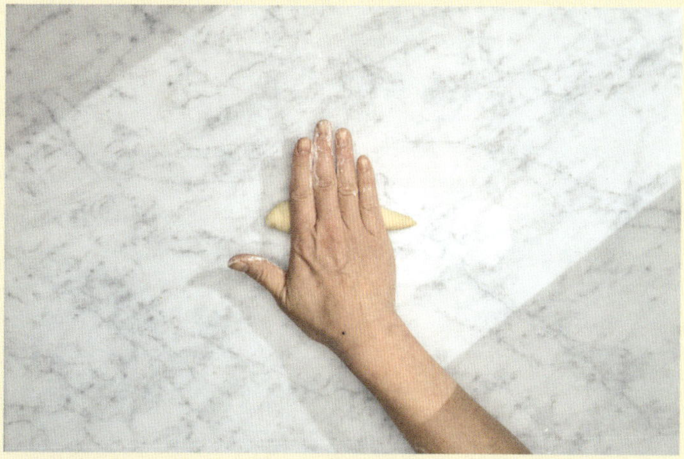

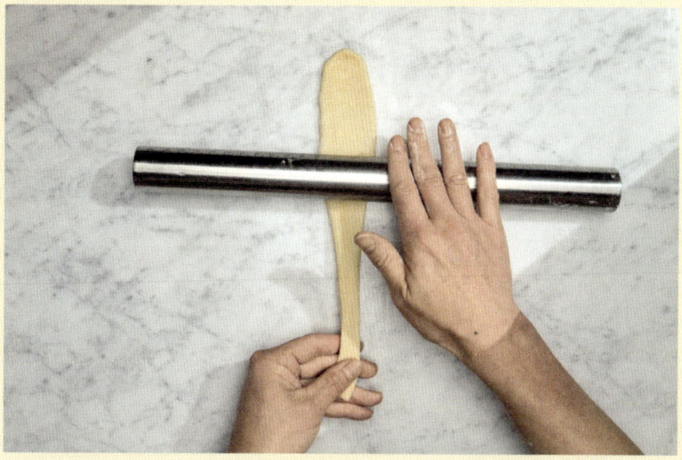
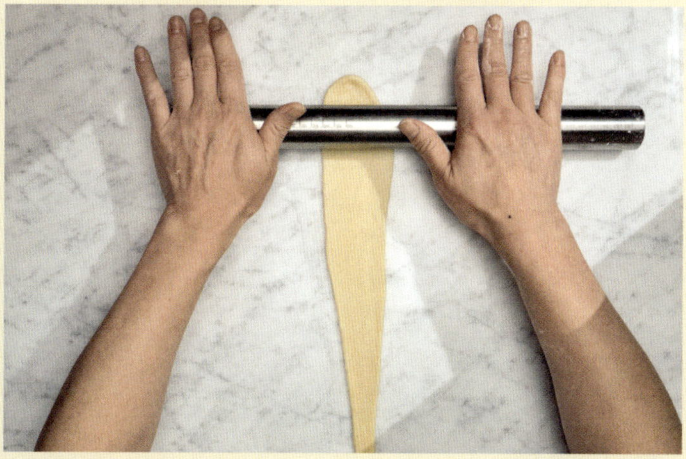

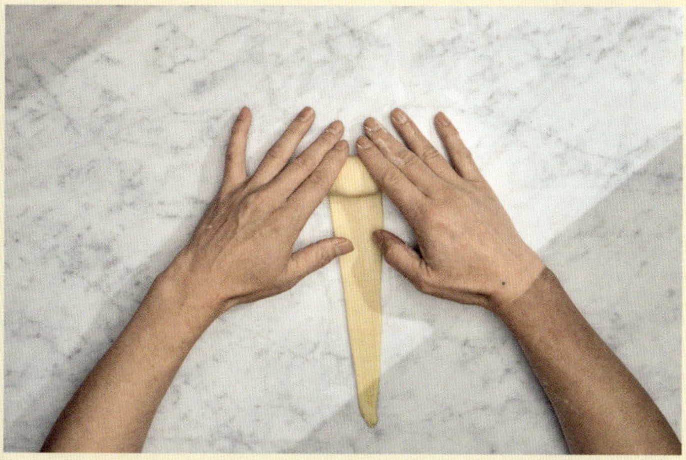

BLACK SUGAR ROLL

KOKUTO RORU

黒糖ロール

'Kokuto' literally means 'black sugar', but it's closer to an unrefined cane sugar with deep caramel and mineral notes. Often from Okinawa, it is made by boiling down pure sugarcane juice until it hardens into syrup-like blocks. It retains its natural molasses and minerals, such as calcium, potassium and iron, giving it a rich, earthy sweetness and a faint bitterness that white sugar lacks. If you have trouble sourcing kokuto, look for muscovado, Barbados sugar or dark unrefined cane sugar – anything that still carries a hint of molasses and grit.

This bread, with the deep sweetness and rustic flavour of kokuto, evokes a comforting sense of nostalgia. Its gentle sweetness makes you want to reach for another piece. I hope that this kind of simple, heartfelt goodness is something we can pass on to the next generation.

MAKES 8

SPONGE DOUGH (MAKE AHEAD)

125 g (4.41 oz) bread flour	(50%)
8 g (0.28 oz) kokuto (black sugar)	(3%)
3 g (0.11 oz) osmotolerant instant dry yeast	(1.2%)
100 g (3.53 oz) full-cream (whole) milk, lukewarm	(40%)

FINAL DOUGH (ADDITIONS)

20 g (0.71 oz) cream (40% milkfat)	(8%)
40 g (1.41 oz) egg (from approx. 1 egg)	(16%)
15 g (0.53 oz) water	(6%)
125 g (4.41 oz) bread flour, plus extra for dusting	(50%)
5 g (0.18 oz) fine sea salt	(2%)
50 g (1.76 oz) kokuto (black sugar)	(20%)
35 g (1.23 oz) cultured unsalted butter, softened	(14%)

(Values in parentheses indicate baker's percentages)

EGG WASH

50 g (1.76 oz) egg (from approx. 1 egg)
15 g (0.53 oz) water or full-cream (whole) milk

Day 1

MAKE THE SPONGE DOUGH

1 Combine the flour, kokuto and yeast in a bowl. Add the lukewarm milk and mix until no dry flour remains. Cover and proof at room temperature until doubled in size, about 1 hour. Refrigerate overnight (up to 16 hours).

Desired final sponge dough temperature before refrigeration: 26°C (79°F).

Day 2

MIX THE FINAL DOUGH

2 Place the cream, egg and water into the bowl of a stand mixer fitted with a dough hook, followed by the flour and salt. Tear the sponge dough into pieces and add to the bowl. Mix on speed 3 (low) for 5 minutes. Increase to speed 6 (medium–high) and mix for 10 minutes. Add the kokuto and mix on speed 6 for a further 10 minutes, or until the dough starts coming together. Gradually add the softened butter and continue mixing. In the final stage of mixing, the dough will come together into a lump and begin slapping against the bowl as it separates from the side. The finished dough should be glossy and pass a windowpane test (stretching it thin enough to let light through without tearing).

Desired final dough temperature: 26°C (79°F).

FIRST PROOF

3 Cover the bowl with a damp tea towel and proof the dough for 30 minutes. Perform a fold by stretching one side of the dough up out of the bowl and folding it down over the remaining dough in the bowl.

DIVIDE AND REST

4 Turn the dough out onto the bench and divide into 8 × 65 g (2.29 oz) portions. Round each piece gently by placing your palm over the dough and rolling it taut against the surface of the bench. Cover with the tea towel and rest on the bench for 20 minutes to relax the gluten.

SHAPE

5 Lightly flour the bench and place the dough seam side up. Flatten each piece of dough into a rectangle shape. Working with one piece of dough at a time, with a long edge facing you, fold the dough into thirds by bringing the top and bottom edges into the middle, then fold it in half. Pinch the seam tightly to seal, then roll the dough gently back and forth until it stretches to about 25 cm (10 in) in length.

6 Twist the dough to make a loop in the middle, then slip one end underneath the loop and bring the other end over the top to form a loose coil. Place the dough on a baking tray lined with baking paper.

FINAL PROOF

7 Proof at 30°C (86°F) for 40 minutes (see page 27) or until the dough looks puffy and light.

BAKE AND SERVE

8 Preheat the oven to 180°C (356°F) fan-forced.

9 Whisk together the egg wash ingredients in a small bowl, then strain the mixture through a sieve. Brush the surface of the rolls lightly with the egg wash.

10 Bake for 9 minutes, or until evenly browned. Cool on a wire rack.

11 Enjoy the rich, deep sweetness of the black sugar by biting into the bun as soon as it's cooled – you won't be able to resist! If it starts to dry out a little, toast it and spread with butter. It's also perfect for a veggie-packed sandwich.

STORE

12 Wrap each roll individually in plastic wrap or store in an airtight container and keep at room temperature for up to 2 days. For longer storage, freeze individually wrapped rolls in a freezer-safe bag for up to 2 weeks. Thaw at room temperature, then toast or warm in the oven before serving.

THE STORY OF KOKUTO

Okinawa's relationship with sugar runs deep. Sugarcane arrived from China in the early Edo period, and by the 1600s, the subtropical islands of Okinawa and Amami were producing kokuto – dark, mineral-rich sugar made by boiling down pure cane juice. It became one of Okinawa's most important trade goods and a taste that defined the region's sweets, from chinsuko biscuits to sata andagi doughnuts. Even today, each island's kokuto tastes slightly different, depending on the island's soil and climate. Kokuto is used in both sweet and savoury dishes, including desserts and braised pork, and can also be eaten as a snack or dissolved to make a syrup.

MISO BUN

MISOPAN

味噌パン

The story goes that in the early 1970s, at Friand Pan–Yogashiten in Numata, a baker borrowed the sauce from the region's beloved yakimanju (grilled manju) and brushed it onto bread instead of dumplings. The result was misopan: part pastry, part souvenir.

Gunma, a wheat-growing prefecture, took it personally. Bakeries competed over whose misopan was the 'true' one – some baked the miso inside, others glazed it on top, a few worked it into the dough. In neighbouring Nagano, the same name describes a completely different bread: miso-flavoured, not miso-filled.

Our version tilts traditional. We fold miso inside the dough so the flavour blooms gently as it bakes. It tastes like an onigiri that wandered into a bakery and decided to never leave. The miso gives the bread a deep, savoury backbone – almost a Vegemite-like richness – and you can use whichever style of miso you prefer. Lighter miso will bake to a soft golden hue with mellow sweetness; darker miso will give a deeper colour and a more assertive, roasted flavour.

MAKES 8

SPONGE DOUGH (MAKE AHEAD)

125 g (4.41 oz) bread flour	(50%)
8 g (0.28 oz) raw (demerara) sugar	(3%)
3 g (0.11 oz) osmotolerant instant dry yeast	(1.2%)
100 g (3.53 oz) full-cream (whole) milk, lukewarm	(40%)

FINAL DOUGH (ADDITIONS)

20 g (0.71 oz) cream (40% milkfat)	(8%)
40 g (1.41 oz) egg (from approx. 1 egg)	(16%)
15 g (0.53 oz) water	(6 %)
30 g (1.06 oz) miso	(12%)
85 g (3.0 oz) bread flour	(34%)
40 g (1.41 oz) plain (all-purpose) flour	(16%)
2 g (0.07 oz) fine sea salt	(0.8%)
25 g (0.88 oz) raw (demerara) sugar	(10%)
35 g (1.23 oz) cultured unsalted butter, softened	(14%)

(Values in parentheses indicate baker's percentages)

Day 1

MAKE THE SPONGE DOUGH

1 Combine the bread flour, sugar and yeast in a bowl. Add the lukewarm milk and mix until no dry flour remains. Cover and proof at room temperature until doubled in size, about 1 hour. Refrigerate overnight (up to 16 hours).

Desired final sponge dough temperature before refrigeration: 26°C (79°F).

Day 2

MIX THE FINAL DOUGH

2 Place the cream, egg, water and miso into the bowl of a stand mixer fitted with a dough hook, followed by the flours and salt. Tear the sponge dough into pieces and add to the bowl. Mix on speed 3 (low) for 5 minutes. Increase to speed 6 (medium–high) and mix for 10 minutes. Add the sugar and mix on speed 6 for a further 10 minutes, or until the dough starts coming together. Gradually add the softened butter and continue mixing. In the final stage of mixing, the dough will come together into a lump and begin slapping against the bowl as it separates from the side. The finished dough should be glossy and pass a windowpane test (stretching it thin enough to let light through without tearing).

Desired final dough temperature: 26°C (79°F).

FIRST PROOF

3 Cover the bowl with a damp tea towel and proof the dough for 30 minutes. Perform a fold by stretching one side of the dough up out of the bowl and folding it down over the remaining dough in the bowl.

DIVIDE AND REST

4 Turn the dough out onto the bench and divide into 8 × 65 g (2.29 oz) portions. Round each piece gently by placing your palm over the dough and rolling it taut against the surface of the bench. Cover with the tea towel and rest on the bench for 20 minutes to relax the gluten.

SHAPE

5 Gently round each piece of dough again, then place seam side down on a baking tray lined with baking paper.

EGG WASH

50 g (1.76 oz) egg (from approx. 1 egg)
15 g (0.53 oz) water or full-cream (whole) milk

FINAL PROOF

6 Proof at 30°C (86°F) for 45 minutes (see page 27) or until the dough looks puffy and light.

BAKE AND SERVE

7 Preheat the oven to 185°C (365°F) fan-forced.

8 Whisk together the egg wash ingredients until smooth, then strain the mixture through a sieve. Brush the surface of the buns lightly with the egg wash.

9 Bake for 9 minutes, or until evenly browned. Cool on a wire rack.

10 Enjoy the buns on their own to appreciate the subtle miso flavour that melts in your mouth, or use to make protein-packed sandwiches such as tuna or egg.

STORE

11 Wrap each bun individually in plastic wrap or store in an airtight container and keep at room temperature for up to 2 days. For longer storage, freeze individually wrapped buns in a freezer-safe bag for up to 2 weeks. Thaw at room temperature, then toast or warm in the oven before serving.

WALNUT BUN

KURUMIPAN

クルミパン

For most of Japan's food history, kurumi (walnuts) had little to do with bread. They appeared in sweets, sauces or regional cooking, but not the daily loaf. That changed in 1984 when the Omiya branch of the bakery chain Andersen developed kurumipan as an original product.

By the 1990s, kurumipan was appearing in bakeries and supermarkets across Japan, helped along by the California Walnut Association, which designated the third day of every month as 'Kurumi Pan Day'.

The original kurumipan had a small round shape, often with five or six curved segments like a flower, baked golden and dusted lightly with flour. Inside, the crumb was soft and pale, laced with roasted walnuts that gave a quiet crunch in every bite.

MAKES 8

SPONGE DOUGH (MAKE AHEAD)

125 g (4.41 oz) bread flour	(50%)
8 g (0.28 oz) raw (demerara) sugar	(3%)
3 g (0.11 oz) osmotolerant instant dry yeast	(1.2%)
100 g (3.53 oz) full-cream (whole) milk	(40%)

FINAL DOUGH (ADDITIONS)

100 g (3.53 oz) walnuts	(40%)
20 g (0.71 oz) cream (40% milkfat)	(8%)
40 g (1.41 oz) egg (from approx. 1 egg)	(16%)
15 g (0.53 oz) water	(6%)
85 g (3.0 oz) bread flour	(34%)
40 g (1.41 oz) plain (all-purpose) flour	(16%)
5 g (0.18 oz) fine sea salt	(2%)
27 g (0.95 oz) raw (demerara) sugar	(11%)
35 g (1.23 oz) cultured unsalted butter, softened	(14%)

(Values in parentheses indicate baker's percentages)

↓ MORE INGREDIENTS

Day 1

MAKE THE SPONGE DOUGH

1 Combine the bread flour, sugar and yeast in a bowl. Add the lukewarm milk and mix until no dry flour remains. Cover and proof at room temperature until doubled in size, about 1 hour. Refrigerate overnight (up to 16 hours).

Desired final sponge dough temperature before refrigeration: 26°C (79°F).

Day 2

ROAST THE WALNUTS

2 Preheat the oven to 150°C (300°F) fan-forced. Line a baking tray with baking paper.

3 Spread the walnuts on the prepared tray in a single layer.

4 Bake for 10–15 minutes, then set aside to cool completely.

MIX THE FINAL DOUGH

5 Place the cream, egg and water into the bowl of a stand mixer fitted with a dough hook, followed by the flours and salt. Tear the sponge dough into pieces and add to the bowl. Mix on speed 3 (low) for 5 minutes. Increase to speed 6 (medium–high) and mix for 10 minutes. Add the sugar and mix on speed 6 for a further 10 minutes, or until the dough starts coming together. Gradually add the softened butter and continue mixing. In the final stage of mixing, the dough will come together into a lump and begin slapping against the bowl as it separates from the side. Add the cooled roasted walnuts and mix on speed 2 (low) for 30–45 seconds – just enough to distribute the walnuts without breaking them. The finished dough should be glossy and pass a windowpane test (stretching it thin enough to let light through without tearing).

Desired final dough temperature: 26°C (79°F).

FIRST PROOF

6 Cover the bowl with a damp tea towel and proof the dough for 30 minutes. Perform a fold by stretching one side of the dough up out of the bowl and folding it down over the remaining dough in the bowl.

DIVIDE AND REST

7 Turn the dough out onto the bench and divide into 8 × 75 g (2.65 oz) portions. Round each piece gently by placing your palm over the dough and rolling it taut against the surface of the bench. Cover with the tea towel and rest on the bench for 15 minutes to relax the gluten.

↓ RECIPE CONTINUES

EGG WASH (OPTIONAL)

50 g (1.76 oz) egg (from approx. 1 egg)
15 g (0.53 oz) water or full-cream (whole) milk

CUT THE TOP PETALS

8 Using a dough scraper or scissors held at a slight angle, make five or six evenly spaced cuts around the top of each dough ball. Cut from the outside towards the centre, stopping 5 mm–1 cm (¼–½ in) before the middle so the petals stay connected. The cuts should be 2.5–3 cm (1–1¼ in) deep.

HORIZONTAL SIDE-SNIPS (CLASSIC JAPANESE METHOD)

9 Hold your scissors parallel to the bench, with the blades pointing straight in. Make a small horizontal snip (5–8 mm/¼–⅓ in deep) into the side of each petal, going around the dough. These side-snips help the petals 'bloom' and expose the walnuts during baking.

OPEN THE PETALS GENTLY

10 Using your fingertips, nudge each petal slightly outwards. Do not push them too much; the oven spring will finish the job. Place the shaped buns seam side down on a baking tray lined with baking paper.

FINAL PROOF

11 Proof at 30°C (86°F) for 45 minutes (see page 27) or until the dough looks puffy and light.

BAKE AND SERVE

12 Preheat the oven to 185°C (365°F) fan-forced.

13 If you like a glossy finish, whisk together the egg wash ingredients until smooth, then strain the mixture through a sieve and lightly brush the surface of the buns – kurumipan are often baked without it.

14 Bake for 9 minutes, or until the tops are evenly golden and the walnuts smell fragrant. Cool on a wire rack.

15 Try this hearty bread on its own first to appreciate the flavour and its satisfying chew. Toast and spread with plenty of butter, use it to make your favourite sandwiches, or pair it with cheeses such as gorgonzola or camembert for a delicious cheese platter.

STORE

16 Wrap each bun individually in plastic wrap or store in an airtight container and keep at room temperature for up to 2 days. For longer storage, freeze individually wrapped buns in a freezer-safe bag for up to 2 weeks. Thaw at room temperature, then toast or warm in the oven before serving.

FROM BUN TO BOOK

When their daughter was born, Harvard's wife craved kurumipan, so he began baking it at home – a dozen rolls every few days. I spotted the buns on Instagram and left a simple comment: *I'd like to try one.*

That was the beginning of my visits to Harvard's house on Little Cardigan Street. Looking back, Harvard laughs at the thought – the rolls were nowhere near good enough for a professional baker. But that's what bread does: when you miss something badly enough, you'll travel to a stranger's kitchen for it.

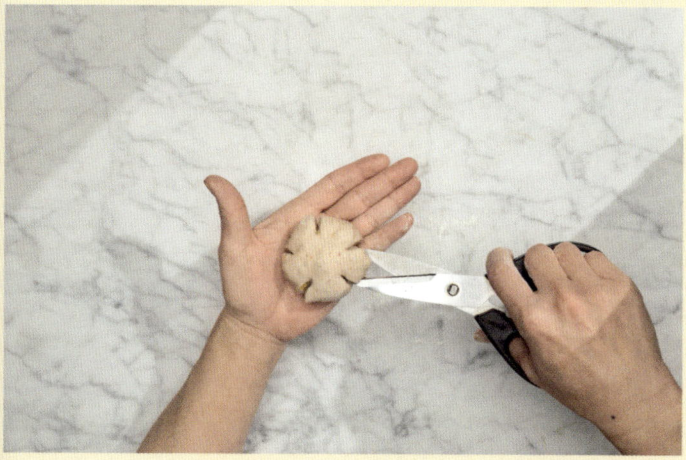

SWEETCORN BUN

KONPAN

コーンパン

Sweetcorn's first visit to Japan came with the Portuguese in the 1500s, likely as livestock feed – coarse, not exactly beloved. That began to change in the Meiji era, when imported varieties took root, and again in the postwar decades, as Japan's appetite for soft, sweet produce grew.

In the 1970s, Sakata Seed released Honey Bantam and then Peter Corn, a bi-colour hybrid – three parts yellow, one part white – that combined sweetness with tender texture. Within three years, Peter Corn made up almost 90 per cent of Japan's sweetcorn crop. Its secret was Sakurast, a seed-coating treatment that made it resistant to soil disease. For a time, it defined the flavour of Japanese summers. Eventually, it too was replaced, as the market shifted back towards single-colour yellow corn varieties like Gold Rush.

Somewhere along that timeline, corn found its way into bakeries. One story credits Donq, in Shizuoka's Seibu department store, where bakers lacking soft-bread ovens improvised by folding corn and syrup into a milky dough. The result was light, fragrant and instantly popular.

From there, konpan took on many forms – round buns stuffed with kernels, open-faced rolls glazed with butter and mayonnaise, and neat rectangular versions designed for convenience-store trays.

With every bite, you get the delightful pop of the corn, and the more you chew, the sweeter the corn tastes – making it a truly delicious bread. It's wonderful toasted with plenty of butter, and it also makes a tasty base for sandwiches with ham and lettuce.

MAKES 8

SPONGE DOUGH (MAKE AHEAD)

125 g (4.41 oz) bread flour	(50%)
8 g (0.28 oz) raw (demerara) sugar	(3%)
3 g (0.11 oz) osmotolerant instant dry yeast	(1.2%)
100 g (3.53 oz) full-cream (whole) milk, lukewarm	(40%)

Day 1

MAKE THE SPONGE DOUGH

1 Combine the bread flour, sugar and yeast in a bowl. Add the lukewarm milk and mix until no dry flour remains. Cover and proof at room temperature until doubled in size, about 1 hour. Refrigerate overnight (up to 16 hours).

Desired final sponge dough temperature before refrigeration: 26°C (79°F).

Day 2

STEAM THE SWEETCORN

2 Remove the husks and silks from the sweetcorn. Steam for 10–12 minutes, until tender, then allow to cool and cut off the kernels.

MIX THE FINAL DOUGH

3 Place the cream, egg and water into the bowl of a stand mixer fitted with a dough hook, followed by the flours and salt. Tear the sponge dough into pieces and add to the bowl. Mix on speed 3 (low) for 5 minutes. Increase to speed 6 (medium–high) and mix for 10 minutes. Add the sugar and mix on speed 6 for a further 10 minutes, or until the dough starts coming together. Gradually add the softened butter and continue mixing. In the final stage of mixing, the dough will come together into a lump and begin slapping against the bowl as it separates from the side. Add the sweetcorn and mix on speed 2 (low) for 30–45 seconds – just enough to distribute the kernels without breaking them. The finished dough should be glossy and pass a windowpane test (stretching it thin enough to let light through without tearing).

Desired final dough temperature: 26°C (79°F).

FIRST PROOF

4 Cover the bowl with a damp tea towel and proof the dough for 30 minutes. Perform a fold by stretching one side of the dough up out of the bowl and folding it down over the remaining dough in the bowl.

FINAL DOUGH (ADDITIONS)

125 g (4.41 oz) sweetcorn kernels (from about 1½ cobs)	(50%)
20 g (0.71 oz) cream (40% milkfat)	(8%)
40 g (1.41 oz) egg (from approx. 1 egg)	(16%)
8 g (0.28 oz) water	(3%)
85 g (3.0 oz) bread flour	(34%)
40 g (1.41 oz) plain (all-purpose) flour	(16%)
5 g (0.18 oz) fine sea salt	(2%)
27 g (0.95 oz) raw (demerara) sugar	(11%)
35 g (1.23 oz) cultured unsalted butter, softened	(14%)

(Values in parentheses indicate baker's percentages)

EGG WASH

50 g (1.76 oz) egg (from approx. 1 egg)
15 g (0.53 oz) water or full-cream (whole) milk

DIVIDE AND REST

5 Turn the dough out onto the bench and divide into 8 × 77 g (2.72 oz) portions. Round each piece gently by placing your palm over the dough and rolling it taut against the surface of the bench. Cover with the tea towel and rest on the bench for 20 minutes to relax the gluten.

SHAPE

6 Gently round each piece of dough again, then place seam side down on a baking tray lined with baking paper.

FINAL PROOF

7 Proof at 30°C (86°F) for 45 minutes (see page 27) or until the dough looks puffy and light.

BAKE AND SERVE

8 Preheat the oven to 185°C (365°F) fan-forced.

9 Whisk together the egg wash ingredients until smooth, then strain the mixture through a sieve. Brush the surface of the buns lightly with the egg wash.

10 Bake for 9 minutes, or until the tops are evenly golden brown. Cool on a wire rack.

11 Enjoy this fun, sweet bread with the crunch of corn on its own, slice it in half and make a cheesy toast, or make a sandwich with ham and veggies – they're all delicious.

STORE

12 Wrap each bun individually in plastic wrap or store in an airtight container and keep at room temperature for up to 2 days. For longer storage, freeze individually wrapped buns in a freezer-safe bag for up to 2 weeks. Thaw at room temperature, then toast or warm in the oven before serving.

SWEET POTATO BUN

SATSUMAIMOPAN

さつまいもパン

Autumn in Japan offers many seasonal flavours, but when it comes to the three most popular sweet ingredients, sweet potatoes, chestnuts and pumpkins (winter squash) top the list, so much so that there's even a Japanese phrase – imo-kuri-kabocha – to remember them by. Each one has a comforting, gentle sweetness and is incredibly versatile, appearing in countless confections on the shelves of pastry shops and supermarkets. While it would be wonderful to introduce all three, here we will focus on sweet potato bread, which is relatively easy to work with.

MAKES 8

SPONGE DOUGH (MAKE AHEAD)

125 g (4.41 oz) bread flour	(50%)
8 g (0.28 oz) raw (demerara) sugar	(3%)
3 g (0.11 oz) osmotolerant instant dry yeast	(1.2%)
100 g (3.53 oz) full-cream (whole) milk, lukewarm	(40%)

SWEET SIMMERED SWEET POTATO (KANRO-NI)

200 g (7.05 oz) Japanese sweet potato (about 1 small)
165 g (5.82 oz) water
130 g (4.59 oz) raw (demerara) sugar

SWEET POTATO YIELD

150 g (5.29 oz)

Day 1

MAKE THE SPONGE DOUGH

1 Combine the bread flour, sugar and yeast in a bowl. Add the lukewarm milk and mix until no dry flour remains. Cover and proof at room temperature until doubled in size, about 1 hour. Refrigerate overnight (up to 16 hours).

Desired final sponge dough temperature before refrigeration: 26°C (79°F).

Day 2

PREPARE THE SWEET POTATO

2 Wash the sweet potato well and dice into 1.5 cm (½ in) cubes. Soak in water for about 15 minutes to remove excess starch and prevent discolouration. Drain.

3 Place the sweet potato cubes in a saucepan and add the water and sugar.

4 Bring to the boil over medium heat, then reduce the heat to low and simmer, turning the pieces occasionally, for 5–10 minutes, until just before tender and the liquid is reduced to a glossy syrup.

5 Remove from the heat and allow the sweet potato to cool. The flavour will deepen as it rests. Store the sweet potato and syrup in an airtight container in the fridge for 2–3 days. Bring the sweet potato to room temperature before straining the syrup and adding the sweet potato to the dough.

MIX THE FINAL DOUGH

6 Place the cream, egg and water into the bowl of a stand mixer fitted with a dough hook, followed by the flours and salt. Tear the sponge dough into pieces and add to the bowl. Mix on speed 3 (low) for 5 minutes. Increase to speed 6 (medium–high) and mix for 10 minutes. Add the sugar and mix on speed 6 for a further 10 minutes, or until the dough starts coming together. Gradually add the softened butter and continue mixing. In the final stage of mixing, the dough will come together into a lump and begin slapping against the bowl as it separates from the side. Add 125 g (4.41 oz) of well-drained room-temperature sweet potato and mix on speed 2 (low) for 30–45 seconds – just enough to distribute the sweet potato without breaking it. The finished dough should be glossy and pass a windowpane test (stretching it thin enough to let light through without tearing).

Desired final dough temperature: 26°C (79°F).

SATSUMAIMO: A ROOT WITH A BIRTHPLACE

Sweet potato first arrived in Japan via the Ryukyu Islands and Satsuma (modern-day Kagoshima) in the 17th century.

The name 'satsumaimo' literally means 'Satsuma potato', named after the region where its cultivation took root and flourished.

It was a resilient crop, thriving where rice could not, and became a symbol of self-sufficiency through times of famine. Over the centuries, it moved from field food to beloved ingredient – the star of yaki-imo, imo yokan and countless nostalgic sweets.

In Kagoshima, bakeries still treat the sweet potato with local pride. Many make satsumaimopan with their own regional produce, folding in roasted cubes or swirling sweet potato paste through soft dough. Walk into a Kyushu bakery in autumn, and you'll see trays of them lined up next to anpan and melonpan: a seasonal ritual that connects farm, oven and comfort in one bite.

In Tokyo and its surrounding prefectures, sweet potato breads mark the arrival of autumn. Known as aki gentei satsumaimopan, they are small pull-apart buns filled with sweet potato and sometimes topped with streusel to evoke nostalgia.

FINAL DOUGH (ADDITIONS)

20 g (0.71 oz) cream (40% milkfat)	(8%)
40 g (1.41 oz) egg (from approx. 1 egg)	(16%)
15 g (0.53 oz) water	(6%)
85 g (3.0 oz) bread flour	(34%)
40 g (1.41 oz) plain (all-purpose) flour	(16%)
5 g (0.18 oz) fine sea salt	(2%)
27 g (0.95 oz) raw (demerara) sugar	(11%)
35 g (1.23 oz) cultured unsalted butter, softened	(14%)

(Values in parentheses indicate baker's percentages)

EGG WASH

50 g (1.76 oz) egg (from approx. 1 egg)
15 g (0.53 oz) water or full-cream (whole) milk

TO ASSEMBLE

black sesame seeds, for sprinkling (optional)

FIRST PROOF

7 Cover the bowl with a damp tea towel and proof the dough for 30 minutes. Perform a fold by stretching one side of the dough up out of the bowl and folding it down over the remaining dough in the bowl.

DIVIDE AND REST

8 Turn the dough out onto the bench and divide into 8 × 77 g (2.72 oz) portions. Round each piece gently by placing your palm over the dough and rolling it taut against the surface of the bench. Cover with the tea towel and rest on the bench for 20 minutes to relax the gluten.

SHAPE

9 Gently round each piece of dough again, then place seam side down on a baking tray lined with baking paper.

FINAL PROOF

10 Proof at 30°C (86°F) for 45 minutes (see page 27) or until the dough looks puffy and light.

BAKE AND SERVE

11 Preheat the oven to 185°C (365°F) fan-forced.

12 Whisk together the egg wash ingredients in a small bowl, then strain the mixture through a sieve. Brush the surface of the buns lightly with the egg wash and score a cross in the top of each bun. Sprinkle generously with black sesame seeds, if desired.

13 Bake for 9 minutes, or until the tops are evenly golden brown. Cool on a wire rack.

14 Serve the sweet potato buns on their own for breakfast or a quick lunch. Spread with jam for a sweet treat or top with hummus or cheese for something savoury.

STORE

15 Wrap each bun individually in plastic wrap or store in an airtight container and keep at room temperature for up to 2 days. For longer storage, freeze individually wrapped buns in a freezer-safe bag for up to 2 weeks. Thaw at room temperature, then toast or warm in the oven before serving.

PUMPKIN BUN

KABOCHAPAN

かぼちゃパン

As seen in our shokupan recipes in chapter one, Japanese bakeries often knead extra ingredients into the dough – seeds, teas or vegetables – to add colour, flavour, or both. Vegetable breads made with spinach, carrot or tomato aren't just meant to be eye-catching; it's also a quiet way to sneak a little extra nutrition into everyday bread. Pumpkin works especially well – it's easy to handle, widely available and gives a natural yellow hue without overpowering the dough.

MAKES 8

SPONGE DOUGH (MAKE AHEAD)

125 g (4.41 oz) bread flour	(50%)
8 g (0.28 oz) raw (demerara) sugar	(3%)
3 g (0.11 oz) osmotolerant instant dry yeast	(1.2%)
100 g (3.53 oz) full-cream (whole) milk	(40%)

FINAL DOUGH (ADDITIONS)

100 g (3.53 oz) Japanese pumpkin (winter squash)	(40%)
20 g (0.71 oz) cream (40% milkfat)	(8%)
40 g (1.41 oz) egg (from approx. 1 egg)	(16%)
8 g (0.28 oz) water	(3%)
85 g (3.0 oz) bread flour, plus extra for dusting	(34%)
40 g (1.41 oz) plain (all-purpose) flour	(16%)
5 g (0.18 oz) fine sea salt	(2%)
27 g (0.95 oz) raw (demerara) sugar	(11%)
35 g (1.23 oz) cultured unsalted butter, softened	(14%)

(Values in parentheses indicate baker's percentages)

Day 1

MAKE THE SPONGE DOUGH

1 Combine the bread flour, sugar and yeast in a bowl. Add the lukewarm milk and mix until no dry flour remains. Cover and proof at room temperature until doubled in size, about 1 hour. Refrigerate overnight (up to 16 hours).

Desired final sponge dough temperature before refrigeration: 26°C (79°F).

Day 2

PREPARE THE PUMPKIN

2 Peel, deseed and dice the pumpkin into bite-sized chunks. Steam for 8–10 minutes, until tender, then pass it through a sieve to make a smooth paste. Allow to cool.

MIX THE FINAL DOUGH

3 Place the cream, egg, water and pumpkin paste into the bowl of a stand mixer fitted with a dough hook, followed by the flours and salt. Tear the sponge dough into pieces and add to the bowl. Mix on speed 3 (low) for 5 minutes. Increase to speed 6 (medium–high) and mix for 10 minutes. Add the sugar and mix on speed 6 for a further 10 minutes, or until the dough starts coming together. Gradually add the softened butter and continue mixing. In the final stage of mixing, the dough will come together into a lump and begin slapping against the bowl as it separates from the side. The finished dough should be glossy and pass a windowpane test (stretching it thin enough to let light through without tearing).

Desired final dough temperature: 26°C (79°F).

FIRST PROOF

4 Cover the bowl with a damp tea towel and proof the dough for 30 minutes. Perform a fold by stretching one side of the dough up out of the bowl and folding it down over the remaining dough in the bowl.

DIVIDE AND REST

5 Turn the dough out onto the bench and divide into 8 × 75 g (2.65 oz) portions. Round each piece gently by placing your palm over the dough and rolling it taut against the surface of the bench. Cover with the tea towel and rest for 15 minutes.

SHAPE

6 Gently round each piece of dough again, then place seam side down on a baking tray lined with baking paper.

FINAL PROOF

7 Proof at 30°C (86°F) for 45 minutes or until the dough looks puffy and light.

BAKE AND SERVE

8 Preheat the oven to 185°C (365°F) fan-forced. Lightly dust the buns with flour and score the top, if desired.

9 Bake for 9 minutes, or until the tops are evenly golden brown. Cool on a wire rack.

10 Serve as a snack, either plain or as a sandwich filled with salad and cheese.

STORE

11 Wrap each bun individually in plastic wrap or store in an airtight container and keep at room temperature for up to 2 days. For longer storage, freeze individually wrapped buns in a freezer-safe bag for up to 2 weeks. Thaw at room temperature, then toast or warm in the oven before serving.

CHAPTER FIVE

CHAPTER FIVE

COPPEPAN

コッペパン

Coppepan is one of Japan's simplest breads, a soft roll that fed the nation after World War II.

Its name comes from the French word 'coupé' – 'to cut' – describing the slit down the middle where fillings are tucked in.

Japan's school lunch program still uses coppepan as a standard carb option. When I was growing up, for many children it was their daily encounter with bread, eaten alongside a drink of milk and a small portion of jam, margarine or curry.

Some bakeries let customers choose their own fillings for coppepan, and those shops were always the busiest. As a child, picking the filling felt exciting, and seeing the baker generously pack mine to order always felt special.

Unlike shokupan, which invites comparison to European loaves, or kashipan, adorned with cream or decorative tops, coppepan is made to carry fillings tied to nostalgia – peanut butter cream, croquettes, even noodles.

COPPEPAN

KOPPEPAN

コッペパン

Coppepan is all about balance: a fine, even crumb with just enough structure to slice and fill. This foundational dough is lightly enriched for softness, then shaped into simple ovals and baked until barely golden. The goal is a roll that stays pillowy, not crusty. Once you have the base, the variations are endless.

MAKES 8

YUDANE (MAKE AHEAD)

59 g (2.08 oz) bread flour with 12% protein	(20%)
6 g (0.21 oz) raw (demerara) sugar	(2%)
88 g (3.1 oz) boiling water	(30%)

FINAL DOUGH (ADDITIONS)

29 g (1.02 oz) cream (40% milkfat)	(10%)
147 g (5.19 oz) water	(50%)
235 g (8.29 oz) bread flour with 12% protein, plus extra for dusting	(80%)
18 g (0.63 oz) raw (demerara) sugar	(6%)
6 g (0.21 oz) fine sea salt	(2%)
4 g (0.14 oz) osmotolerant instant dry yeast	(1.2%)
24 g (0.85 oz) unsalted butter, softened	(8%)

(Values in parentheses indicate baker's percentages)

↓ MORE INGREDIENTS

Day 1

MAKE THE YUDANE

1 Warm a bowl using hot water, then drain and dry it thoroughly.

2 Place the flour and sugar in the bowl and mix well. Add the boiling water in one swift motion, ensuring it evenly coats the flour.

3 While the bowl is still warm, mix the dough with a wooden spatula until it comes together into a cohesive lump. Cover with plastic wrap, pressing it directly onto the surface of the yudane to prevent a crust forming. Once cooled to body temperature, refrigerate overnight to rest. (Yudane can be stored in the fridge for up to 3 days.)

Day 2

MIX THE FINAL DOUGH

4 Place the yudane, cream and water in the bowl of a stand mixer fitted with a dough hook, followed by the flour, sugar, salt and yeast. Mix on speed 3 (low) for 5 minutes. Increase to speed 6 (medium–high) and mix for 20 minutes, or until the dough starts coming together. Gradually add the softened butter and continue mixing. In the final stage of mixing, the dough will come together into a lump and begin slapping against the bowl as it separates from the side. The finished dough should be glossy and pass a windowpane test (stretching thin enough to let light through without tearing).

Desired final dough temperature: 26°C (79°F).

FIRST PROOF

5 Cover the bowl with a damp tea towel and proof the dough for 30 minutes. Perform a fold by stretching one side of the dough up out of the bowl and folding it down over the remaining dough in the bowl.

DIVIDE AND REST

6 Turn the dough out onto the bench and divide into 8 × 75 g (2.65 oz) portions. Form each piece into an oval by gently by placing your palm over the dough and rolling it taut against the surface of the bench. Cover with the tea towel and rest on the bench for 20 minutes to relax the gluten.

↓ RECIPE CONTINUES

EGG WASH

50 g (1.76 oz) egg (from approx. 1 egg)
15 g (0.53 oz) cream (40% milkfat) or full-cream (whole) milk

SHAPE

7 Lightly flour the bench and place the dough seam side up. Flatten each piece of dough into a rectangle shape. Working with one piece of dough at a time, with a long edge facing you, fold the dough into thirds by bringing the top and bottom edges into the middle, then fold it in half. Press the seam tightly to seal, then roll the dough gently back and forth until it stretches to about 18 cm (7 in) in length. Arrange seam side down on a baking tray lined with baking paper.

FINAL PROOF

8 Proof at 30°C (86°F) for 1 hour (see page 27) or until the dough looks puffy and light.

BAKE AND SERVE

9 Preheat the oven to 190°C (374°F) fan-forced.

10 Whisk together the egg wash ingredients until smooth, then strain the mixture through a sieve. Brush the surface of the buns lightly with the egg wash.

11 Bake for 9 minutes, or until the tops of the coppepan are evenly golden brown. Cool on a wire rack.

12 Serve on their own or use as a canvas for sweet and savoury fillings. See the following coppepan recipes for some delicious ideas.

STORE

13 Wrap each bun individually in plastic wrap or store in an airtight container and keep at room temperature for up to 2 days. For longer storage, freeze individually wrapped buns in a freezer-safe bag for up to 2 weeks. Thaw at room temperature, then toast or warm in the oven before serving.

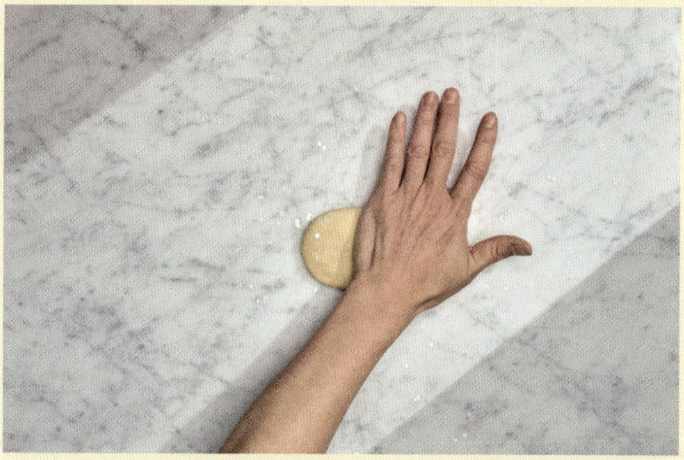
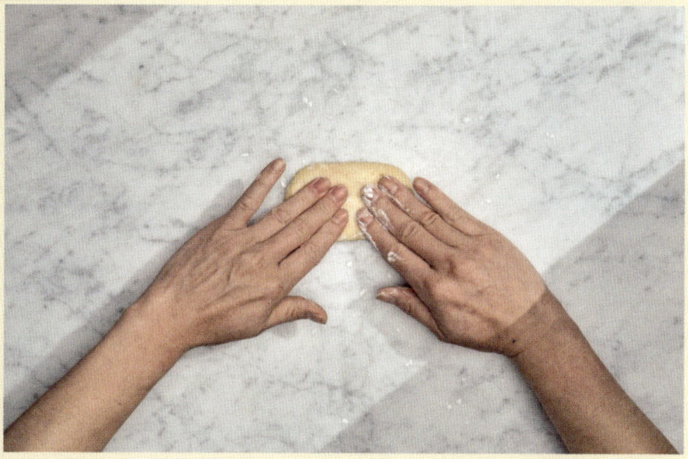

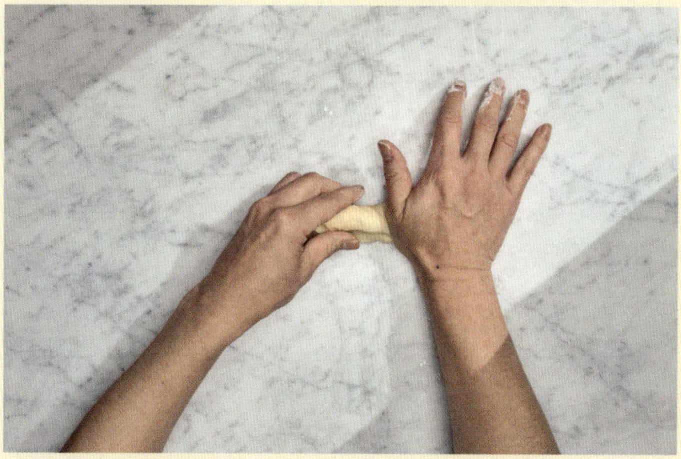
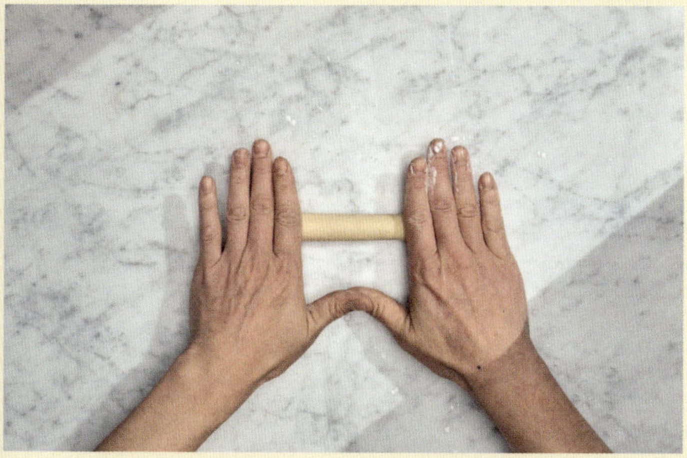

JAM COPPEPAN

JYAMU COPPEPAN

ジャムコッペパン

I will repeat what I said in the jam bun recipe on page 102: when it comes to jam in Japan, it's almost always strawberry jam.

For our jam coppepan, the filling is the same as it has been for decades: strawberry jam, bright and familiar.

It also needs butter – or more accurately, margarine. In the Showa era, jam and margarine were staples of school lunches. I remember getting a small jam sachet with my daily coppepan and trying to work out the ideal ratio as I spread it on.

Even today, packaged coppepan in supermarkets and convenience stores keep the classic jam-and-margarine pairing. It has a flavour that's completely different from jam on toasted bread – softer, sweeter, a little nostalgic – and surprisingly addictive.

MAKES 4

- 4 × Coppepan (see page 193)
- 60 g (2.12 oz) margarine or chilled sliced salted butter
- 120 g (4.23 oz) (or more) Strawberry jam (jelly) (see page 102), for spreading

1. Make a horizontal cut along the length of each coppepan and gently open them.
2. Spread the inside with margarine (or add slices of butter), then generously layer strawberry jam on top.

ANKO BUTTER COPPEPAN

AN BATA COPPEPAN

あんバターコッペパン

Anko is an essential spread for coppepan. What sets it apart from a typical anpan is, without a doubt, the butter. It transforms a simple anpan idea into something richer and more grown-up. The creamy saltiness of the butter against the sweetness of the anko is instantly addictive. Some bakeries swap the butter for whipped cream; at convenience stores you'll even find anko–margarine versions. But the combination of anko and butter – simple, balanced and a little decadent – is the one that never loses its appeal.

MAKES 4

- 4 × Coppepan (see page 193)
- 240 g (8.47 oz) Anko (see page 80)
- 60 g (2.12 oz) chilled sliced salted butter

1. Make a horizontal cut along the length of each coppepan and gently open them.
2. Spread a generous layer of anko, then top with slices of chilled butter.

PEANUT BUTTER COPPEPAN

PEE NATSU BATAA COPPEPAN

ピーナッツバターコッペ

The peanut butter for coppepan should be soft, spreadable and fluffy. Some versions include chunky peanuts for texture, but here we're making a sweet, whipped peanut butter that's light and easy to spread.

MAKES 6

WHIPPED PEANUT BUTTER

- 100 g (3.53 oz) cream (35% milkfat)
- 25 g (0.88 oz) icing (confectioners') sugar
- 50 g (1.76 oz) smooth peanut butter

TO ASSEMBLE

- 6 × Coppepan (see page 193)

WHIPPED PEANUT BUTTER YIELD

150 g (5.29 oz); 90 g (3.17 oz) used for piping

MAKE THE WHIPPED PEANUT BUTTER

1. In a bowl, combine the cream and icing sugar and whip until soft peaks form (about 80 per cent whipped).
2. Add the peanut butter in two or three batches and whip until stiff peaks form.
3. Transfer the whipped peanut butter to a piping bag fitted with a round nozzle.

ASSEMBLE

4. Make a horizontal cut along the length of each coppepan and gently open them.
5. Pipe generous layer of whipped peanut butter inside the coppepan and serve.

STIR-FRIED NOODLE BUN

YAKISOBAPAN

焼きそばパン

Yakisobapan is Japan's most iconic 'carb-on-carb' invention. It was born in 1950s Tokyo, when a candy-shop owner slid sauce-fried noodles into a coppepan so hungry students could eat on the run. Crucially, the bun matters: coppepan is softer and lighter than brioche, sweet enough to counter the sauce but never rich enough to overpower it, making it the ideal cradle for the noodles. The real magic sits in the supporting cast – the fruity Worcestershire-style sauce that caramelises the noodles, the sharp beni shoga cutting through the richness and the whisper of katsuobushi or aonori on top. These small details turn a simple lunch into a classic of Japan's B-kyu gurume (B-grade gourmet) world.

You can add any vegetables or protein you like to the yakisoba, but even the noodles on their own – without any veggies or protein at all – are plenty delicious. The beni shoga is a must, though.

MAKES 3

YAKISOBA

- 1 cabbage leaf (about 20 g/0.71 oz)
- 30 g (1.06 oz) thinly sliced pork belly
- 150 g (5.29 oz) yakisoba noodles
- 2 tablespoons neutral oil
- katsuobushi (bonito flakes), to taste

YAKISOBA SAUCE

- 2 tablespoons sake
- 1 tablespoon soy sauce
- 1 tablespoon Worcestershire sauce
- 1 tablespoon oyster sauce

TO ASSEMBLE

- 3 × Coppepan (see page 193)
- dijon mustard, for spreading
- mayonnaise, for spreading
- aonori (seaweed powder), for topping
- beni shoga (red pickled ginger), for topping

MAKE THE YAKISOBA

1. Cut the cabbage and pork belly into bite-sized pieces. Loosen the yakisoba noodles. Mix all the sauce ingredients together.
2. Heat 1 tablespoon of the oil in a frying pan over medium–high heat. Add the noodles and cook until browned on one side, then flip and brown the other side. Remove the noodles from the pan and set aside.
3. Wipe the pan clean, add the remaining 1 tablespoon of oil and stir-fry the pork over medium–high heat until the colour changes. Add the cabbage and continue stir-frying.
4. Push the pork and cabbage to one side, add the noodles to the empty space and pour the sauce over the noodles. Use a spatula to loosen them as they heat.
5. Stir everything together until evenly coated, add the katsuobushi and toss gently.

ASSEMBLE

6. Make a cut along the top of each coppepan, slicing only halfway through – just like a hot dog bun.
7. Spread the mustard and mayonnaise inside the coppepan.
8. Fill generously with the yakisoba.
9. Top with the aonori and beni shoga.

WHAT IS B-KYU GURUME?

B-kyu gurume – 'B-grade gourmet' – is Japan's celebration of the common people's food. These are the dishes born in factory towns, school canteens and festival stalls: cheap, filling, unpretentious plates once eaten by students, labourers and anyone who needed maximum satisfaction for minimum yen. Think yakisoba, takoyaki, curry rice, katsu sandwiches – foods judged not by refinement, but by nostalgia, regional pride and sheer joy.

The movement exploded nationally with the launch of the B-1 Grand Prix in 2006, a festival where towns compete for bragging rights over their local specialty. Fujinomiya yakisoba became the star early on, winning the first two Grand Prix titles back-to-back (2006 and 2007) with its ultra-chewy noodles, crunchy nikukasu (pork-back fat cracklings) and signature dashiko (sardine powder).

B-kyu gurume also thrives in pop culture. In the manga *Ranma ½*, the chaotic lunchtime scramble for bread – often featuring yakisobapan – became a recurring gag, cementing these foods as icons of school life: fast, messy, competitive, gloriously anti-fine dining.

CROQUETTE BUN

KOROKKEPAN

コロッケパン

French-style croquettes, made with bechamel and minced meat, arrived in the Meiji era through hotel restaurants and elite dining rooms in Tokyo and Yokohama. But dairy was expensive, butter was rare, and most households didn't own the equipment to make a proper roux. Potatoes, on the other hand, were cheap, local and familiar. By the Taisho period, home cooks and butchers' shops had transformed the French croquette into something distinctly Japanese: mashed potatoes seasoned with a little onion and meat, coated in panko and fried until golden brown.

Korokke is now an everyday comfort food, and every Japanese person knows the one truth: the best ones come from the local butcher, still hot from the fryer. A bakery's korokke may never quite reach that level, but there's a particular joy in a coppepan stuffed with a korokke and drenched in thick, sweet–savoury tonkatsu sauce.

The recipe below is my vegetarian take on the original korokke.

MAKES 6

CROQUETTES

- 600 g (21.16 oz) potatoes, such as sebago or desiree
- 80 g (2.82 oz) finely diced carrot
- 80 g (2.82 oz) shelled edamame
- 1 tablespoon rice bran oil
- 200 g (7.06 oz) finely chopped onion
- 20 g (0.71 oz) butter
- 20 g (0.71 oz) sugar
- black pepper, to taste
- 2 eggs, lightly beaten
- 100 g (3.53 oz) plain (all-purpose) flour
- 100 g (3.53 oz) water
- panko breadcrumbs, for coating
- neutral oil, for deep-frying

TO ASSEMBLE

- 6 × Coppepan (see page 193)
- dijon mustard, for spreading
- Japanese mayonnaise, for spreading
- 8 cabbage leaves (about 180 g/6.35 oz), shredded
- tonkatsu sauce, for drizzling

MAKE THE KOROKKE

1. Place the potatoes in a saucepan in a single layer. Cover with water, season generously with salt and bring to a gentle boil over medium heat. Reduce the heat to low and simmer for 30–40 minutes, until the potatoes are easily pierced with a knife.
2. Meanwhile, bring another saucepan of salted water to the boil, add the carrot and edamame and cook for about 5 minutes, until tender. Drain and set aside.
3. Heat the rice bran oil in a frying pan over medium heat. Add the onion and a pinch of salt and saute for 3–4 minutes, until translucent. Stir in the butter until melted, then remove the pan from the heat.
4. Drain the potatoes and carefully peel while hot. Transfer the potatoes to a bowl, add a pinch of salt and mash roughly with a rubber spatula – don't overwork the potatoes or they will become sticky.
5. Add the cooked onion, carrot and edamame to the mashed potato, along with the sugar and black pepper, to taste. Mix thoroughly until combined, then flatten the mixture slightly and cover tightly with plastic wrap to prevent drying. Allow to cool, then refrigerate for 1 hour.
6. Shape the korokke mixture into six oval patties, making a slight indentation in the centre for even frying.

BATTER AND CRUMB

7. In a bowl, whisk together the egg, flour and water to make a smooth batter. Place the panko breadcrumbs in another bowl.
8. Dip each patty into the batter, then coat evenly with panko. Make sure there are no exposed spots – the korokke burst easily during frying.

DEEP-FRY

9. Heat enough oil for deep-frying in a large saucepan to 180°C (356°F). Working in batches, fry the korokke for 2–3 minutes, until golden brown. Drain well and season with a little salt. Cut the korokke in half.

ASSEMBLE

10. Make a horizontal cut along the length of each coppepan and gently open them.
11. Spread mustard and mayonnaise inside the roll and add a layer of shredded cabbage. Place two korokke halves inside each roll and drizzle generously with tonkatsu sauce.
12. Serve immediately while the korokke are still crisp.

FRIED FISH COPPEPAN

HIROMIZAKANA NO FURAI KOPPEPAN

白身魚のフライコッペ

Among all the savoury breads and sandwiches you'll find in a bakery, the fried fish coppepan is one of the most classic, always-reliable items. At the Japanese bakery where I used to work, it sold exceptionally well. Even though it was priced a bit higher, it clearly had an appeal that set it apart from other sandwiches and savoury items.

You can certainly use store-bought frozen crumbed fish, but since we're here, I'm including a recipe for making it from scratch. And once you get used to preparing homemade tartar sauce, you'll find that nothing beats its freshness and flavour.

MAKES 4

TARTAR SAUCE (MAKES 200 G (7.05 OZ)

- 2 tablespoons finely chopped onion
- finely chopped parsley, to taste
- 2 tablespoons finely chopped cornichon
- 2 hard-boiled eggs, finely chopped
- 1 tablespoon freshly squeezed lemon juice
- 50 g (1.76 oz) mayonnaise

CRUMBED FISH

- 3 × 150 g (5.20 oz) skinless firm white fish fillets, such as cod, haddock or pollock
- ½ teaspoon salt
- 100 g (3.53 oz) plain (all-purpose) flour, plus extra for dusting
- 2 eggs, lightly beaten
- 100 g (3.53 oz) water
- panko breadcrumbs, for coating
- neutral oil, for deep-frying

TO ASSEMBLE

- 4 × Coppepan (see page 193)
- dijon mustard, for spreading
- mayonnaise, for spreading
- 8 lettuce leaves (any soft leafy variety works well)
- tonkatsu sauce, for drizzling
- salted potato chips (crisps), to serve (optional)

MAKE THE TARTAR SAUCE

1. Sprinkle a little salt over the chopped onion and massage with your hands. Rinse the onion under cold water and squeeze to remove excess moisture.
2. Mix the onion, parsley, cornichon and hard-boiled egg in a bowl, then add the lemon juice, mayonnaise and a pinch of salt and pepper and stir well to combine.

MAKE THE CRUMBED FRIED FISH

3. Cut each fish fillet into 2–3 pieces. Season with the salt and set aside to rest for 10 minutes – this lightly cures the flesh and improves its texture.
4. Pat the fish dry with paper towel, then season with pepper and dust lightly with flour.
5. In a bowl, whisk together the flour, egg and water to make a smooth batter. Place the panko breadcrumbs in another bowl.
6. Dip the fish in the batter before coating generously with panko. Rest for 5 minutes.
7. Heat enough oil for deep-frying in a large saucepan to 180°C (356°F). Working in batches, fry the fish for 2–3 minutes, turning once, until golden and crisp. Drain well.

ASSEMBLE

8. Make a horizontal cut along the length of each coppepan and gently open them.
9. Spread mustard and mayonnaise inside the roll, then add a layer of lettuce.
10. Place 2–3 pieces of fried fish in each coppepan and drizzle with tonkatsu sauce.
11. Spoon some of the tartar sauce on top and serve with potato chips, if you like.

WHAT IS YOSHOKU? AND HOW IS IT DIFFERENT FROM B-KYU GURUME?

Yoshoku (洋食) is Japan's homegrown genre of 'Western-style' cooking – European dishes reimagined through Japanese tastes, ingredients and techniques. It emerged in the late 19th and early 20th centuries, when chefs took unfamiliar Western ideas and rebuilt them for local palates. Butter-heavy stews became curry rice using spice blends and flour roux. Beef cutlets evolved into tonkatsu with crisp panko and shredded cabbage. Omelettes grew into omurice, stuffed with ketchup rice and shaped for schoolkids. These dishes look Western at first glance, but they follow Japanese logic: lighter, sweeter, softer and designed for rice-eating culture.

B-kyu gurume, on the other hand, isn't about origin at all – it's about status and attitude: cheap, accessible, nostalgic everyday food eaten by the common people.

DEEP-FRIED COPPEPAN

AGEPAN

揚げパン

Agepan – Japanese fried bread – began life in the early 1950s as a clever way to turn leftover or slightly stale bread into a sweet, comforting treat for school children. A cook in Tokyo discovered that deep-frying the bread and dusting it with sugar made it irresistible, even when the bread had lost its freshness. For decades it remained a beloved staple of school lunches, and surveys still rank agepan as a favourite childhood memory.

But in recent years, many schools have stopped serving it due to rising costs, labour shortages and stricter nutritional rules. That only makes each serving feel more precious – for those who grew up with it and for anyone discovering it now.

Agepan is still widely adored, and making it at home lets you enjoy that nostalgic flavour anytime, which may be the greatest pleasure of all. Here we are offering two classic flavours – kinako and cacao – both deeply nostalgic in their own way. Just a heads-up: things might get a little messy when you eat it!

MAKES 4

- neutral oil, for shallow-frying
- 4 × Coppepan (see page 193)

KINAKO MIXTURE

- 40 g (1.41 oz) kinako powder (roasted soybean powder)
- 40 g (1.41 oz) icing (confectioners') sugar

CACAO MIXTURE

- 40 g (1.41 oz) pure cacao
- 40 g (1.41 oz) icing (confectioners') sugar

1. In a shallow tray, combine the kinako or cacao mixture ingredients and mix well.
2. Pour 2 cm (¾ in) oil in a large frying pan and heat to 180°C (356°F). Fry the coppepan for 1–2 minutes, turning once, until golden brown.
3. Transfer the hot coppepan to the kinako or cacao mixture and coat evenly while still warm.
4. Serve immediately.

CHAPTER SIX

CHAPTER SIX

SOUZAIPAN

惣
菜
パ
ン

Souzaipan (惣菜パン) – literally 'side-dish bread' – began as an attempt to make bread more familiar to a rice-eating nation and evolved into a complete genre of its own, one that now defines Japanese bakeries as much as shokupan or kashipan.

The foundations were laid in the early 20th century. Curry bread (karepan) came first – a deep-fried bun filled with curry, perfectly matching the yoshoku (Western-style Japanese cuisine) boom of the Taisho and Showa eras. Soon after came korokkepan (croquette buns), yakisobapan (stir-fried noodle buns) and sausage rolls. These were foods you could hold in one hand, born from lunch counters, school tuckshops and train kiosks.

By the 1970s, new combinations joined the canon: konmayopan (sweetcorn and mayonnaise buns), tunamayopan (tuna and mayonnaise buns) and tamagopan (egg buns). Cheap, creamy and satisfying, they became comfort food for everyone – the weekday snack that needed no occasion.

Souzaipan kept evolving with Japan itself. Bakeries began borrowing from Europe in form and flavour – focaccia-based pizza breads, quiche-like tarts, gratin-filled rolls.

At the same time, another branch grew in the opposite direction: wa-souzaipan (和惣菜パン) – breads filled with unmistakably Japanese foods. Think kinpira gobo (braised burdock root), hijiki (seaweed), karaage (fried chicken) or miso pork. These hybrids don't imitate the West or return to tradition; they meet halfway, a love child of globalisation.

Souzaipan now covers everything from nostalgic to new-wave – from fried curry buns to kinpira baguettes.

What unites them is purpose: bread that isn't decoration or dessert, but everyday food.

CURRY BUN

KAREPAN

カレーパン

Karepan sits at the intersection of two things Japan has made its own: curry and bread. Japanese curry has evolved into a style loved worldwide, and within Japan it's long been considered a kind of soul food – familiar, comforting and universal. Because of that, curry bread inspires strong opinions. Every bakery has its own version, and the differences in filling, texture and seasoning are surprisingly wide.

The recipe here aims for a standard, well-balanced karepan – the kind you might think of as the 'baseline' in the best possible sense. Once you learn it, feel free to adjust it however you like: change the protein, tweak the spice level, or fold in ingredients that suit your own curry preferences.

MAKES 8

SPONGE DOUGH (MAKE AHEAD)

125 g (4.41 oz) bread flour	(50%)
8 g (0.28 oz) raw (demerara) sugar	(3%)
3 g (0.11 oz) osmotolerant instant dry yeast	(1.2%)
100 g (3.53 oz) full-cream (whole) milk, lukewarm	(40%)

CURRY FILLING

70 g (2.47 oz) potato, peeled
100 g (3.53 oz) onion
60 g (2.12 oz) carrot
100 g (3.53 oz) beef chuck or minced (ground) beef
1 tablespoon vegetable oil
280 g (9.88 oz) water
70 g (2.47 oz) Japanese curry roux

CURRY FILLING YIELD

500 g (17.64 oz)

Day 1

MAKE THE SPONGE DOUGH

1 Combine the bread flour, sugar and yeast in a bowl. Add the lukewarm milk and mix until no dry flour remains. Cover and proof at room temperature until doubled in size, about 1 hour. Refrigerate overnight (up to 16 hours).

Desired final sponge dough temperature before refrigeration: 26°C (79°F).

Day 2

MAKE THE CURRY FILLING

2 Finely chop the vegetables in a food processor (or finely chop them by hand). Remove and set aside.

3 If using beef chuck, finely chop the meat in the food processor to roughly the same size as the vegetables.

4 Heat the vegetable oil in a large frying pan over medium–high heat, add the beef and cook, stirring frequently, until browned. Add the vegetables and saute for 2–3 minutes, until starting to soften, then add the water and cook for about 10 minutes, until the vegetables are tender, the beef is cooked through and the water has reduced.

5 Remove the pan from the heat. Add the curry roux and stir until dissolved, then return the pan to low heat and simmer gently for about 5 minutes for the flavours to develop.

6 Transfer to a bowl and set aside to cool. Once cold, the curry filling should be firm enough to hold its shape when rolled by hand and wrapped inside the dough. If the curry contains too much moisture, it will be difficult to handle and may leak through the dough and cause it to burst.

MIX THE FINAL DOUGH

7 Place the cream and egg into the bowl of a stand mixer fitted with a dough hook, followed by the flours and salt. Tear the sponge dough into pieces and add to the bowl. Mix on speed 3 (low) for 5 minutes. Increase to speed 6 (medium–high) and mix for 10 minutes. Add the sugar and mix on speed 6 for a further 10 minutes, or until the dough starts coming together. Gradually add the softened butter and continue mixing. In the final stage of mixing, the dough will come together into a lump and begin slapping against the bowl as it separates from the side. The finished dough should be glossy and pass a windowpane test (stretching it thin enough to let light through without tearing).

Desired final dough temperature: 26°C (79°F).

TWO 'Y'S MAKE A 'K'

Japanese curry is considered yoshoku (洋食, Western-style food), and bread-making also came from the West. So karepan is, in a sense, yoshoku × yoshoku. Yet once the two were combined, the result became unmistakably Japanese.

One of the strongest origin stories points to Meika-do (名花堂), a bakery in Fukagawa, Tokyo. In 1927, its owner, Nakada Toyoharu, created a Western-style bread (洋食パン), filled it with curry, coated it in panko, deep-fried it and even registered a utility model for the idea. The logic was simple: curry was too moist to bake cleanly, but frying made everything crisp and contained. Other shops, such as Denmark Brot in Nerima in the 1930s, are also named as early innovators.

What's clear is that karepan is a product of convergence: Tokyo's inventive bread-makers, the arrival of British curry and the modern embrace of deep-frying.

FINAL DOUGH (ADDITIONS)

20 g (0.71 oz) cream (40% milkfat)	(8%)
40 g (1.41 oz) egg (from approx. 1 egg)	(16%)
85 g (3.0 oz) bread flour, plus extra for dusting	(34%)
40 g (1.41 oz) plain (all-purpose) flour	(16%)
5 g (0.18 oz) fine sea salt	(2%)
27 g (0.95 oz) raw (demerara) sugar	(11%)
35 g (1.23 oz) cultured unsalted butter, softened	(14%)

(Values in parentheses indicate baker's percentages)

BATTER AND CRUMB

- 80 g (2.82 oz) plain (all-purpose) flour
- 120 g (4.23 oz) egg (from approx. 3 eggs), beaten
- 120 g (4.23 oz) panko breadcrumbs

DEEP-FRYING

- neutral oil, for deep-frying

FIRST PROOF

8 Cover the bowl with a damp tea towel and proof the dough for 30 minutes. Perform a fold by stretching one side of the dough up out of the bowl and folding it down over the remaining dough in the bowl.

DIVIDE AND REST

9 Turn the dough out onto the bench and divide into 8 × 60 g (2.12 oz) portions. Round each piece gently by placing your palm over the dough and rolling it taut against the surface of the bench. Cover with the tea towel and rest for 20 minutes.

SHAPE

10 Lightly flour the bench and place the dough seam side up. Flatten the dough pieces into 8–10 cm (3¼–4 in) discs, keeping the edges thinner and the centre slightly thicker to prevent the curry filling from breaking through the dough.

11 Scoop a portion of curry filling (50–60 g/1.76–2.12 oz) onto the centre of one dough disc. Lift the edge of the dough up and around the filling, pleating and pinching firmly to seal completely. Make sure no curry is exposed. Turn the dough seam side down and gently round the bun between your palms until smooth and dome-shaped. Place on a baking tray lined with baking paper. Repeat with the remaining dough and filling.

FINAL PROOF

12 Proof at 30°C (86°F) for 30 minutes (see page 27) or until the dough looks slightly puffy and light.

BATTER AND CRUMB

13 Place the plain flour in a bowl, the beaten egg in a second bowl and the panko breadcrumbs in a third bowl.

14 Lightly dust each karepan with flour, then dip into the beaten egg and roll in the panko until evenly coated.

DEEP-FRY

15 Meanwhile, heat enough oil for deep-frying in a small saucepan to 170–180°C (338–356°F).

16 Working in batches, deep-fry the karepan, turning once, until golden brown and crisp (about 3–4 minutes each side). Transfer to a wire rack lined with paper towel to drain. Allow to cool slightly.

SERVE

17 Enjoy the karepan while warm or eat them cold – they're delicious either way. They also pair well with beer or wine.

STORE

18 Store the karepan in an airtight container at room temperature for 1–2 days.

CURRY AND BOILED EGG BUN

MARUGOTO TAMAGO KAREPAN

丸ごとたまごカレーパン

This is a twist on the classic karepan: place a boiled egg inside the dough along with the curry filling. The result is reminiscent of a Scotch egg: crisp on the outside, the soft egg pairing beautifully with the savoury curry, like an onsen tamago added on curry rice. It feels unexpectedly luxurious, making each bite even more satisfying.

MAKES 8

SPONGE DOUGH (MAKE AHEAD)

125 g (4.41 oz) bread flour	(50%)
8 g (0.28 oz) raw (demerara) sugar	(3%)
3 g (0.11 oz) osmotolerant instant dry yeast	(1.2%)
100 g (3.53 oz) full-cream (whole) milk, lukewarm	(40%)

FINAL DOUGH (ADDITIONS)

20 g (0.71 oz) cream (40% milkfat)	(8%)
40 g (1.41 oz) egg (from approx. 1 egg)	(16%)
85 g (3.0 oz) bread flour, plus extra for dusting	(34%)
40 g (1.41 oz) plain (all-purpose) flour	(16%)
5 g (0.18 oz) fine sea salt	(2%)
27 g (0.95 oz) raw (demerara) sugar	(11%)
35 g (1.23 oz) cultured unsalted butter, softened	(14%)

(Values in parentheses indicate baker's percentages)

Day 1

MAKE THE SPONGE DOUGH

1 Combine the bread flour, sugar and yeast in a bowl. Add the lukewarm milk and mix until no dry flour remains. Cover and proof at room temperature until doubled in size, about 1 hour. Refrigerate overnight (up to 16 hours).

Desired final sponge dough temperature before refrigeration: 26°C (79°F).

Day 2

2 Boil the eggs until they are as soft or as hard as you like. Drain, remove the shells and set aside to cool.

MIX THE FINAL DOUGH

3 Place the cream and egg into the bowl of a stand mixer fitted with a dough hook, followed by the flours and salt. Tear the sponge dough into pieces and add to the bowl. Mix on speed 3 (low) for 5 minutes. Increase to speed 6 (medium–high) and mix for 10 minutes. Add the sugar and mix on speed 6 for a further 10 minutes, or until the dough starts coming together. Gradually add the softened butter and continue mixing. In the final stage of mixing, the dough will come together into a lump and begin slapping against the bowl as it separates from the side. The finished dough should be glossy and pass a windowpane test (stretching it thin enough to let light through without tearing).

Desired final dough temperature: 26°C (79°F).

FIRST PROOF

4 Cover the bowl with a damp tea towel and proof the dough for 30 minutes. Perform a fold by stretching one side of the dough up out of the bowl and folding it down over the remaining dough in the bowl.

DIVIDE AND REST

5 Turn the dough out onto the bench and divide into 8 × 60 g (2.12 oz) portions. Round each piece gently by placing your palm over the dough and rolling it taut against the surface of the bench. Cover with the tea towel and rest for 20 minutes.

TO ASSEMBLE

8 eggs
400 g (14.1 oz) Curry filling (see page 214)

BATTER AND CRUMB

80 g (2.82 oz) plain (all-purpose) flour
120 g (4.23 oz) egg (from approx. 3 eggs), beaten
120 g (4.23 oz) panko breadcrumbs

DEEP-FRYING

neutral oil, for deep-frying

SHAPE

6 Lightly flour the bench and place the dough seam side up. Flatten the dough pieces into 10–12 cm (4–4¾ in) discs, keeping the edges thinner and the centre slightly thicker to prevent the curry filling from breaking through the dough.

7 Scoop a portion of curry filling (around 50–60 g/1.76–2.12 oz) onto the centre of one dough disc and top with an egg. Lift the edge of the dough up and around the filling, pleating and pinching firmly to seal completely. Make sure no curry is exposed. Turn the dough seam side down and gently round the bun between your palms until smooth and dome-shaped. Place on a baking tray lined with baking paper. Repeat with the remaining dough, filling and eggs.

FINAL PROOF

8 Proof at 30°C (86°F) for 30 minutes (see page 27) or until the dough looks slightly puffy and light.

BATTER AND CRUMB

9 Place the plain flour in a bowl, the beaten egg in a second bowl and the panko breadcrumbs in a third bowl.

10 Lightly dust each bun with flour, then dip into the beaten egg and roll in the panko until evenly coated.

DEEP-FRY

11 Meanwhile, heat enough oil for deep-frying in a small saucepan to 170–180°C (338–356°F).

12 Working in batches, deep-fry the buns, turning once, until golden brown and crisp (about 3–4 minutes each side). Transfer to a wire rack lined with paper towel to drain. Allow to cool slightly.

SERVE

13 Enjoy these satisfying buns as a meal on their own. They are also a crowd-pleaser at potlucks or picnics.

STORE

14 Store the buns in an airtight container at room temperature for 1–2 days.

SWEETCORN AND MAYONNAISE BUN

KONMAYOPAN

コーンマヨパン

Konmayopan might be the simplest of all souzaipan, and that's what makes it so enduring. A soft roll topped with sweetcorn and a swirl of Japanese mayonnaise, sometimes finished with cheese or parsley.

Every bakery still sells some version of it – sometimes puffed and golden, sometimes shaped like an open tart. Konmayopan tends to be on the larger side, and the packaged ones sold in convenience stores are affordable and filling, making it a popular choice among hungry teenagers with growing appetites.

In recent years, more sophisticated versions have also appeared, crafted with carefully selected ingredients and with elegant presentation. But I encourage you to try making the classic, straightforward version – it's simple, comforting and endlessly satisfying; the kind of bun you'll keep coming back to.

MAKES 8

SPONGE DOUGH (MAKE AHEAD)

125 g (4.41 oz) bread flour	(50%)
8 g (0.28 oz) raw (demerara) sugar	(3%)
3 g (0.11 oz) osmotolerant instant dry yeast	(1.2%)
100 g (3.53 oz) full-cream (whole) milk, lukewarm	(40%)

SWEETCORN AND MAYONNAISE FILLING

200 g (7.05 oz) sweetcorn, husks and silks removed
120 g (4.23 oz) Japanese mayonnaise

Day 1

MAKE THE SPONGE DOUGH

1 Combine the bread flour, sugar and yeast in a bowl. Add the lukewarm milk and mix until no dry flour remains. Cover and proof at room temperature until doubled in size, about 1 hour. Refrigerate overnight (up to 16 hours).

Desired final sponge temperature before refrigeration: 26°C (79°F).

Day 2

MAKE THE SWEETCORN AND MAYONNAISE FILLING

2 Steam the sweetcorn for 10–12 minutes, until tender. Cut off the kernels and set aside in a bowl to cool. Stir through the mayonnaise.

MIX THE FINAL DOUGH

3 Place the cream, egg and water into the bowl of a stand mixer fitted with a dough hook, followed by the flours and salt. Tear the sponge dough into pieces and add to the bowl. Mix on speed 3 (low) for 5 minutes. Increase to speed 6 (medium–high) and mix for 10 minutes. Add the sugar and mix on speed 6 for a further 10 minutes, or until the dough starts coming together. Gradually add the softened butter and continue mixing. In the final stage of mixing, the dough will come together into a lump and begin slapping against the bowl as it separates from the side. The finished dough should be glossy and pass a windowpane test (stretching it thin enough to let light through without tearing).

Desired final dough temperature: 26°C (79°F).

FIRST PROOF

4 Cover the bowl with a damp tea towel and proof the dough for 30 minutes. Perform a fold by stretching one side of the dough up out of the bowl and folding it down over the remaining dough in the bowl.

DIVIDE AND REST

5 Turn the dough out onto the bench and divide into 8 × 60 g (2.12 oz) portions. Round each piece gently by placing your palm over the dough and rolling it taut against the surface of the bench. Cover with the tea towel and rest for 20 minutes to relax the gluten.

SHAPE

6 Lightly flour the bench and place the dough seam side up. Flatten each dough piece, then roll each one out to a 10–12 cm (4–4¾ in) disc. Place the discs seam side down on a baking tray lined with baking paper.

FINAL PROOF

7 Proof at 30°C (86°F) for 45 minutes (see page 27) or until the dough looks puffy and light.

FINAL DOUGH (ADDITIONS)

20 g (0.71 oz) cream (40% milkfat)	(8%)
40 g (1.41 oz) egg (from approx. 1 egg)	(16%)
15 g (0.53 oz) water	(6%)
85 g (3.0 oz) bread flour, plus extra for dusting	(34%)
40 g (1.41 oz) plain (all-purpose) flour	(16%)
5 g (0.18 oz) fine sea salt	(2%)
27 g (0.95 oz) raw (demerara) sugar	(11%)
35 g (1.23 oz) cultured unsalted butter, softened	(14%)

(Values in parentheses indicate baker's percentages)

EGG WASH

- 50 g (1.76 oz) egg (from approx. 1 egg)
- 15 g (0.53 oz) cream (40% milkfat) or full-cream (whole) milk

GARNISH

shredded mozzarella or cheddar and chopped parsley (optional)

BAKE AND SERVE

8 Preheat the oven to 185°C (365°F) fan-forced.

9 Whisk together the egg wash ingredients in a small bowl, then strain the mixture through a sieve. Brush the surface of the buns lightly with the egg wash.

10 Make a light indentation in the centre of each dough disc, then divide the sweetcorn filling evenly among the indentations. Scatter with a little shredded cheese, if desired, and smooth the surface with a spatula.

11 Bake for 9 minutes, or until the tops of the buns are evenly golden brown. Cool on a wire rack. Sprinkle with chopped parsley, if desired.

12 Enjoy for breakfast or pop one into a packed lunch. Back when I was a growing teen, I'd snack on a big konmayopan from the convenience store before dinner. As an adult, I'd sometimes grab one as a late-night snack to fill my stomach after a night at an izakaya.

STORE

13 Wrap each bun individually in plastic wrap or store in an airtight container and keep at room temperature for up to 2 days. For longer storage, freeze individually wrapped buns in a freezer-safe bag for up to 2 weeks. Thaw at room temperature, then toast or warm in the oven before serving.

JAPANESE VS. WESTERN MAYONNAISE

Japanese mayonnaise – most famously Kewpie – differs fundamentally from its Western counterpart. It uses only egg yolks (not whole eggs), rice vinegar or apple cider vinegar instead of distilled white vinegar, a higher ratio of oil for richness, and MSG. The result is creamier, deeper and more savoury, with a distinct umami tang.

Western mayonnaise, by contrast, is lighter, sharper and more acidic – designed to cut through fat, not blend into it. In Japan, mayonnaise doesn't just accompany food; it completes it. That's why, in breads like konmayopan, it's baked into the surface rather than spread on top. The tang burns off in the oven, and what's left is a shallow-fried, golden crust. It's condiment doing the work of seasoning.

SAUSAGE ROLL

MARUGOTO SOSEJI PAN

まるごとソーセージパン

Unlike British-style sausage rolls – sausage meat wrapped in puff pastry – the Japanese version often uses soft, milky bread dough, hugging a full sausage (usually a German-influenced wiener – ウィンナー).

One documented example is Yamazaki's (まるごとソーセージ), introduced in 1987. The product uses a long sausage placed whole atop or inside soft bread, often finished with a touch of mustard or dressing. Yamazaki cites consistent sales over decades and notes that the core formula hasn't changed much.

The charm of the roll is its simplicity – savoury protein and sweet carbs – no frills, no fuss. The sausage is the hero, the bread its cushion. In bakeries, you'll sometimes find variants: cheese added around the sausage, coated in breadcrumbs, or topped with sauces.

At home, you can replicate it easily. Wrap your favourite sausage in enriched dough, allow it to proof and bake until golden. You might brush with butter or mustard before serving. The result is a sandwich hybrid: part bun, part sausage, fully satisfying.

MAKES 8

SPONGE DOUGH (MAKE AHEAD)

125 g (4.41 oz) bread flour	(50%)
8 g (0.28 oz) raw (demerara) sugar	(3%)
3 g (0.11 oz) osmotolerant instant dry yeast	(1.2%)
100 g (3.53 oz) full-cream (whole) milk, lukewarm	(40%)

FINAL DOUGH (ADDITIONS)

20 g (0.71 oz) cream (40% milkfat)	(8%)
40 g (1.41 oz) egg (from approx. 1 egg)	(16%)
15 g (0.53 oz) water	(6%)
85 g (3.0 oz) bread flour, plus extra for dusting	(34%)
40 g (1.41 oz) plain (all-purpose) flour	(16%)
5 g (0.18 oz) fine sea salt	(2%)
27 g (0.95 oz) raw (demerara) sugar	(11%)
35 g (1.23 oz) cultured unsalted butter, softened	(14%)

(Values in parentheses indicate baker's percentages)

Day 1

MAKE THE SPONGE DOUGH

1 Combine the bread flour, sugar and yeast in a bowl. Add the lukewarm milk and mix until no dry flour remains. Cover and proof at room temperature until doubled in size, about 1 hour. Refrigerate overnight (up to 16 hours).

Desired final sponge dough temperature before refrigeration: 26°C (79°F).

Day 2

MIX THE FINAL DOUGH

2 Place the cream, egg and water into the bowl of a stand mixer fitted with a dough hook, followed by the flours and salt. Tear the sponge dough into pieces and add to the bowl. Mix on speed 3 (low) for 5 minutes. Increase to speed 6 (medium–high) and mix for 10 minutes. Add the sugar and mix on speed 6 for a further 10 minutes, or until the dough starts coming together. Gradually add the softened butter and continue mixing. In the final stage of mixing, the dough will come together into a lump and begin slapping against the bowl as it separates from the side. The finished dough should be glossy and pass a windowpane test (stretching it thin enough to let light through without tearing).

Desired final dough temperature: 26°C (79°F).

FIRST PROOF

3 Cover the bowl with a damp tea towel and proof the dough for 30 minutes. Perform a fold by stretching one side of the dough up out of the bowl and folding it down over the remaining dough in the bowl.

DIVIDE AND REST

4 Divide the dough into 8 × 60 g (2.12 oz) portions. Form each piece into an oval by gently placing your palm over the dough and rolling it taut against the surface of the bench. Cover with the tea towel and rest on the bench for 20 minutes to relax the gluten.

TO ASSEMBLE

- 8 frankfurter sausages
- Japanese mayonnaise, for spreading
- shredded mozzarella or cheddar, for topping
- chopped parsley, to serve
- tomato ketchup, to serve (optional)

EGG WASH

- 50 g (1.76 oz) egg (from approx. 1 egg)
- 15 g (0.53 oz) cream (40% milkfat) or full-cream (whole) milk

SHAPE

5 Lightly flour the bench and place the dough seam side up. Flatten each piece of dough into a rectangle shape. Working with one piece of dough at a time, with a long edge facing you, fold the dough into thirds by bringing the top and bottom edges into the middle, then fold it in half. Pinch the seam tightly to seal, then roll the dough gently back and forth until it stretches to about 43 cm (17 in) in length. Wrap the rolled dough strip around the length of a sausage, tucking the ends of the dough securely between the sausage and the dough. Place on a baking tray lined with baking paper. Repeat with the remaining dough and sausages.

FINAL PROOF

6 Proof at 30°C (86°F) for 45 minutes (see page 27) or until the dough looks puffy and light.

BAKE AND SERVE

7 Preheat the oven to 185°C (365°F) fan-forced.

8 Whisk the egg wash ingredients together in a small bowl, then strain the mixture through a sieve.

9 Score the rolls lengthways along the length of each sausage. Brush the surface lightly with the egg wash and fill the scored space with mayonnaise and shredded cheese.

10 Bake for 9 minutes, or until the tops of the rolls are evenly golden brown. Sprinkle chopped parsley over the top and cool on a wire rack. Drizzle with ketchup, if desired.

11 These sausage rolls are great at any time of day – morning, noon or night. The savoury bread is perfect to serve at parties and a sure hit with beer, wine or your favourite drink.

STORE

12 Wrap each roll individually in plastic wrap or store in an airtight container and keep at room temperature for up to 2 days. For longer storage, freeze individually wrapped rolls in a freezer-safe bag for up to 2 weeks. Thaw at room temperature, then warm in the oven before serving.

BACON AND CHEESE BUN

BEKON CHIZU PAN

ベーコンチーズパン

If you pop into a neighbourhood bakery in Japan, you'll be amazed at just how many kinds of savoury breads they have. The shelves are packed with all sorts of shapes and fillings, almost bursting with variety. Bacon and cheese bread is a staple you'll find everywhere, but each bakery puts its own spin on it. Some add tomato ketchup to the classic bacon-and-cheese combo, while others knead herbs into the dough – showing off their creativity while still keeping it familiar and delicious. My version includes caramelised onions cooked until they're sweet and deep in flavour. They bridge the smoky bacon and cheese, giving the bread a rounder flavour that is easy to come back to.

MAKES 8

SPONGE DOUGH (MAKE AHEAD)

125 g (4.41 oz) bread flour	(50%)
8 g (0.28 oz) raw (demerara) sugar	(3%)
3 g (0.11 oz) osmotolerant instant dry yeast	(1.2%)
100 g (3.53 oz) full-cream (whole) milk, lukewarm	(40%)

FINAL DOUGH (ADDITIONS)

20 g (0.71 oz) cream (40% milkfat)	(8%)
40 g (1.41 oz) egg (from approx. 1 egg)	(16%)
15 g (0.53 oz) water	(6%)
85 g (3.0 oz) bread flour, plus extra for dusting	(34%)
40 g (1.41 oz) plain (all-purpose) flour	(16%)
5 g (0.18 oz) fine sea salt	(2%)
27 g (0.95 oz) raw (demerara) sugar	(11%)
35 g (1.23 oz) cultured unsalted butter, softened	(14%)

(Values in parentheses indicate baker's percentages)

↓ MORE INGREDIENTS

Day 1

MAKE THE SPONGE DOUGH

1 Combine the bread flour, sugar and yeast in a bowl. Add the lukewarm milk and mix until no dry flour remains. Cover and proof at room temperature until doubled in size, about 1 hour. Refrigerate overnight (up to 16 hours).

Desired final sponge dough temperature before refrigeration: 26°C (79°F).

Day 2

MIX THE FINAL DOUGH

2 Place the cream, egg and water into the bowl of a stand mixer fitted with a dough hook, followed by the flours and salt. Tear the sponge dough into pieces and add to the bowl. Mix on speed 3 (low) for 5 minutes. Increase to speed 6 (medium–high) and mix for 10 minutes. Add the sugar and mix on speed 6 for a further 10 minutes, or until the dough starts coming together. Gradually add the softened butter and continue mixing. In the final stage of mixing, the dough will come together into a lump and begin slapping against the bowl as it separates from the side. The finished dough should be glossy and pass a windowpane test (stretching it thin enough to let light through without tearing).

Desired final dough temperature: 26°C (79°F).

FIRST PROOF

3 Cover the bowl with a damp tea towel and proof the dough for 30 minutes. Perform a fold by stretching one side of the dough up out of the bowl and folding it down over the remaining dough in the bowl.

DIVIDE AND REST

4 Divide the dough into 8 × 60 g (2.12 oz) portions. Form each piece into an oval by gently placing your palm over the dough and rolling it taut against the surface of the bench. Cover with the tea towel and rest on the bench for 20 minutes to relax the gluten.

↓ RECIPE CONTINUES

FILLINGS AND TOPPINGS

Japanese mayonnaise
8 bacon slices
1 × quantity Caramelised onion (see page 246)
shredded mozzarella or cheddar
chopped parsley (optional)

EGG WASH

50 g (1.76 oz) egg (from approx. 1 egg)
15 g (0.53 oz) cream (40% milkfat) or full-cream (whole) milk

SHAPE

5 Lightly flour the bench and place the dough seam side up. Flatten each piece of dough, then use a rolling pin to elongate the shape until it is about 17 cm (6½ in) long.

6 Spread mayonnaise over the dough, then tear a slice of bacon into bite-sized pieces and place on top of the mayonnaise. Finally, dot a few blobs of caramelised onion on top. Roll up the dough from the bottom to the top and seal.

7 Using a pair of scissors, cut a slit on the opposite side of the seam, but don't cut all the way through. Gently open up the dough so you can see two connected spirals. Place on a baking tray lined with baking paper. Repeat with the remaining dough and filling ingredients.

FINAL PROOF

8 Proof at 30°C (86°F) for 45 minutes (see page 27) or until the dough looks puffy and light.

BAKE AND SERVE

9 Preheat the oven to 185°C (365°F) fan-forced.

10 Whisk the egg wash ingredients together in a small bowl, then strain the mixture through a sieve. Brush the surface of the buns lightly with egg wash and sprinkle with shredded cheese.

11 Bake for 9 minutes, or until the tops of the buns are evenly golden brown. Cool on a wire rack. Sprinkle with chopped parsley, if desired.

12 Enjoy this classic combination of bacon and cheese at breakfast, lunch or dinner – it's sure to become a staple in your household.

STORE

13 Wrap each bun individually in plastic wrap or store in an airtight container and keep at room temperature for up to 2 days. For longer storage, freeze individually wrapped buns in a freezer-safe bag for up to 2 weeks. Thaw at room temperature, then warm in the oven before serving.

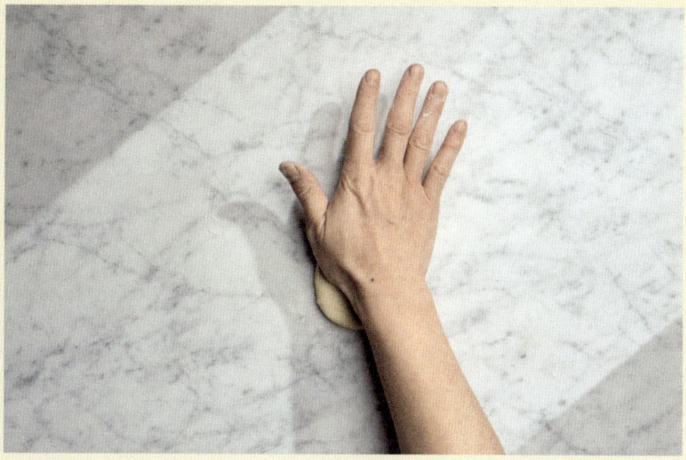

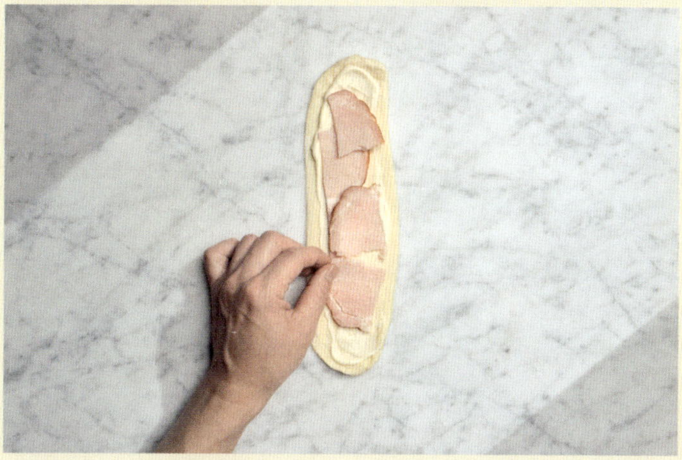

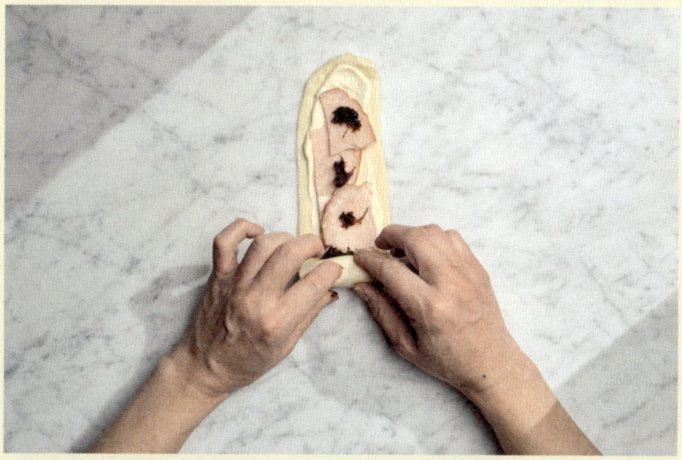

POTATO, BUTTER, CHEESE AND MAYO BUN

JAGA BATA CHIZU PAN

じゃがバターチーズパン

If yakisobapan is the Asian take on carb-on-carb, then this is its Western cousin. Once you taste it, the logic is obvious.

Soft potato, a little cheese, a little mayo, a little butter – nothing fancy, just a combination that always works. In Japan, potato and dairy have quietly become a natural pairing: butter-shoyu potatoes, croquettes, gratins, jaga butter (boiled potatoes with butter).

At some point it stopped feeling Asian or Western. With Hokkaido producing so much of Japan's milk and potatoes, this pairing has simply become part of everyday Japanese culture.

MAKES 8

SPONGE DOUGH (MAKE AHEAD)

125 g (4.41 oz) bread flour	(50%)
8 g (0.28 oz) raw (demerara) sugar	(3%)
3 g (0.11 oz) osmotolerant instant dry yeast	(1.2%)
100 g (3.53 oz) full-cream (whole) milk, lukewarm	(40%)

FINAL DOUGH (ADDITIONS)

20 g (0.71 oz) cream (40% milkfat)	(8%)
40 g (1.41 oz) egg (from approx. 1 egg)	(16%)
15 g (0.53 oz) water	(6%)
85 g (3.0 oz) bread flour, plus extra for dusting	(34%)
40 g (1.41 oz) plain (all-purpose) flour	(16%)
5 g (0.18 oz) fine sea salt	(2%)
27 g (0.95 oz) raw (demerara) sugar	(11%)
35 g (1.23 oz) cultured unsalted butter, softened	(14%)

(Values in parentheses indicate baker's percentages)

Day 1

MAKE THE SPONGE DOUGH

1 Combine the bread flour, sugar and yeast in a bowl. Add the lukewarm milk and mix until no dry flour remains. Cover and proof at room temperature until doubled in size, about 1 hour. Refrigerate overnight (up to 16 hours).

Desired final sponge dough temperature before refrigeration: 26°C (79°F).

Day 2

BOIL THE POTATOES

2 Put the potatoes in a saucepan and cover with cold water. Season well with salt and bring to the boil. Reduce the heat to medium and simmer for 10–15 minutes, until slightly tender. Drain and allow to cool. Peel the potatoes, if desired, and cut into quarters.

MIX THE FINAL DOUGH

3 Place the cream, egg and water into the bowl of a stand mixer fitted with a dough hook, followed by the flours and salt. Tear the sponge dough into pieces and add to the bowl. Mix on speed 3 (low) for 5 minutes. Increase to speed 6 (medium–high) and mix for 10 minutes. Add the sugar and mix on speed 6 for a further 10 minutes, or until the dough starts coming together. Gradually add the softened butter and continue mixing. In the final stage of mixing, the dough will come together into a lump and begin slapping against the bowl as it separates from the side. The finished dough should be glossy and pass a windowpane test (stretching it thin enough to let light through without tearing).

Desired final dough temperature: 26°C (79°F).

FIRST PROOF

4 Cover the bowl with a damp tea towel and proof the dough for 30 minutes. Perform a fold by stretching one side of the dough up out of the bowl and folding it down over the remaining dough in the bowl.

DIVIDE AND REST

5 Divide the dough into 8 × 60 g (2.12 oz) portions. Form each piece into an oval by gently placing your palm over the dough and rolling it taut against the surface of the bench. Cover with the tea towel and rest on the bench for 20 minutes to relax the gluten.

FILLINGS AND TOPPINGS
600 g (21.16 oz) small potatoes
80 g (2.82 oz) Japanese mayonnaise
salted butter
shredded cheese mozzarella or cheddar
chopped parsley (optional)

EGG WASH
50 g (1.76 oz) egg (from approx. 1 egg)
15 g (0.53 oz) cream (40% milkfat) or full-cream (whole) milk

SHAPE

6 Lightly flour the bench and place the dough seam side up. Flatten the dough pieces into 8–10 cm (3¼–4 in) discs, keeping the edges thinner and the centre slightly thicker to prevent the filling from breaking through the dough.

7 Place a couple of pieces of potato in the centre of one of the dough pieces. Lift the edge of the dough up and around the filling, pleating and pinching firmly to seal completely. Make sure no potato is exposed. Turn the dough seam side down and gently round the dough between your palms until smooth and dome-shaped. Place on a baking tray lined with baking paper. Repeat with the remaining dough and potato.

FINAL PROOF

8 Proof at 30°C (86°F) for 45 minutes (see page 27) or until the dough looks puffy and light.

BAKE AND SERVE

9 Preheat the oven to 185°C (365°F) fan-forced.

10 Whisk the egg wash ingredients together in a small bowl, then strain the mixture through a sieve. Brush the surface of the buns lightly with egg wash and score a cross in the top of each bun.

11 Place the mayonnaise in a piping bag with a round nozzle. Pipe 10 g (0.35 oz) mayonnaise on top of each bun, followed by a slice of salted butter and some shredded cheese.

12 Bake for 9 minutes, or until the tops of the buns are evenly golden brown. Cool on a wire rack. Sprinkle with chopped parsley, if desired.

13 Eat while still warm. They will still be delicious once cooled, but it's best to enjoy them soon after baking.

STORE

14 Wrap each bun individually in plastic wrap or store in an airtight container and keep at room temperature for up to 2 days.

CHAPTER SEVEN

CHAPTER SEVEN

SANDO

サ
ン
ド

Bread arrived as part of the West's influence on Japan in the late 19th century, and with bread came sandwiches. Early versions appeared in cafes during the Taisho and early Showa eras, when 'Western food' still felt aspirational. But over time, the Japanese sandwich shed its rough edges to become an altogether more refined affair.

You can eat one neatly, one-handed, without crumbs or resistance. What mattered wasn't what went inside, but how evenly it sat. Instead of stacking more, we are aiming for perfection.

If Western sandwiches are about structure – bread with personality, crusts that fight back, fillings that try to escape – then sando are about harmony and control.

Sandwiches in Japan – whether served in hotels, ordered in cafes, sold at bakeries or convenience stores, or made at specialty shops – take on the character of where they're made, each chasing its own idea of perfection. In this chapter, I focus on sandwiches made at home. Whether you use shokupan from a bakery or a loaf you've baked yourself, you can create a sandwich tuned precisely to your own taste. For me, that's the meaning of indulgence.

EGG SANDO

TAMAGO SANDO

たまごサンド

Egg sandwiches exist everywhere; Japan just perfected them. By the Taisho era, magazines were already printing egg-sandwich recipes (often without mayonnaise), and by the 1930s cafes like Tokyo's Kayaba had their own versions. After the war, when eggs and mayo became affordable, the modern style emerged: soft shokupan, trimmed crusts and a finely chopped egg filling bound with bright, vinegared mayonnaise.

Convenience stores amplified the sando's availability by being within twenty steps of any train gate. Visitors rave; locals barely notice it. Tamago sando is there, like oxygen.

Because it's a simple dish, small details – how the eggs are cooked and chopped, and how much mayonnaise is added – can dramatically change the final result. It's important to start by deciding on your own preferred texture and flavour. Here, I will show you how to make the egg salad that I believe pairs perfectly with the fluffy bread I bake.

MAKES 2

- butter, for spreading
- dijon mustard, for spreading
- 4 slices Shokupan, sliced 1.5–2 cm (½–¾ in) thick (see page 34)

EGG SALAD

- 3 eggs
- pinch of salt
- white pepper, to taste
- 15 g (0.53 oz) Japanese mayonnaise
- 20 g (0.71 oz) sour cream

MAKE THE EGG SALAD

1. Bring a saucepan of water to the boil. Pierce each egg with an egg piercer or thumbtack (this helps prevent cracking).
2. Gently lower the eggs into the water and cook for 9 minutes.
3. Transfer the eggs immediately to cold water to stop cooking. Peel once cooled.
4. Mash the eggs through a large-mesh sieve (with holes about 6 mm/¼ in) into a bowl. (An egg slicer works too, though the texture will be slightly finer.)
5. Season with the salt and white pepper to taste.
6. Add the mayonnaise and sour cream, folding gently until just combined. Avoid overmixing – too much stirring will turn the egg pasty. Leaving small, irregular pieces gives the salad a soft, homemade character.
   For a creamier texture, chop the eggs more finely, or separate the yolks and whites before chopping. If omitting sour cream, replace with 12 g (0.42 oz) mayonnaise per egg as a guide.

ASSEMBLE

7. Lightly spread butter and mustard on one side of each shokupan slice.
8. Spoon half the egg salad into the centre of one bread slice, allowing it to mound slightly higher in the middle.
9. Hold the slice in your palm and, using the back of a spoon, lightly push the filling outwards from the centre towards the corners. Avoid pressing too hard, as this will flatten the texture – use a soft touch, as if you're simply guiding the filling into place. This creates a fluffy, even layer. If trimming the crusts, keep the filling about 1 cm (½) inside the edges so you don't cut it off.
10. Place a second slice of bread on top. Press gently to settle everything. (Keeping the filling domed rather than flat preserves the soft, cloud-like texture that defines a good egg sando.) Repeat to make the second egg sando.
11. Cut the sando in half and serve.

FRIED CUTLET SANDO

KATSU SANDO

カツサンド

In the early 20th century, with the rise of yoshoku (Western-style dishes), it was only a matter of time before someone decided to sandwich pork cutlets – borrowed from the European schnitzel – between two slices of bread. The earliest record points to Rengatei, a Ginza restaurant often credited with inventing tonkatsu, which began serving a portable version of its creation in the Taisho period.

If egg sandwiches were delicate, the katsu sando was masculine. It became the sandwich that defined a modern kind of food craving: quick, deep-fried, satisfying.

Over the decades, it's also become a shorthand for luxury. High-end versions swap pork for wagyu, panko for finer crumbs, even gold leaf for garnish. You can find katsu sando behind the counter at convenience stores for 300 yen, or at Ginza Bairin and Maisen for ten times that. Chefs from Sydney to London to New York now serve their interpretations – sometimes sloppy, sometimes reverent – but always chasing the same equation: softness, crunch, umami.

One thing I want to emphasise is this: *katsu sandwiches are incredible eaten cold*. When warm, they're undeniably satisfying, but a cooled katsu sando has its own charm – the cutlet firms slightly, the sauce seeps into the crumb and the cabbage softens just enough to blend into the whole. I hope more people discover the irresistible appeal of a cold katsu sandwich.

MAKES 2

- 4 slices Shokupan sliced 1.5–2 cm (½–¾ in) thick (see page 34)
- butter, for spreading
- dijon mustard, for spreading
- 60 g (2.12 oz) shredded cabbage

TONKATSU

- 2 × 150–200 g (5.29–7.05 oz) thick-cut pork loins
- white pepper, to taste
- plain (all-purpose) flour, for dusting
- 1 egg, beaten
- panko breadcrumbs, for coating
- neutral oil, for deep-frying

TONKATSU SAUCE

- 100 g (3.53 oz) tonkatsu sauce
- 20 g (0.71 oz) tomato ketchup
- 10 g (0.35 oz) honey

MAKE THE TONKATSU

1. Lightly score the fat on the pork, then tenderise the meat using a mallet, flattening it until the pork roughly matches the size of your bread.
2. Season both sides generously with salt and white pepper.
3. Place the flour in a bowl, the beaten egg in a second bowl and the panko in a third bowl.
4. Lightly dust the pork in the flour, then dip it in the beaten egg and thoroughly coat in the panko, pressing to adhere the breadcrumbs to the pork. Set aside for 30 minutes.
5. Heat enough oil for deep-frying to 180°C (356°F). Add the tonkatsu and fry for 5–6 minutes, turning halfway through cooking, until both sides are golden and the centre is cooked through.

MAKE THE TONKATSU SAUCE

6. Mix the ingredients in a bowl until combined. (The touch of honey adds gentle sweetness, while the ketchup brings a bright tang that helps the sauce meld beautifully with the bread.)

ASSEMBLE

7. Lightly toast the shokupan.
8. Spread butter and dijon mustard on one side of two slices. Top with the shredded cabbage.
9. Spoon the tonkatsu sauce generously over both sides of the tonkatsu – don't be shy. A slightly excessive amount is ideal: freshly made, it's punchy; later, once absorbed into the crumb and coating, it becomes even better. Lay the tonkatsu on the cabbage.
10. Place the remaining bread slices on top. Press gently to settle everything.
11. Cut in half, keeping the crusts on – they help keep the structure of the sando, and for me, shokupan crust is always the best part.

TUNA SANDO

TSU NA SANDO

ツナサンド

Like egg sandwiches, tuna sandwiches are another staple beloved in Japanese households. If you have a tin of tuna in the pantry, then you can make a tuna sandwich for breakfast or a snack. Children can make them without using the stove. Each family often has its own way of preparing them – some add onions, some don't; some like to season with extra pepper – which gives each tuna sandwich its own character.

In cafes, the tuna sando often appears as part of the 'mix sandwich', sharing a plate with egg, ham, and cucumber sando. In convenience stores, it's an anchor – a safe option in a sea of seasonal experiments. It's the sandwich you can eat half-asleep on the Shinkansen, or quietly in an office between meetings.

This recipe is not a regular tuna sandwich recipe; it takes a little extra time and effort, but it yields a smoother, more flavourful filling that brings the tuna sando to the next level.

MAKES 2

butter, for spreading

dijon mustard, for spreading

4 slices Shokupan, sliced 1.5–2 cm (½–¾ in) thick (see page 34)

TUNA FILLING

1 tablespoon neutral oil

80 g (2.82 oz) onion, finely chopped

40 g (1.41 oz) shredded mozzarella or cheddar

10 g (0.35 oz) miso paste

140 g (4.94 oz) tinned tuna in oil, drained

10 g (0.35 oz) cornichon, chopped

30 g (1.06 oz) Japanese mayonnaise

MAKE THE TUNA FILLING

1. Heat the oil in a frying pan over medium heat, add the onion, along with a pinch of salt, and saute until lightly brown. Gradually add small splashes of water, letting each addition evaporate before adding the next, until the onion becomes deeply caramelised. This builds sweetness, richness and a toasty aroma – and helps prevent the bread becoming soggy from the onion.
2. Transfer the caramelised onion to a bowl, add the shredded cheese and miso and mix thoroughly while the onion is still warm. The heat melts the cheese and helps the miso dissolve, creating a smooth, flavourful base that adds depth to the filling.
3. Add the tuna, cornichon and mayonnaise, season with black pepper and mix well until fully combined. The result should be creamy, savoury, lightly sweet – a perfect match for soft shokupan.

ASSEMBLE

4. Spread butter and mustard on one side of each shokupan slice. Spoon the tuna filling on top, letting it mound slightly in the middle.
5. Hold a tuna-topped slice in your palm and, using the back of a spoon, lightly push the filling outwards from the centre towards the corners. Avoid pressing too hard, as this will flatten the texture – use a soft touch, as if you're simply guiding the filling into place. This creates a fluffy, even layer. If trimming the crusts, keep the filling about 1 cm (½ in) inside the edges so you don't cut it off.
6. Place an unspread slice of bread on top. Press gently to settle everything. (Keeping the filling domed rather than flat preserves the soft texture that defines a good tuna sando.) Repeat to finish the second tuna sando.
7. Cut the sando in half and enjoy.

MIX SANDO

MIKKU SU SANDO

ミックスサンド

If the tamago sando is about texture and the tuna sando is about comfort, the mix sando is about delegation. You can't decide, so you let the cafe do the thinking – the 'omakase' of sandwiches.

When I was a kid in Japan, mixed sandwiches were everywhere: movie theatres, playhouses, station kiosks, Shinkansen carts, local events. Because the box always held favourites and not-so-favourites, I remember trading pieces with my parents or friends. These days, I'm not sure kids even choose mixed sandwiches, and the chances to encounter them feel rare.

Every cafe has its own approach. Some toast one layer; others butter the bread; some add a piece of fruit. What matters is proportion – how one bite is creamy, the next crisp, the next slightly sweet.

You can take the same approach at home. Open the fridge, see what you have and stack your sando in an order that makes sense. A mix sando isn't about rules; it's about balance. Here, I'm offering one version – simple fillings prepared properly and arranged logically.

MAKES 1 SET OF 3 SANDWICHES

- 6 thin slices Shokupan (see page 34)

CREAMY EGG FILLING

- 2 eggs
- 10 g (0.35 oz) Japanese mayonnaise
- 15 g (0.53 oz) sour cream
- 6 g (0.21 oz) butter
- 1 g (0.04 oz) chopped dill
- 10 g (0.35 oz) cream cheese, softened

LEMON BUTTER

- 100 g (3.53 oz) salted butter, at room temperature
- 1½ teaspoons lemon zest
- 1 teaspoon lemon juice

HAM FILLING

- 14 g (0.49 oz) lemon butter (see recipe above)
- 40 g (1.41 oz) ham
- white pepper, to taste

CUCUMBER FILLING

- 45 g (1.59 oz) short cucumber
- white pepper, to taste
- white wine vinegar, to taste
- 14 g (0.49 oz) lemon butter (see recipe above)

MAKE THE CREAMY EGG SANDO

1 Pierce each egg with an egg piercer or thumbtack. Add the eggs gently to a saucepan of boiling water and cook for 9 minutes. Transfer to cold water and peel.

2 Finely chop the egg and place in a bowl. Season with salt and pepper, then fold in the mayonnaise and sour cream until combined. Avoid overmixing – it will make the egg too smooth and it will lose its character.

3 Spread the butter on one slice of bread. Place the egg salad in the centre, mounding it slightly higher in the middle.

4 Mix the dill with the cream cheese, spread it onto a second slice of bread and place it on top of the egg salad.

MAKE THE LEMON BUTTER

5 Mix the butter with the lemon zest and lemon juice.

6 The butter will keep in an airtight container in the fridge for 3 days or in the freezer for up to 1 month.

MAKE THE HAM SANDO

7 Spread the lemon butter on two bread slices, right to the edges.

8 Cut the ham in half and place it on one bread slice, about 1 cm (½ in) inside the crust, with the straight edge facing out. Season with white pepper. Top with the second slice.

MAKE THE CUCUMBER SANDO

9 Trim the ends of the cucumber, halve lengthways and finely slice into ribbons. Place in a shallow bowl and season with salt, white pepper and a drizzle of white wine vinegar. Mix gently to coat, then leave the cucumber to marinate for 5 minutes.

10 Place the cucumber between two pieces of paper towel and press lightly to remove moisture. Spread the lemon butter on the two remaining slices of bread, all the way to the edges. Arrange the cucumber slices lengthways, slightly overlapping to create a beautiful contrast between the cucumber's dark green skin and pale interior in the cross-section. Top with the second slice of bread.

ASSEMBLE

11 Stack all three sandwiches and wrap them tightly in plastic wrap. This keeps their height even when cutting. Cut off all the crusts.

12 To slice, hold your knife at a 45 degree angle and use long, smooth strokes, pivoting on the knife tip rather than pressing straight down. Cut the sando into thirds, then serve cut side up.

VEGETABLE SANDO

YASAI SANDO

野菜サンド

Salad in a sandwich may feel obvious now, but historically, raw greens were not a regular part of Japanese meals. Until the early 20th century, vegetables were usually cooked, pickled or simmered.

Today, yasai sando are becoming mainstream in cafes across Japan – Tabelog lists over a thousand places that sell it – a sign that the once-novel 'sandwich with raw greens' is steadily becoming normalised.

In Australia, the salad sandwich is part of everyday life – a ritual of tomato, beetroot, cheese, lettuce and sometimes a slice of egg; a full summer, held by buttered white bread.

Whoever controls moisture controls the sandwich. Putting fresh vegetables between slices of shokupan is essentially a battle against moisture. The trick is to keep the fluffy 'bed' of bread intact while still keeping the vegetables crisp. When you think about it, it's a small engineering challenge.

You can, of course, put anything between bread and call it a sandwich, but since we're here, why not aim for a yasai sando that's delicious, enjoyable and beautiful to look at when cut?

MAKES 1

HERB MAYONNAISE

- 50 g (1.76 oz) Japanese mayonnaise
- 40 g (1.41 oz) sour cream
- 1 g (0.04 oz) dill, finely chopped
- 1 g (0.04 oz) chervil, finely chopped
- 1 g (0.04 oz) parsley, finely chopped

CARROT SALAD

- 50 g (1.76 oz) carrot
- 8 g (0.28 oz) olive oil
- 8 g (0.28 oz) white wine vinegar
- pinch of sugar and salt

CUCUMBER SALAD

- 45 g (1.59 oz) short cucumber
- white pepper, to taste
- white wine vinegar, to taste

MAKE THE HERB MAYONNAISE

1. Combine the mayonnaise and sour cream in a bowl, add the herbs, season with salt and pepper and stir to combine. Set aside.

MAKE THE CARROT SALAD

2. Julienne the carrot – the thickness can be adjusted to your preference: finely julienned carrots are easier to eat and blend well with the other ingredients; thicker shreds add more crunch and make the sandwich more substantial.
3. In a small bowl, whisk together the olive oil, white wine vinegar, sugar and salt to make a dressing.
4. Toss the julienned carrot with the dressing and set aside.

PREPARE THE CUCUMBER SALAD

5. Trim the ends of the cucumber, halve lengthways and finely slice into ribbons. Place in a shallow bowl and season with salt, white pepper and a drizzle of white wine vinegar. Mix gently to coat, then leave the cucumber to marinate for 5 minutes.
6. Place the cucumber between two pieces of paper towel and press lightly to remove moisture.

PREPARE THE LETTUCE AND TOMATO

7. Carefully separate the lettuce leaves and wash them thoroughly in plenty of cold water. Spin them dry in a salad spinner, then press with paper towel to remove any remaining moisture. If the leaves are too large, fold them to fit the size of the shokupan.
8. Rinse the tomato and remove the stem. Pat dry with paper towel and slice to your preferred thickness. Place the slices on a tray lined with paper towel and sprinkle with a little salt. Just before assembling the sandwich, press the slices gently with another piece of paper towel to remove any excess moisture.

NO LETTUCE IN SIGHT

In 1928, a Japanese military cooking manual included a recipe for 'vegetable salad', calling for boiled or preserved vegetables such as potato, onion and carrot, mixed with a dressing of vinegar, oil and hand-whipped mayonnaise.

There were no raw greens in sight.

That detail, recorded in agricultural archives, suggests that even into the early Showa era, Japan's concept of 'salad' was closer to Western potato salad than to a leafy mix. Salad leaves were seen as hard to digest, less practical and, before refrigeration became widespread, sometimes even unsafe.

The shift towards fresh greens came later – thanks to improved transport, cold storage and the introduction of mayonnaise in the 1920s. From there, the leap from salad to sandwich was short. By the mid-20th century, the yasai (vegetable) sando offered something new: freshness between bread.

TO ASSEMBLE

2 iceberg lettuce leaves
½ tomato
salted butter, for spreading
dijon mustard, for spreading
2 slices Shokupan, sliced 1.5–2 cm (½–¾ in) thick (see page 34)
2 slices cheese (any kind)

ASSEMBLE

9 Spread butter, mustard and 15 g (0.53 oz) of the herb mayonnaise on one side of each shokupan slice.

10 Add the sliced cheese, then arrange the cucumber slices on top.

11 Lay the tomato slices over the cucumber, then mound the carrot salad in the centre and place the lettuce on top.

12 Top with the second slice of shokupan and press gently on the sandwich with your palms. Wrap it tightly in a large piece of plastic wrap or baking paper.

13 Using a sharp knife, make a clean, confident vertical cut to slice the sandwich in half, sliding the blade straight down through the stacked fillings rather than sawing back and forth.

14 Cut the sando in half and enjoy.

NOTES

For vegetables that tend to release water, such as cucumber and zucchini, salt them lightly and leave for a few minutes, then squeeze out the excess moisture.

If you're using very juicy ingredients like tomatoes, sandwich them between moisture-blocking items such as lettuce.

Place dry ingredients like cheese next to the bread. If you want to add different vegetables, choose ones that don't release too much moisture. Avocado is also a great option.

CLUBHOUSE SANDO

KURABU HAUSU SANDO

クラブハウスサンド

The 1970s marked a turning point for Japan's food-service industry, as American chains like KFC, McDonald's, Mister Donut and Denny's arrived and spurred the growth of Japanese chains such as Skylark, Royal Host and MOS Burger. This period laid the foundation for the family restaurants and fast-food culture that continue to shape Japan's food scene today. Before then, clubhouse sandwiches were the kind of thing you'd find at places like the Imperial Hotel – something fancy, meant for the upper crust of society. But as the food-service industry became more shaped by American culture, the clubhouse sandwich suddenly felt much closer to everyday life.

For people who grew up with simple egg or tuna sando, the clubhouse was almost dazzling: thick-cut, toasted bread stacked high with all kinds of fillings we'd never seen before. It looked exciting, a little glamorous and completely new. FYI, for me, the 'classic' clubhouse will always be the one from Royal Host, the Japanese family restaurant.

MAKES 1

- 1 × 150–200 g (5.29–7.05 oz) piece boneless skinless chicken thigh
- cornflour (cornstarch), for dusting
- vegetable oil, for frying
- 1 egg
- 2 bacon slices
- ½ tomato
- 2 iceberg lettuce leaves
- 3 slices Shokupan, sliced 1.5–2 cm (½–¾ in) thick (see page 34)
- salted butter, for spreading
- dijon mustard, for spreading
- tomato ketchup, for drizzling
- Japanese mayonnaise, for spreading
- 4 cornichons, to garnish

1. Season the chicken with salt and pepper and let it sit for 10 minutes.
2. Dust the chicken lightly with cornflour – this gives the chicken a crisp surface and keeps the inside juicy.
3. Heat the vegetable oil in a frying pan over low heat. Add the chicken, cover and cook for 5 minutes. Flip and cook, covered, for another 5 minutes.
4. Remove the lid and pour off any excess oil. Increase the heat to medium and sear both sides of the chicken for 1 minute each side. Remove from the pan and set aside.
5. Increase the heat to medium–high, crack in the egg and fry it to your liking.
6. When the yolk is halfway set, place the bacon slices on top of the egg. (This keeps the egg and bacon together as one filling.) Flip the egg and bacon together and cook until the bacon is fried to your liking.
7. Slice the tomato into rounds, then cut each round in half.
8. Wash and dry the lettuce thoroughly with paper towel, then fold the leaves to fit the slices of shokupan.

THE HOTEL SANDWICH TRADITION

Few places in Japan carry the pedigree of the Imperial Hotel (帝国ホテル) in Tokyo, long associated with the refined club sandwich served in its bars and lounges.

According to *GINZA* magazine, the story dates back to the late 1920s, when the hotel's eighth head chef, Ishiwata Bunjiro (石渡文治郎), encountered a similar sandwich at the Ritz in Paris. Impressed by its form and flavour, he brought the idea back to Tokyo and introduced it under the name 'American Clubhouse Sandwich'.

Kateigaho magazine notes that the Imperial's version remains a signature in its Old Imperial Bar: thin-sliced bread, roast chicken, bacon, tomato, lettuce and mustard butter, stacked to a precise height of 4.5 cm (1¾ in) – a small feat of balance and proportion.

Note.com calls the Imperial Hotel's rendition 'a benchmark of elegance', where the sandwich is treated less like a casual bite and more like an exercise in craft.

Tokyo Calendar observes that nearly every major hotel in Tokyo now has its own take on the clubhouse – from the Park Hyatt to the Okura – each adjusting the fillings and textures to their house style.

The clubhouse sandwich, along with dishes like curry rice and omelette rice, all passed through these kitchens before filtering down into kissaten menus and home kitchens throughout Japan.

ASSEMBLE

9. Toast all three slices of bread.
10. Spread butter and mustard on one slice of toast and top with the bacon and egg. Drizzle lightly with tomato ketchup.
11. Spread butter and mustard on both sides of a second slice of toast and place it on top of the bacon and egg.
12. Place the tomato slices on top in the centre and season lightly with salt.
13. Add the grilled chicken, then finish with the lettuce.
14. Spread butter and mayonnaise on one side of the third slice of toast and place it mayo side down on top of the chicken.
15. Press the sandwich gently with your palms. Trim away the crusts and cut the sandwich into halves or quarters.
16. Secure each half or quarter with a cocktail stick and garnish with a cornichon.
17. Enjoy straight away.

FRUIT AND WHIPPED CREAM SANDO

FURUTSU SANDO

フルーツサンド

In Japan, fruit is a luxury. A melon can cost more than dinner and a perfect strawberry is often sold individually, wrapped like a small gift.

Fruit sando emerged from Japan's postwar fruit-parlour culture. By the 1950s and 60s, fruit specialty shops like Sembikiya and Takano were turning surplus fruit into cream-filled sandwiches that looked as polished as the cafes they came from. Refrigeration had improved, cream was accessible and Western-style sweets were in demand – the timing was right.

For decades, the fruit sando lived in department-store cafes and tearooms. Then social media changed its place in the world. The clean cross-sections made them instantly recognisable, and bakeries began pushing variations: figs, grapes, melon, mango; mascarpone instead of cream; even ice-cream versions.

Even though they're now sold everywhere – including convenience stores – the fruit sando still feels a little special.

MAKES 2

- 150 g (5.29 oz) cream (40% milkfat)
- 50 g (1.76 oz) plant-based cream (see Notes)
- 15 g (0.53 oz) icing (confectioners') sugar
- 3 g (0.11 oz) vanilla essence
- 1 kiwi fruit, peeled
- 6 strawberries
- 8 segments tinned mandarin
- 4 slices Shokupan, sliced 1.5–2 cm (½–¾ in) thick (see page 34)

1. Whip the cream, plant-based cream, icing sugar and vanilla essence together until stiff peaks form.
2. Cut the kiwi into quarters lengthways. Trim and hull the strawberries. Drain the mandarin segments on paper towel to remove excess moisture.

ASSEMBLE

3. Trim the crusts off the bread.
4. Spread a thick layer of cream on each slice.
5. Arrange the fruit, keeping the cut lines in mind for a clean cross-section, on two slices.
6. Top with the remaining slices of bread.
7. Wrap each sandwich gently in plastic wrap and chill for at least 30 minutes.
8. Remove the plastic wrap and slice into sandwich fingers just before serving.

NOTES

Choose fruits that don't release too much juice. Strawberries, kiwi and pineapple work well; canned fruit is also reliable. Juicy fruits like peaches and oranges can make the bread soggy.

Blending a small amount of plant-based cream with dairy cream results in a lighter texture that requires less sugar.

THE FRUIT PARLOUR LINEAGE

The fruit sando didn't begin in a bakery – it began in a fruit shop.

Japan's famous fruit parlours, like Sembikiya (founded 1834) and Takano (1885), started as purveyors of imported and domestic produce for the wealthy. In the Taisho era, the rise of the mobo and moga – modern boys and modern girls – made cafes and fruit parlours fashionable spaces of urban life. These young Tokyoites embraced Western sweets, cream and coffee, setting the stage for Japan's first fruit desserts.

After the war, department stores adopted the same aesthetic – polished fruit behind glass, seasonal displays, a perfectly sliced fruit sando beside coffee and chiffon cake. These stores defined Japan's idea of 'Western-style' desserts: clean, soft, photogenic, seasonal.

That lineage still shapes the fruit sando today. Whether sold by a high-end patisserie or a corner konbini, it inherits the same philosophy: respect the fruit, protect its texture and make sweetness look elegant.

CHAPTER EIGHT

DONATSU

CHAPTER EIGHT

DONATSU

ドーナツ

Ever wonder why donatsu (doughnut) shops never sell curry doughnuts, only bakeries?

A doughnut shop's system is built around frying: doughs are formulated for the fryer, shapes are controlled with moulds, and consistency is key. That's how chains can reproduce the same doughnut anywhere.

Bakeries run on a completely different rhythm. Mixing, fermenting, shaping and baking happen all day. Frying doughnuts is just one task in that larger cycle, which is why shapes and finishes can vary. That's also where bakery doughnuts shine with character. The dough is fermented, the flavours are fuller, there's texture, substance, a quiet satisfaction. (And fillings like curry – the kind doughnut shops never touch – makes me feel right at home.)

A quick note: fluffy, airy doughnuts are yeast-raised. Crumbly ones, like old-fashioneds, are cake doughnuts made with baking powder. They're cousins, not siblings.

In this chapter, we'll be making bakery-style doughnuts. No fancy, Instagrammable decorations, no frills – just incredibly simple doughnuts that only a bakery would make. A few of these doughnuts might seem almost forgotten, but they have loyal fans who wouldn't trade them for anything else.

TWISTED SUGAR DOUGHNUT

TSUISUTO DONATSU (SHUGA)

ツイストドーナツ（シュガー）

Before the ring-shaped doughnut became standard, Japan's first love was twisted.

The twisted sugar doughnut traces its lineage back to mahua, a fried, twisted rope of dough that originated in Tianjin, China. It's said that a version of it arrived in Japan during the Nara period (710–794 CE) from the Tang Dynasty, known then as 'sakubei' – literally, 'rope cake'.

Fried, yeasted dough rolled in sugar became a symbol of simple happiness – something you could find in a dagashiya (old-fashioned candy store), local bakery or school canteen. It was cheap, filling and universally understood.

Unlike the dense mahua or the airy kkwabaegi in Korea, Japan's twisted doughnut sits somewhere in between: lightly chewy, dusted with fine sugar and slightly bready. It's the kind of sweet that offers comfort, one twist at a time.

MAKES 8

SPONGE DOUGH (MAKE AHEAD)

125 g (4.41 oz) bread flour	(50%)
8 g (0.28 oz) raw (demerara) sugar	(3%)
3 g (0.11 oz) osmotolerant instant dry yeast	1.2%)
100 g (3.53 oz) full-cream (whole) milk, lukewarm	(40%)

FINAL DOUGH (ADDITIONS)

20 g (0.71 oz) cream (40% milkfat)	(8%)
40 g (1.41 oz) egg (from approx. 1 egg)	(16%)
85 g (3.0 oz) bread flour, plus extra for dusting	(34%)
40 g (1.41 oz) plain (all-purpose) flour	(16%)
5 g (0.18 oz) fine sea salt	(2%)
27 g (0.95 oz) raw (demerara) sugar	(11%)
35 g (1.23 oz) cultured unsalted butter, softened	(14%)

(Values in parentheses indicate baker's percentages)

TO FINISH

- neutral oil, for deep-frying
- caster (superfine) sugar or icing (confectioners') sugar, for coating

Day 1

MAKE THE SPONGE DOUGH

1 Combine the bread flour, sugar and yeast in a bowl. Add the lukewarm milk and mix until no dry flour remains. Cover and proof at room temperature until doubled in size, about 1 hour. Refrigerate overnight (up to 16 hours).

Desired final sponge dough temperature before refrigeration: 26°C (79°F).

Day 2

MIX THE FINAL DOUGH

2 Place the cream and egg into the bowl of a stand mixer fitted with a dough hook, followed by the flours and salt. Tear the sponge dough into pieces and add to the bowl. Mix on speed 3 (low) for 5 minutes. Increase to speed 6 (medium–high) and mix for 10 minutes. Add the raw sugar and mix on speed 6 for a further 10 minutes, or until the dough starts coming together. Gradually add the softened butter and continue mixing. In the final stage of mixing, the dough will come together into a lump and begin slapping against the bowl as it separates from the side. The finished dough should be glossy and pass a windowpane test (stretching it thin enough to let light through without tearing).

Desired final dough temperature: 26°C (79°F).

FIRST PROOF

3 Cover the bowl with a damp tea towel and proof the dough for 30 minutes. Perform a fold by stretching one side of the dough up out of the bowl and folding it down over the remaining dough in the bowl.

DIVIDE AND REST

4 Turn the dough out onto the bench and divide into 8 × 60 g (2.12 oz) portions. Round each piece gently by placing your palm over the dough and rolling it taut against the surface of the bench. Cover with the tea towel and rest for 20 minutes.

SHAPE

5 Lightly flour the bench and place the dough seam side up. Flatten each piece of dough into a rectangle shape. Working with one piece of dough at a time, with a long edge facing you, fold the dough into thirds by bringing the top and bottom edges into the middle, then fold it in half. Press the seam tightly to seal, then roll the dough gently back and forth until it stretches to about 35 cm (13¾ in) in length, keeping the centre slightly thicker. Fold the rolled-out dough in half, then twist it by rolling it forwards to create two or three twists. Press the ends firmly to seal. Place on a baking tray lined with baking paper. Repeat with the remaining dough.

↓ RECIPE CONTINUES

FINAL PROOF

6 Proof at 30°C (86°F) for 30 minutes (see page 27) or until the dough looks slightly puffy and light.

DEEP-FRY

7 Heat enough oil for deep-frying in a saucepan to 170–180°C (338–356°F).

8 Working in batches, deep-fry the doughnuts, turning halfway through cooking, for 3–4 minutes on each side, until golden brown and crisp. Transfer to a wire rack lined with paper towel to drain.

9 Place enough sugar to coat the doughnuts in a bowl. Toss the doughnuts in the sugar while they're still hot.

SERVE

10 Enjoy the doughnuts as soon as possible after making, while they're fresh and at their best.

A GLOBAL LEXICON OF THE TWISTED DOUGHNUT

Every culture has its own way of twisting and frying dough. What began as mahua in ancient China travelled through dynasties and trade routes, picking up local flours, oils and meanings along the way. The table below traces that lineage: one idea, many accents.

NAME	PRIMARY REGION / COUNTRY	KEY CHARACTERISTICS
Mahua (麻花)	Taiwan, China	The ancient progenitor; crispy throughout or soft and fluffy inside.
Kkwabaegi (꽈배기)	Korea	Mildly sweet, fluffy and spongy; traditionally coated in sugar and cinnamon.
Sakubei (索餅)	Japan (historical)	Ancient Tang-Dynasty import; a common ancestor to modern doughnuts and noodles.
Twisted Doughnut	Japan (modern)	A nostalgic Showa-era snack, sold in local bakeries and dagashiya (traditional candy stores).
Shakoy / Lubid-Lubid	Philippines	Textural range from soft and fluffy to sticky and chewy; glutinous rice flour versions are prevalent.
Pilipit	Philippines	A smaller, drier and crunchier variant of shakoy.
Treccia	Italy	The Italian iteration, sometimes filled with pastry cream.
Bánh Quẩy Thừng	Vietnam	The Vietnamese name for the 'twisted-rope doughnut'.

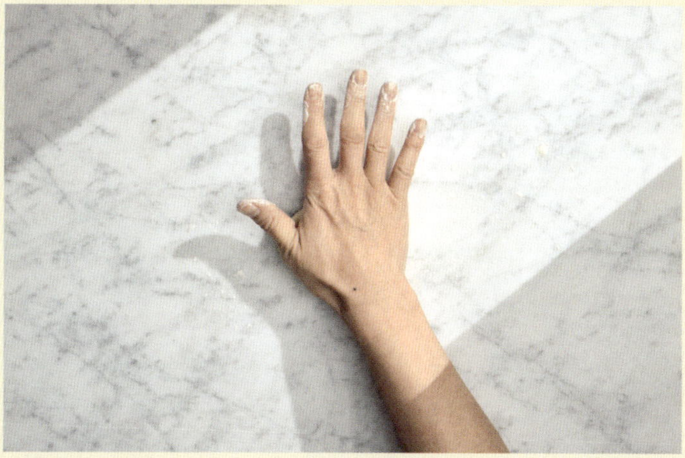

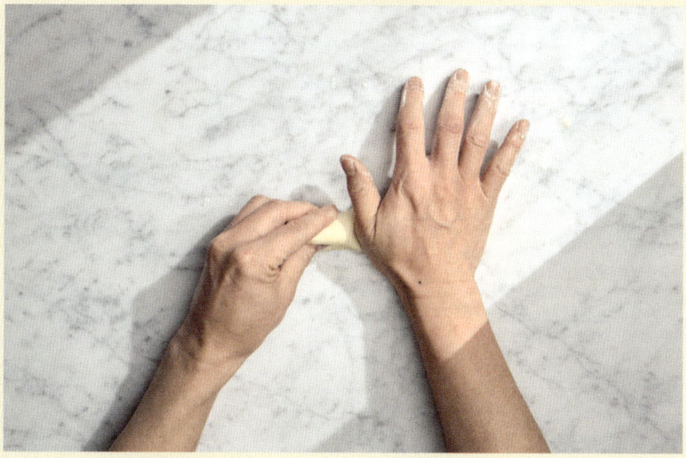
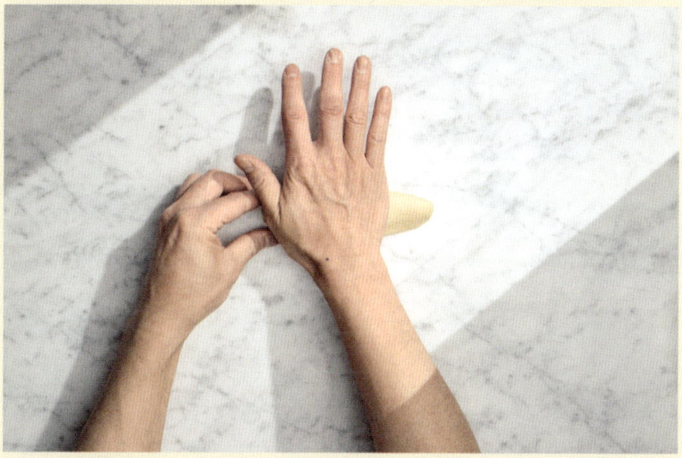
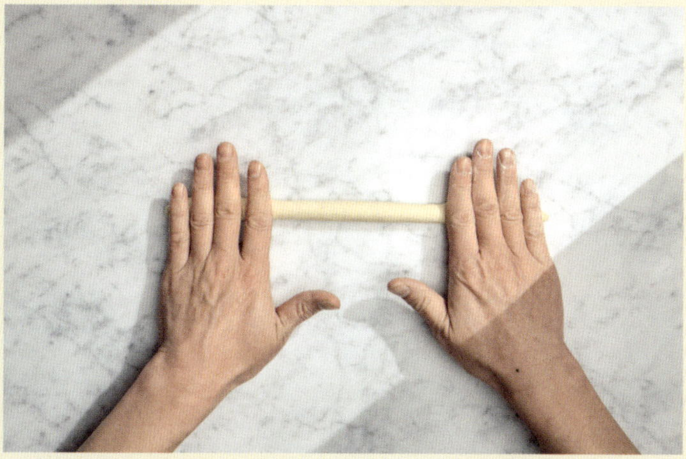

HONEY-GLAZED TWISTED DOUGHNUT

TSUISUTO DONATSU (HANI GUREZU)

ツイストドーナツ（ハニーグレーズ）

This is the same doughnut as the sugar twist on page 264 – only dressed differently.

A sugar twist is coated while the doughnut is still warm, so the crystals cling loosely to the surface. This gives a grainy crunch and a dry sweetness that disappears as the doughnut cools.

A glazed doughnut is different: sugar and honey are melted and the doughnut is brushed or dipped into the sticky liquid. Once it sets, it forms a thin, glossy shell that softens with each bite. It's smoother, stickier and remains sweet for longer.

It's not about better or worse; it just depends on the mood. Bakeries often choose sugar because it's quicker to apply during a busy production run. And of course, you don't have to sweeten it at all. Sometimes, the doughnut itself is enough.

MAKES 8

SPONGE DOUGH (MAKE AHEAD)

125 g (4.41 oz) bread flour	(50%)
8 g (0.28 oz) raw (demerara) sugar	(3%)
3 g (0.11 oz) osmotolerant instant dry yeast	(1.2%)
100 g (3.53 oz) full-cream (whole) milk, lukewarm	(40%)

FINAL DOUGH (ADDITIONS)

20 g (0.71 oz) cream (40% milkfat)	(8%)
40 g (1.41 oz) egg (from approx. 1 egg)	(16%)
85 g (3.0 oz) bread flour, plus extra for dusting	(34%)
40 g (1.41 oz) plain (all-purpose) flour	(16%)
5 g (0.18 oz) fine sea salt	(2%)
27 g (0.95 oz) raw (demerara) sugar	(11%)
35 g (1.23 oz) cultured unsalted butter, softened	(14%)

(Values in parentheses indicate baker's percentages)

Day 1

MAKE THE SPONGE DOUGH

1 Combine the bread flour, raw sugar and yeast in a bowl. Add the lukewarm milk and mix until no dry flour remains. Cover and proof at room temperature until doubled in size, about 1 hour. Refrigerate overnight (up to 16 hours).

Desired final sponge dough temperature before refrigeration: 26°C (79°F).

Day 2

MIX THE FINAL DOUGH

2 Place the cream and egg into the bowl of a stand mixer fitted with a dough hook, followed by the flours and salt. Tear the sponge dough into pieces and add to the bowl. Mix on speed 3 (low) for 5 minutes. Increase to speed 6 (medium–high) and mix for 10 minutes. Add the raw sugar and mix on speed 6 for a further 10 minutes, or until the dough starts coming together. Gradually add the softened butter and continue mixing. In the final stage of mixing, the dough will come together into a lump and begin slapping against the bowl as it separates from the side. The finished dough should be glossy and pass a windowpane test (stretching it thin enough to let light through without tearing).

Desired final dough temperature: 26°C (79°F).

FIRST PROOF

3 Cover the bowl with a damp tea towel and proof the dough for 30 minutes. Perform a fold by stretching one side of the dough up out of the bowl and folding it down over the remaining dough in the bowl.

DIVIDE AND REST

4 Turn the dough out onto the bench and divide into 8 × 60 g (2.12 oz) portions. Round each piece gently by placing your palm over the dough and rolling it taut against the surface of the bench. Cover with the tea towel and rest for 20 minutes.

SHAPE

5 Lightly flour the bench and place the dough seam side up. Flatten each piece of dough into a rectangle shape. Working with one piece of dough at a time, with a long edge facing you, fold the dough into thirds by bringing the top and bottom edges into the middle, then fold it in half. Press the seam tightly to seal, then roll the dough gently back and forth until it stretches to about 35 cm (13¾ in) in length, keeping the centre slightly thicker. Fold the rolled-out dough in half, then twist it by rolling it forwards to create two or three twists. Press the ends firmly to seal. Place on a baking tray lined with baking paper. Repeat with the remaining dough.

GLAZE:
EAST AND WEST

In Japan, doughnut glaze tends to be thinner and more restrained – more syrup than icing. It's usually made from dissolved sugar (sometimes with a touch of honey or mirin), then applied to the doughnut while they're still warm. The coating sets into a translucent sheen that softens the surface of the doughnut without overwhelming it. You can still taste the bread.

Western glazes, especially in American-style doughnuts, are thicker and opaque, often made with powdered sugar and milk. They dry to a firm shell, adding crunch and sweetness that dominate the bite.

The difference isn't just taste but philosophy: Japan's glaze aims for balance; Western glaze aims for indulgence. One highlights the dough; the other steals the show. Both have their place – it just depends on whether you want your twist to whisper or to sing.

HONEY GLAZE

- 200 g (7.05 oz) icing (confectioners') sugar
- 20 g (0.71 oz) honey
- 20–30 g (0.71–1.06 oz) water

TO FINISH

- neutral oil, for deep-frying

FINAL PROOF

6 Proof at 30°C (86°F) for 30 minutes (see page 27) or until the dough looks slightly puffy and light.

MAKE THE HONEY GLAZE

7 Place the icing sugar, honey and water in a heatproof bowl and mix well. Set the bowl over a small saucepan of simmering water and warm, stirring frequently, until the glaze reaches 30–40°C (86–104°F).

DEEP-FRY

8 Heat enough oil for deep-frying in a saucepan to 170–180°C (338–356°F).

9 Working in batches, deep-fry the doughnuts, turning halfway through cooking, for 3–4 minutes on each side, until golden brown and crisp. Transfer to a wire rack lined with paper towel to drain.

10 Coat the surface of the doughnuts in the honey glaze while they're still hot by either dipping them into the glaze or brushing the glaze over the surface of the doughnuts.

SERVE

11 Enjoy the doughnuts as soon as possible after making, while they're fresh and at their best.

RED BEAN PASTE DOUGHNUT

ANDONATSU

あんドーナツ

Red bean paste doughnuts are a common sight in Japanese bakeries.

The 'an' (sweet red bean paste) comes from wagashi tradition, so in a sense it belongs to Japanese confectionery. However, you won't find red bean paste doughnuts at wagashi shops, and doughnut chains rarely make them either. They really are an invention that bridges the two worlds.

I can almost picture how it started: leftover anko from making anpan, a bit of dough from the morning batch – let's not waste it and fry it instead. That's the kind of practical decision a bakery makes without thinking.

Dusted with sugar on the outside and filled with firm, slightly earthy anko, an-doughnuts are simple, honest and unpretentious, a classic through and through.

MAKES 8

SPONGE DOUGH (MAKE AHEAD)

125 g (4.41 oz) bread flour	(50%)
8 g (0.28 oz) raw (demerara) sugar	(3%)
3 g (0.11 oz) osmotolerant instant dry yeast	(1.2%)
100 g (3.53 oz) full-cream (whole) milk, lukewarm	(40%)

FINAL DOUGH (ADDITIONS)

20 g (0.71 oz) cream (40% milkfat)	(8%)
40 g (1.41 oz) egg (from approx. 1 egg)	(16%)
85 g (3.0 oz) bread flour, plus extra for dusting	(34%)
40 g (1.41 oz) plain (all-purpose) flour	(16%)
5 g (0.18 oz) fine sea salt	(2%)
27 g (0.95 oz) raw (demerara) sugar	(11%)
35 g (1.23 oz) cultured unsalted butter, softened	(14%)

(Values in parentheses indicate baker's percentages)

Day 1

MAKE THE SPONGE DOUGH

1 Combine the bread flour, raw sugar and yeast in a bowl. Add the lukewarm milk and mix until no dry flour remains. Cover and proof at room temperature until doubled in size, about 1 hour. Refrigerate overnight (up to 16 hours).

Desired final sponge dough temperature before refrigeration: 26°C (79°F).

Day 2

MIX THE FINAL DOUGH

2 Place the cream and egg into the bowl of a stand mixer fitted with a dough hook, followed by the flours and salt. Tear the sponge dough into pieces and add to the bowl. Mix on speed 3 (low) for 5 minutes. Increase to speed 6 (medium–high) and mix for 10 minutes. Add the raw sugar and mix on speed 6 for a further 10 minutes, or until the dough starts coming together. Gradually add the softened butter and continue mixing. In the final stage of mixing, the dough will come together into a lump and begin slapping against the bowl as it separates from the side. The finished dough should be glossy and pass a windowpane test (stretching it thin enough to let light through without tearing).

Desired final dough temperature: 26°C (79°F).

FIRST PROOF

3 Cover the bowl with a damp tea towel and proof the dough for 30 minutes. Perform a fold by stretching one side of the dough up out of the bowl and folding it down over the remaining dough in the bowl.

DIVIDE AND REST

4 Turn the dough out onto the bench and divide into 8 × 60 g (2.12 oz) portions. Round each piece gently by placing your palm over the dough and rolling it taut against the surface of the bench. Cover with the tea towel and rest for 20 minutes.

FILLING

400 g (14.11 oz) Anko (see page 80)

TO FINISH

neutral oil, for deep-frying
caster (superfine) sugar or icing (confectioners') sugar, for coating

SHAPE

5 Lightly flour the bench and place the dough seam side up. Flatten the dough pieces into 8–10 cm (3¼–4 in) discs, keeping the edges thinner and the centre slightly thicker to prevent the filling from breaking through the dough.

6 Scoop a portion of anko (around 50 g/1.76 oz) onto the centre of one dough disc. Lift the edge of the dough up and around the filling, pleating and pinching firmly to seal completely. Make sure no bean paste is exposed. Turn the dough seam side down and gently round the dough between your palms until smooth and dome-shaped. Place on a baking tray lined with baking paper. Repeat with the remaining dough and filling.

FINAL PROOF

7 Proof at 30°C (86°F) for 30 minutes (see page 27) or until the dough looks slightly puffy and light.

DEEP-FRY

8 Heat enough oil for deep-frying in a saucepan to 170–180°C (338–356°F).

9 Working in batches, deep-fry the doughnuts, turning halfway through cooking, for 3–4 minutes on each side, until golden brown and crisp. Transfer to a wire rack lined with paper towel to drain.

10 Place enough sugar to coat the doughnuts in a bowl. Toss the doughnuts in the sugar while they're still hot.

SERVE

11 Enjoy the doughnuts as soon as possible after making, while they're fresh and at their best. They pair beautifully with a cup of strong green tea.

KARINTO DOUGHNUT

KARINTO DONATSU

かりんとうドーナツ

Karinto is a time-tested Japanese fried snack: dough made from flour, sugar, water (and often a leavening agent) is shaped into sticks or ropes, deep-fried, then coated in sugar or kokuto (black sugar).

Its name may come from the crunchy 'kari-kari' sound or from a resemblance to the karin (quince) fruit in colour and form.

Many karinto products already exist – karinto doughnuts, karinto cookies, even karinto senbei (rice crackers). The doughnut is a natural extension: a sweet bridge linking traditional fried snacks and the contemporary world of doughnuts. Karinto doughnuts may look like chubby little karinto snacks, but inside they're soft and fluffy. Their easy-to-grab shape makes them perfect for snacking, and they're usually sold in generously filled bags at an affordable price, making them a beloved snack and gift by food lovers of all ages, to food lovers of all ages!

MAKES 30

- 65 g (2.29 oz) egg (from approx. 1 large egg)
- 70 g (2.47 oz) raw (demerara) sugar
- 5 g (0.18 oz) vegetable oil
- 140 g (4.94 oz) plain (all-purpose) flour
- 2 g (0.07 oz) baking powder
- neutral oil, for deep-frying

BLACK SUGAR GLAZE

- 150 g (5.29 oz) kokuto (black sugar)
- 50 g (1.76 oz) raw (demerara) sugar
- 45 g (1.59 oz) water

MAKE THE DOUGH

1 In a bowl, beat the egg. Add the sugar and vegetable oil and whisk until the mixture is smooth and the sugar has mostly dissolved. Sift the flour and baking powder together. Gradually add the dry ingredients to the egg mixture. Fold gently with a spatula until a sticky dough forms. Do not overmix, or the doughnuts will be tough.

DIVIDE AND SHAPE

2 Divide the dough into bite-sized portions (12–15 g/0.42–0.53 oz each). Roll between your palms and shape into sticks.

DEEP-FRY

3 Heat enough oil for deep-frying to 160–170°C (320–338°F) in a small saucepan.

4 Working in batches, deep-fry the dough, turning halfway through cooking, for about 2 minutes on each side, until golden brown and crisp. Transfer to a wire rack lined with paper towel to drain.

MAKE THE BLACK SUGAR GLAZE

5 Place the kokuto, raw sugar and water in a small saucepan. Warm over medium heat while stirring with a spatula until the sugar dissolves. Bring to the boil, then reduce the heat to low and simmer for 1–2 minutes, until slightly thickened.

6 Remove the pan from the heat, add the doughnuts and toss to coat. Spread the doughnuts on a tray lined with baking paper and allow to cool.

SERVE

7 Enjoy the doughnuts as soon as possible after making, while they're fresh and at their best.

STORE

8 Although best enjoyed straight away, the karinto doughnuts will keep in an airtight container at room temperature for up to 2 days.

SWEET BEGINNINGS

Karinto's roots possibly date back to the Nara era, arriving as togashi (sweets) from Tang-Dynasty China. It became a popular snack in the Edo period, especially in Tokyo's karinto sellers' streets. One landmark moment came in 1875, when a shop in Asakusa began selling fried dough sticks coated in black sugar. That version spread through the downtown streets and became what most people today recognise as karinto.

CHAPTER NINE

CHAPTER NINE

MUSHIPAN

蒸しパン

Mushipan, also known as steamed buns, sit at the meeting point of different traditions. The method originates from Chinese steamed cakes, such as fa gao, but the batter is more similar to a Western muffin.

Where the conventional oven uses dry heat to build crust and colour, steaming retains the moisture of the bread. The result is a soft and springy texture from edge to centre, with no browning or Maillard reaction. The crumb feels closer to a sponge cake than bread, pale and uniform throughout.

Mushipan gained popularity in the 1950s and 1960s, when ovens were still rare in Japanese homes. Bakeries and street stalls sold mushipan as an affordable, everyday snack. Sweet potato was a common addition, both for flavour and as a natural sweetener at a time when sugar supply was still limited.

Mushipan's appeal was not only taste but practicality: anyone could make it with just a saucepan and steam.

At bakeries, mushipan are, of course, sometimes made using a traditional steamer, but in reality, most are made using unique methods suited to each bakery's workflow. Here, in addition to the steaming method, we'll also introduce a bakery-style way to make mushipan in the oven.

CHEESE MUSHIPAN

CHIZU MUSHIPAN

チーズ蒸しパン

Cheese mushipan is a soft, wobbly, steamed little cake that somehow tastes like cheesecake, custard and pancake batter all at once. The flavour is gentle: a warm dairy sweetness with a faint tang from the cheese, almost pudding-like when you tear it open. In Japan it's a childhood classic, the kind of snack you'd find in school lunchboxes or on convenience-store shelves between the melonpan and chocolate coronet.

MAKES 8

- 60 g (2.12 oz) grated cheddar
- 50 g (1.76 oz) grated parmesan
- 50 g (1.76 oz) cream cheese
- 210 g (7.41 oz) full-cream (whole) milk
- 165 g (5.82 oz) egg (from approx. 3 large eggs)
- 180 g (6.35 oz) raw (demerara) sugar
- 60 g (2.12 oz) white sesame oil or neutral oil
- 240 g (8.47 oz) plain (all-purpose) flour
- 18 g (0.63 oz) baking powder
- butter, for melting (optional)

MOULD DIMENSIONS

10 × 6.5 × 3 cm (4 × 2½ × 1¼ in)

1. Preheat a large steamer over medium–high heat.
2. Place the cheddar, parmesan, cream cheese and milk in a saucepan. Warm gently over low heat, whisking until the cheese melts and the mixture becomes smooth. Do not let it boil. Remove from the heat and leave to cool slightly.
3. In a heatproof bowl, whisk together the eggs and sugar until fully combined.
4. Slowly pour the warm cheese mixture into the egg mixture while whisking continuously. Add the sesame oil and whisk until combined.
5. Sift the flour and baking powder together. Add to the batter in two stages, folding gently with a spatula until no dry flour remains. Do not overmix – the batter should be smooth but not elastic.
6. Lightly oil eight 10 × 6.5 × 3 cm (4 ×2½ × 1¼ in) moulds and line with paper cases of the same size. (You don't need to do this if you have silicone moulds.) Fill each mould to 70 per cent capacity – they will rise significantly during steaming.
7. Place the moulds in the steamer. Steam over medium–high heat for 12–15 minutes, or until a skewer inserted into the centre of a mushipan comes out clean. The steaming time may vary based on heat and steamer size. Lift the lid slightly for the last 15 seconds of cooking to reduce surface wrinkles (this is optional but it gives the mushipan a smooth finish).
8. If you'd like your mushipan to have a golden finish, melt a little butter in a frying pan over medium heat. Sear the tops of the mushipan while pressing down gently to achieve an even golden brown.
9. Serve warm or at room temperature.
10. Wrap the mushipan individually in plastic wrap, then place in an airtight container and store at room temperature for up to 4 days.

BLACK SUGAR MUSHIPAN

KOKUTO MUSHIPAN

黒糖蒸しパン

Japan stretches a long way from north to south, which means the climate – and the local food – can differ hugely depending on where you are. This kokuto mushipan is a classic local treat on the southern island of Kyushu, especially in the city of Kagoshima and Miyazaki prefecture, and in Okinawa, which makes sense since they've historically produced sugar. Surprisingly, it's also popular in Tohoku, the northern part of Honshu (Japan's main island), including Iwate and Miyagi prefectures. It's funny when you think about it – northern Japan is much colder and not where sugarcane grows, yet people there have embraced this simple sweet as a local favourite. Either way, it has always been a humble snack people love to make at home.

In Kagoshima, it's called 'fukuregashi', named for the baking soda that makes the cake more than double in size when steamed – hence sometimes it's also called 'soda cake'. Families have been making it at home as a snack for kids since the Showa era, though it didn't store well and had to be eaten fresh. Nowadays, factory production and better distribution mean it keeps a bit longer, so you can find it in supermarkets alongside other sweet breads.

Bakeries still make kokuto mushipan in big trays and cut it up casually, or bake individual portions in muffin cups. You don't usually go to a bakery just for kokuto mushipan, but having some in your kitchen always feels comforting.

This recipe uses a muffin tray and steam-bakes the mushipan in the oven using a water bath. If you are using a steamer instead, refer to the steaming time for the Cheese mushipan on page 283 as a guide.

MAKES 6

- 60 g (2.12 oz) kokuto (black sugar)
- 50 g (1.76 oz) full-cream (whole) milk
- 1 egg
- 1 tablespoon rice bran oil
- 1½ teaspoons vinegar
- 1 tablespoon honey
- 100 g (3.53 oz) plain (all-purpose) flour
- 4 g (0.14 oz) baking soda
- black sesame seeds, to garnish

1. Preheat the oven to 160–170°C (320–338°F) fan-forced. Fill a baking tray with about 1 cm (½ in) water and place it in the bottom of the oven.
2. Place the kokuto in a bowl. If it's clumped, break up any large pieces with the back of a spoon.
3. Warm the milk to just less than body temperature (32–34°C/90–93°F). Pour half the milk into the kokuto and stir to dissolve the kokuto. Press any remaining clumps against the bowl with the back of a spoon until mostly dissolved.
4. Add the remaining milk, the egg, rice bran oil, vinegar and honey to the bowl. Whisk until well combined.
5. Sift the flour and baking soda together. Add to the batter and fold in gently with a whisk until the batter is smooth and lump-free.
6. Line a six-hole muffin tray with paper cases and fill each one 70–80 per cent full. Sprinkle black sesame seeds on top.
7. Place the muffin tray in the oven and steam-bake the mushipan for 20–25 minutes, until a bamboo skewer inserted into the centre of a mushipan comes out clean. Avoid opening the oven door during baking to retain the steam.
8. If there are still crumbs clinging to the bamboo skewer, cover the tray with foil and bake for an additional 5 minutes. Allow to cool.
9. Kokuto mushipan are lovely as an afternoon snack, especially with strong tea.
10. Wrap the mushipan individually in plastic wrap, then place in an airtight container and store at room temperature for up to 4 days.

ARIGATO GOZAIMASU
THANK YOU

ありがとうございます

SATOSHI NARUSAWA

I would like to express my gratitude especially to the following people who passed the baton to me in my life and work: Brendan Liew, Harvard Wang, Andrea Brabazon, Vina Nurina Pranata, Jodie Myers, Daniel Moses, David Latimer, Benise To, Frankie Tan, Nick Chen, Josh Crasti, Elio Crasti, Wan-yu Chen, team LITTLE CARDIGAN and team BENCH COFFEE CO. Last but not least, I sincerely thank my wife, Asako, and my daughter, Yuma, and my son, Sparkles. Their support and understanding have made me who I am.

HARVARD WANG

I get a thank you too? Awesome. I would like to thank the following people for test-baking the recipes in this book: Joan Tran, MeiHuii Lee, Saw Xiao Rui, Ange Yang, Vivian Ly, Jo Chen, Tian Ong and Sayaka Treeve. To Satoshi and Asako: thank you for never doubting my ability to help knead this project to life. My goshujin Chika: during our wedding reception I thanked everyone but you, so this is a small part of my redemption. Thank you and Hana for being the reason I'm anywhere near the kitchen. Thank you Brendan Liew, Tim White for the 'in', Lucy Heaver, Ana Jacobson, Daniel Herrmann-Zoll, Vicki Valsamis, Susan Le, and everyone at Smith Street Books. Thank you to everyone who supported *Soy Sauce, Sugar, Mirin*. Lastly, thank you to all the bakers for keeping the ovens warm and the tradition alive.

ABOUT THE AUTHORS

SATOSHI NARUSAWA

Born in Tokyo, Satoshi has been a baker for more than 20 years. After a decade of honing his craft in both traditional and French bakeries in Japan, he moved to Australia to reconnect with the simple joy of handmade bread. In Melbourne, he joined Loafer Bread in Fitzroy North, where he embraced the art of sourdough and a community-focused philosophy. While baking shokupan through the night, he rediscovered his true 'panyasan' spirit. In 2022, he opened Little Cardigan in Brunswick in partnership with Bench Coffee Co. Even though his main ingredients are flour and butter, his ultimate comfort is a bowl of Japanese rice cooked in a donabe.

HARVARD WANG

For the last twenty-three years, Harvard has navigated Melbourne as an art director, photographer and food critic, though his most demanding boss is his daughter, who requires a bento box every morning. Born in Malaysia and married into a Japanese family from Kyushu, his life has been a long conversation between cultures and the nuances of Asian cuisine. As a reluctant ramen expert, he believes the best way to eat noodles is to slurp loud, finish quickly and keep your opinions to yourself.

INDEX

Smith Street Books

Published in 2026 by Smith Street Books
Naarm (Melbourne) | Australia
smithstreetbooks.com

Distributed outside of ANZ, North & Latin America by
Thames & Hudson Ltd, 6–24 Britannia Street, London, WC1X 9JD
thamesandhudson.com

EU Authorised Representative: Interart S.A.R.L.
19 rue Charles Auray, 93500 Pantin, Paris, France
productsafety@thameshudson.co.uk; www.interart.fr

ISBN: 978-1-9235-0339-7

Smith Street Books respectfully acknowledges the Wurundjeri People of the Kulin Nation, who are the Traditional Owners of the land on which we work, and we pay our respects to their Elders past and present.

Publisher: Lucy Heaver
Additional text: Harvard Wang
Editor: Ana Jacobson
Design and layout: Susan Le
Photographer: Daniel Herrmann-Zoll
Food stylist: Vicki Valsamis
Photography chefs: Satoshi Narusawa and Asako Narusawa
Proofreader: Pamela Dunne
Indexer: Helena Holmgren
Production manager: Aisling Coughlan

Printed & bound in China by C&C Offset Printing Co., Ltd.

Book 489
10 9 8 7 6 5 4 3 2 1

FSC www.fsc.org MIX Paper | Supporting responsible forestry FSC® C008047